A Guide to
the Backpacking and
Day-hiking
Trails of Kentucky

Other Thomas Outdoor Guides

A Canoeing and Kayaking Guide to the Streams
of Kentucky
by Bob Sehlinger

A Guide to Kentucky Outdoors
by Arthur B. Lander, Jr.

A GUIDE TO
THE BACKPACKING AND
DAY-HIKING
TRAILS OF KENTUCKY

by Arthur B. Lander, Jr.

THOMAS PRESS
Ann Arbor, Michigan

Book designed by Joanne E. Kinney
Trail drawings by Kathleen Jackson and Ellen Koloff

Copyright © 1979 by Arthur B. Lander, Jr.

Printed in the United States of America
Published by Thomas Press, Inc.
Ann Arbor, Michigan 48106
ISBN 0-89732-002-6

Library of Congress Cataloging in Publication Data

Lander, Arthur B
    A guide to the backpacking and day-hiking trails
of Kentucky.

    Includes index.
    1. Backpacking--Kentucky--Guide-books.
2. Hiking--Kentucky--Guide-books. 3. Kentucky--
Description and travel--1951-   --Guide-books.
4. National parks and reserves--Kentucky--Guide-
books. I. Title.
GV199.42.K4L36   917.69'04'4   79-16188
ISBN 0-89732-002-6

The slopes will be thickly shrubbed with rhododendron, darkened by the heavy green shade of hemlocks . . . where water leaps off the rock lip, catching the sunlight as it falls. And always on the wet faces of the rock there will be liverwort and meadow rue and mosses and ferns. These places are fresh, and they stay as fresh in the memory as a clear, cold drink of water.

WENDELL BERRY

Contents

Preface

Although the automobile has been the dominant means of personal transportation for more than three generations, large segments of the population are walking for sheer recreation. Putting one foot in front of the other, the most rudimentary form of human locomotion, has become nothing short of a major recreational pursuit. There's been a boom in hiking during the past decade in the United States.

Hiking is not only good exercise, it is the most ecologically desirable way to visit our wild lands and leave behind the 55 mph world with its noise, fumes, and rapid change. Hiking instills independence and self-confidence by making a person keenly aware of things that too many people in this country take for granted—food, shelter, transportation, and the natural environment. There are lessons to be learned from living with just the basic necessities. The slower pace can bring inner peace and reconciliation with the body. A week or so on the trail can be a fulfilling experience and pure escapism, a respite from the rigors of responsibility and decision making, a time to put things in their proper perspective.

A narrow footpath winding through deep woods, a rainbow in a misty waterfall, waiting out a thunderstorm in a rockhouse at the base of a cliffline—these experiences are vivid in my mind. They are part of why I backpack.

I like to be away from the grind of modern life, to feel adventurous and as free as the wind, to feel the weight of the pack in rhythm with each step, the taste of hot chocolate on a cold morning, a gentle wisp of steam rising from my tin cup like the fog lifting from the creek beside my campsite.

The rewards of hiking in remote lands are many if you just look for them. They are simple experiences of observation and appreciation. The ingredients may be quiet woods, the shrill cry of a hawk circling overhead, or soft rays of sun filtering through a pine thicket. The unhurried pace encourages contemplation; the sights and sounds arouse feelings. It is the life-style of the outdoor romantic.

Perhaps we would not be as conscious of the need to preserve what wild lands are left in America today if it were not for John Muir, the naturalist, explorer and mountaineer, whose writings we think of today as a celebration of the bountiful gifts of nature and our heritage of the simple pleasures of the wilderness life-style.

Muir, the father of the American wilderness consciousness, and guiding light of the national park movement, was a preservation pioneer driven by a thirst for scientific knowledge, and mellowed by aesthetic contemplation. It is ironic that he came along at a time when the westward push caused great waste of our natural resources.

A Thousand-Mile Walk to the Gulf, published posthumously in 1916 from his journals, describes his journey on foot to Florida, an adventure that preceded his extensive travels in California's High Sierra range and the establishment of Yosemite National Park, the consequence of this exhausting solo exploration.

Muir's trek through the southeastern United States took him to Cumberland Gap, a mountain pass thrust into historical prominence by settlers on their way west. It is easy to imagine Muir, sketchbook in hand, leaning against a tree and gazing out over the rocky crest of Cumberland Mountain. He is an inspiration to those who love the freedom and self-sufficiency of exploring wild lands.

Arthur B. Lander, Jr.
January, 1979
St. Matthews, Kentucky

ACKNOWLEDGEMENTS

This guide to the backpacking and day-hiking trails of Kentucky is the result of months and months of field investigations, verifying trail routes on topographic maps, writing trail descriptions, and researching the introductory unit. Without the help of the following persons, the job would have been immensely more difficult.

First of all, I would like to thank Leon Lipscomb, backcountry ranger at Mammoth Cave National Park; Donald Burchfield and John Charron at Tennessee Valley Authority's Land Between the Lakes, and William O. Nichols at Cumberland Gap National Historical Park. Mike Loveless, a former historian at the park, was also a big help by providing me with information on some of the trails. The collective knowledge and experience of many individuals have significantly enriched this book.

I also appreciate the cooperation I received from the U.S. Forest Service—Daniel Boone National Forest district rangers and their staff. My personal thanks to Bill Conger for his work on the trails in Red River Gorge Geological Area, and Edgar Spitzke for his descriptions of some of the trails in the Somerset, London, and Stearns Ranger Districts. To Verne Orndorff, landscape architect for Daniel Boone National Forest, thank you for helping me obtain the most comprehensive data on the Sheltowee Trace and Redbird Crest trails, both of which are now under construction. Larry Smith and Dr. Fred Pipkin also helped with descriptions of some of the trails in Daniel Boone National Forest.

My thanks to Bryan Mattingly and Ben Pipkin for their help in the descriptions of the Jenny Wiley, Michael Tygart, and Simon Kenton trails, which are detailed in Chapter 6, "Trails of Special Mention."

Several persons were a big help in providing me with information for Chapter 8, "Nature and Scenic Areas." Among them were Ed Puterbaugh and Tim Williams.

My thanks also to Doug Billips of the Kentucky Department of Parks for his cooperation in organizing information for Chapter 7, "Selected State and Municipal Park Trails." And to Gerry Rau, assistant supervisor at Otter Creek Park, thank you for helping me prepare the material on that City of Louisville–owned park. My thanks also go to the many Kentucky state park system naturalists and park supervisors who graciously provided me with their collective trail experience in their respective parks.

I would also like to thank Jack Gedmark, M.D., for providing me with advice on the unit on personal preparedness at the beginning of the guidebook.

My personal thanks go to Philip Hayes for fighting the bushes with me on hikes in Mammoth Cave National Park and the Pioneer Weapons Area of Daniel Boone National Forest. Also, I would like to thank Renée Holsclaw, my typist on this project, for such neat and efficient work.

Ridge Trail, Cumberland Gap National Historical Park. Photograph by the author.

1
Introduction

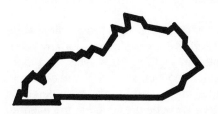

At this writing, there are approximately 950 miles of backpacking and day-hiking trails in Kentucky. Major trail systems can be found in Mammoth Cave National Park, Cumberland Gap National Historical Park, Land Between the Lakes, and Daniel Boone National Forest. The Jenny Wiley Trail and the Sheltowee Trace, both major trails over 150 miles long, are now under development. They attest to the rapid expansion of Kentucky's trail system.

But the recent development of all the trails in Kentucky could not have been possible without the efforts of many individuals (through volunteer work), and agencies coordinating their efforts with the Kentucky Trails Association. Securing funds for planning, construction, and negotiating right-of-ways across private property have been major obstacles to expansion.

The purpose of this guide to the backpacking and day-hiking trails of Kentucky is to identify and describe the hiking opportunities in Kentucky. Introductory sections deal with personal preparedness, equipment, backpacking foods, backcountry photography, orienteering, the terrain and weather, the best seasons for hiking, ecological considerations, and rating the trails. Historical material accompanies the chapters on national parks and nature and scenic areas. The introduction that accompanies each chapter presents an overview of the number of trails and their mileage. Trail sheets list where each individual trail starts, ends, the USGS topographic quadrangles on which it is found, water availability, mileage, trail connections, gain or loss in elevation, fauna and flora, and other pertinent information. Selected equipment outlets are found in the Appendix.

The difficulty in compiling such a guide is that trails are constantly being built, erased, or altered. Vandalism of trailhead signs makes it hard for hikers to find trails. All efforts have been made to write as comprehensive a guide as possible. Since not every foot of every trail was hiked and some information was supplied to the author, there may be some omissions and errors noted by readers. Please send corrections to Thomas Press, P. O. Box 2210, Ann Arbor, Michigan 48106.

PERSONAL PREPAREDNESS

Wilderness-related recreation—rock climbing, long-distance backpacking, hang gliding, white-water canoeing, and mountaineering—demands physical and mental preparedness, specialized abilities, and proper equipment. Wilderness skills take time to learn—it is a process of successfully completing increasingly difficult maneuvers. Unfortunately, many of the accidents that occur in the outdoors happen because a person is not prepared for what is encountered.

Familiarity with terrain and weather conditions and the physical abilities needed to complete a hike are imperative considerations for any hiker, especially a group leader. Proper clothing, sleeping bags, tents, and foodstuffs must be decided on, and potential dangers, as well as the course of action to be taken in the event of an accident must also be considered. In remote areas immediate rescue cannot always be presumed in the event of illness, hypothermia, or injury. Advising friends or park and forest rangers of your trip plan is the only assurance of rescue in the event that you become injured or lost. Follow up on your itinerary by checking out with proper authorities when you leave the backcountry. It may take a little extra effort, but you never know when it may pay off.

Planning cannot be stressed enough. Anyone who has ever forgotten a knife, matches, proper clothing, or whatever will tell you that it just takes one or two oversights to ruin a trip. Likewise, being overloaded with gear on a short trip can be just as unpleasant. There's a fine line between carrying enough equipment and needless overloading, forgetting an essential and hauling around a lot of gear that's never taken out of the pack. No backpacker can therefore dismiss planning as a waste of time.

Planning includes picking a trail, scouting it on paper by consulting topographic maps, and making out a checklist of foods and equipment after deciding how many days and nights the trip will last. Proper preparations for weather conditions that might be encountered and a knowledge of special regulations, if any, for backcountry use should be reviewed. (In Kentucky's national parks, for example, all hikers must have fire permits in their possession before taking to the trail if they plan to stay overnight.) Studying up on the area's history and geology may also add to the pleasure of the trip.

Getting in shape before leaving on a long, arduous trek through the wilds is something that all of us sedentary city dwellers must accept. The transition from a slightly plump office worker to a bronze, hardened wilderness traveler will not happen overnight, and without a proper tune-up, there's going to be a great deal of suffering and muscle strain. A person who gets very little exercise fifty weeks out of the year and then expects to strike out on a two-week adventure, sleep on the ground, endure stinging cold winds or exposure to intense summer sun without some sort of warm-up is asking for a miserable time. The best investment a hiker can make in anticipation of a long trip is a gradual conditioning program, sensible eating, and rest—all the basics of good health. Running, swimming laps and racquetball are all good ways to increase your wind and build up stamina. Backpacking was meant to be fun, not work. If you're out of shape and plodding along the trail, it's easy to feel like a beast of burden rather than a self-sufficient, hardened, backcountry traveler.

I have always felt at home in the wilds, safer than when I drive to the neighborhood grocery store, but nonetheless there are potential dangers in the wilds that all hikers should be aware of. Understanding how to deal with hazards such as bites from poisonous snakes and insects, skin ailments like those caused by poisonous plants and sunburn, and more severe predicaments like hypothermia, heat exhaustion, heat stroke, and diarrhea (the "trots") entails not only common sense and good judgement but specific first aid procedures.

Snakes

Encountering poisonous snakes when hiking is a possibility, albeit a remote one. Hikers should be alert and watchful, especially during the spring when snakes seek the warmth of the sun after emerging from hibernation. Through old wives' tales and a seemingly inborn aversion, human encounters with snakes have been dramatized, unfortunately, to the point of causing undue fear of them in a large segment of the population. True, poisonous snakes can inflict potentially fatal bites, but, for the most part, snakes are quick to flee from larger animals, including humans, and will retire unless threatened. But daylight encounters are rare indeed as all species of poisonous snakes found in Kentucky are nocturnal, that is, they're night feeders.

A good way to keep from inviting snakebites is not to put your hands or feet where you can't see them (under rock ledges, in brush piles, under logs). The two most common poisonous snakes in Kentucky are the copperhead (*Adkinstrodon contortrix*) and the timber rattlesnake (*Crotalus horridus*).

Insects

Insect bites or stings are a hazard to summertime hikers. They are more frequently fatal than snake bites, but, for the most part, the misfortune of getting stung by a yellow jacket, wasp, or honey bee doesn't lead to a serious reaction. Bee stings are more a nuisance than a health threat, but localized swelling, pain and severe itching may nontheless ruin a trip. An allergic reaction to a bee sting is rare; fainting or loss of consciousness are telltale symptons. Other systemic (basic body) reactions may include asthma attacks, hives, or skin rashes. Systemic reactions need the attention of a physician immediately.

In the case of nonpoisonous spider bites, localized swelling, itching and pain may accompany the bite. Bites by poisonous spiders are even rarer than allergic reactions to bee stings.

The black widow is the main poisonous spider found in Kentucky. Victims should be promptly taken to a physician. The aggressive female black widow spider, distinguished from the male of the species by its distinctive red "hour glass" markings on the abdomen, inflicts a wicked bite that produces immediate sharp pain at the site, a cramping pain that spreads throughout the body, nausea, vomiting, headaches, sweating, and muscle spasms. The systemic reaction to a black widow bite usually far outweighs the bite itself, that usually appears as no more than a mosquito bite although it can ulcerate.

Another poisonous spider found in Kentucky is the brown recluse. It tends to hide in dark, recessed areas, hence the name "recluse." It injects strong digestive juices when it bites, which causes extensive ulceration.

Mosquitoes, chiggers, no-see-ums, and ticks must also be dealt with if you are hiking between frosts (approximately mid-April through mid-October). A good remedy for mosquito bites is to keep them from biting since once they get you there's not much that can be done! Repellent in lotion form is best for backpacking because it is potent and is packaged in small, unbreakable bottles. A couple of drops on exposed areas will do the trick. The bottles take up little room in your pack and are environmentally better than aerosols. No-see-ums (almost invisible biting flies) may also be discouraged by using repellent. Since they occur in localized swarms, you can frequently move away from them.

Chiggers are tiny arthropods that can be picked up from sitting directly on the ground or by brushing through tall grasses and weeds. They crawl along the skin until they reach a barrier such as a sock top or waistband. At that point they attach themselves to the base of a hair and cause a very irritating bite. Avoiding areas where chiggers are found, tucking pants into boot tops, and dusting with sulfur powder around the ankles and waistband are helpful measures.

Secondary infections caused by scratching the bites of mosquitoes, no-see-ums, and chiggers can cause a greater problem than the original bite.

Ticks are the most worrisome of insects to many people because they're sneaky, slowly crawling up their prospective victim's arms and legs, trying to find just the right place to bite, and, if undetected, sucking blood like tiny vampires. The parasites really aren't that despicable, it's just their modus operandi.

Large numbers of ticks can be found where there's large numbers of mammals. Mammoth Cave National Park and Land Between the Lakes (LBL) have large infestations because of their sizeable deer herds. Ticks are woodland creatures as are their hosts. Humans have little to fear from the bite of a tick, but localized swelling and infection may occur if the tick is not completely removed after it has become firmly attached. In rare cases, Rocky Mountain spotted fever, which causes paralysis, may occur. For the most part, ticks are just a nuisance.

The tick problem in LBL is the young of the year, or seed ticks as they are commonly called. Reddish-brown in color and slightly smaller than the head of a straight pin though somewhat larger than a common chigger, the small critters cause intense itching and irritation. They are found in greatest numbers north of U.S. 68, and usually appear in July and persist until the first killing frost. People are infested with these pests by brushing up against leaves of herbaceous ground plants in low, damp stream valleys and at the edges of fields. A hundred bites may be sustained at one time. When the ticks get on your clothing, they may bite right away or crawl upward before attaching themselves, and, because of their small size, go unde- tected until it's too late.

The best way to prevent infestation is to avoid areas where these ticks live. If you're hiking, stay on prepared trails; avoid low, damp areas. Insect repellent and yellow sulfur powder will provide some protection. If you think they're all over you it might not be a bad idea to take off your pack, take any valuables out of your pockets, and just jump in a lake! Clothes covered with seed ticks should be handled with care because carpeting in your car, house, sleeping bags, and tents can become infested.

Poisonous Plants

Exposure to plants of the genus *Rhus,* commonly known as poison ivy, poison sumac, or poison oak, is more likely to happen to hikers than any other group of outdoors enthusiasts. Reactions caused by these plants are most common in the summer months when the leafy plant grows at trailside. This skin ailment has ruined many a hike. The leaves aren't the only carriers of the plant oil, which, when it comes in contact with the skin, causes the allergic reaction of itching, redness, minor swelling, blis- ters, and oozing. Exposure to vines, which often attach themselves to tree trunks, or smoke from burning plants of the *Rhus* genus, can also cause the rash, which usually begins within twelve to forty-eight hours after exposure and persists for about two weeks regardless of medication. Avoidance of the plants and repeated washing with soap after known exposure are the only preventive steps. Hot baths or showers (a luxury to trail travelers), and some commercial ointments and lotions provide only limited relief. Pre- scribed oral medications or injections may cause drowsiness, ulcers, or emotional changes, and should be taken only under the supervision of a physician.

Blisters

Blisters are an even more serious skin ailment than poison ivy, oak, or sumac. Your best defense against blisters is footwear that fits properly and has been broken in. Don't start on a hike in a brand new pair of boots or shoes—that's just asking for trouble.

If, however, you do begin to develop a blister, there are some things you can do. At the first sign of irritation, remove your footgear and let the area cool off and dry (external applications of rubbing alcohol may help). Then reduce the chances of further irritation by immobilizing the area with a moleskin pad or adhesive tape.

If a blister has already developed but has not yet ballooned out, you can simply immobilize the irritated area and the fluid will be reabsorbed. But if a bubble has appeared, it will have to be burst with a sharp, sterile needle inserted near the base of the blister. Let the fluid drain naturally. If the skin over the area will not lie flat under a bandage, it should be carefully cut away with sterile scissors and the area should then be treated as an open wound—that is, cleaned, protected from infection, and carefully covered and protected from further irritation.

Gastrointestinal Disorders

Bowel infections are a major cause of year-round discomfort to hikers. Proper hygiene, food preparation, toilet habits, and safe drinking water will, in most cases, prevent common diarrhea or bacillary dysentery. With more and more people visiting remote lands, the possibility of picking up harmful "bugs" in drinking water has increased dramatically. In group hikes where food is prepared together, those doing the cooking must keep their hands especially clean and wash dishes properly after each meal. Common diarrhea is no stranger to the traveler.

The more serious bacillary infections (such as amoebic dysentery) are caused by contamination of food or water sources by microorganisms of the *Shigella* group, which cause fever, severe abdominal pain, and swelling of the large intestine. Fecal contamination of water sources can cause such disorders. Plenty of salt, cold liquids, no solid food, and commercially prepared antidiarrhea compounds will forestall the discomfort. Serious cases, such as amoebic dysentery, require treatment by a physician. In severe cases of amoebic dysentery, the single-celled animals destroy living cells and perforate the colon. Water sources should be regarded with suspicion and drinking water should be treated by boiling or by the use of halazone tablets or iodine.

Sun and Heat

Other summertime hazards are, of course, the overheating of the body—heat exhaustion and sun stroke—and overexposure to the sun. The summer sun is often fierce, and those not used to it should be especially careful. Wide-brimmed hats, long-sleeved shirts, long pants, and commercially available chemical sunscreens are adequate preventive steps. Gradual exposure will lessen the risk of a severe sunburn.

The evaporation of perspiration cools the body and keeps internal temperatures stable during hot weather. Dehydration, exhaustion, excessive humidity, and a lack of wind can cause the body to overheat and bring into play a number of potentially harmful reactions. The heat disorders are classified as: heat syncope (fainting and sensations of giddiness); heat edema (localized swelling and puffiness of feet and ankles); water-depletion heat exhaustion (inadequate water intake to offset excessive sweating); salt-depletion heat exhaustion (severe salt loss through sweating); heat cramps (related to salt exhaustion and affecting legs and arms with excrutiating pain); prickly heat (inflamed skin and tiny blisters occuring under clothes); heat stroke (delirium, convulsions, and the absence of sweating); and heat fatigue (a marked deterioration in efficiency). All these disorders are related and based on inadequate salt intake, excessive exercise, and insufficient water intake during hot weather. Noonday temperatures and sun should be avoided unless the hiker is acclimated to them, and then there's no guarantee that these disorders won't occur unless preventive steps are taken. In summer, the morning and evenings are coolest. Hikers can reduce the possibilities of hot weather disorders by resting in the shade at noontime, by carrying salt tablets, and by drinking lots of water.

Hypothermia

Hypothermia (the lowering of the body's core temperature) and frostbite (necrosis of tissue due to freezing) are the major cold weather hazards to hikers. In newspaper accounts, the cause of death in cold weather fatality is usually described as "exposure to the elements." Such generalization oversimplifies a complex series of events that occur when body heat is lost faster than it can be produced, and, in the case of frostbite, when localized areas, usually extremities like toes or fingers, lose their blood supply and become frozen. The two conditions are indeed related, yet they may occur independently.

The body is a heat-producing machine, its temperature is maintained through the metabolism (burning) of fats, carbohydrates, and proteins. A drop in the body's core temperature of just a couple of degrees can break down that efficient heat-producing capability. A further lowering, to about 90° F, leads to sluggishness, irrational behavior, stupor, collapse, and, ultimately, death. This cold weather killer thrives on a number of events— physical exhaustion, inadequate food and water intake, and the psychological elements of fear, despair, or panic. The first sign of hypothermia is shivering, the body's involuntarily exercising to produce heat since physical activity is another way the body's core temperature can be maintained. When the body's reserves are depleted, hypothermia may be right around the corner.

If the insulating properties of clothing are lost through wetness by falling in a creek, a good drenching from a winter rainstorm, or exertion causing a hiker to become saturated in sweat, the body's ability to produce enough heat to keep its vital organs functioning properly may be severely taxed. As a first line of defense, blood is drawn from the extremities to the body's trunk, setting the stage for the possibility of frostbite.

When cotton, down, or some synthetic clothing gets wet, it may lose up to ninety percent of its insulating capability. Wind accelerates this heat loss. (See wind chill chart on page 11.) Most hypothermia cases occur between 30° and 50°F, a temperature range that most people do not consider that cold. Hypothermia has a way of sneaking up on you, and you may not realize that it is happening. Victims may say they're okay, but don't believe them, believe the symptoms. At the first indication that someone in your hiking party is developing hypothermia, make camp and terminate exposure to wetness and cold winds before exhaustion sets in. Uncontrollable fits of shivering, vague, slow, and slurred speech, memory lapses or incoherence, and frequent stumbling are all signs that a person may be going into hypothermia.

The last line of defense is treatment. The key to successfully bringing someone out of hypothermia is heat from an external source—from warm drinks or from direct body heat of another person. Skin-to-skin exposure in a sleeping bag is the best way. Strip off all wet clothes, get in a sleeping bag with the hypothermia victim.

Although frostbite usually occurs in sub-zero conditions that most hikers will never experience, there's danger in neglecting stinging coldness or numbness of the extremities in hikes through the snow at temperatures hovering around freezing. Since the body will react to a drop in its core temperature by cutting the supply of blood to fingers and toes, susceptibility to frostbite is a real possibility in such situations. The symptoms are localized coldness, loss of feeling, and a yellowish-white and waxy tint to the skin. Treatment, again, is accomplished by skin-to-skin exposure. An ear tip can be warmed by the hands, toes by placing the foot on a warm abdomen, or cold fingers stuck under or inside the victim's own jacket and under the armpits or between the legs. In severe cases the skin will become puffy and then take on a hard, woody feeling, rose-violet coloration, blisters, and may develop into gangrene.

EQUIPMENT

Lightweight backpacks and tents; sturdy hiking boots; freeze-dried foods that reconstitute when added to boiling water; sleeping bags and parkas filled with goose down and synthetic fibers; single-burner stoves that weigh less than two pounds, burn unleaded or butane gas, and can heat a quart of water to a boil in less than five minutes—all now enable hikers to travel through backcountry with greater ease and comfort than those hikers of the canvas knapsack and metal cook-kit era.

The last twenty years have seen remarkable advances in the design and manufacture of lightweight backpacks, the largest step in lightening the hiker's burden. The first hikers and backpackers had to contend with the bulky pack boards. Tubular aluminum packframes designed to fit the contour of the body have revolutionized the pack and have, in part, been responsible for the boom in hiking. The framed pack can be fitted comfortably to anyone regardless of height or body size, allowing a greater portion of the pack load to be shifted to the strongest parts of the body—the hips and legs. They have padded belts and shoulder straps that adjust quickly and easily for a custom fit. The modern pack has special compartments for storage of specific equipment—stoves, foodstuffs, tents, sleeping bags and clothes—and comes in various sizes to accommodate the weekend hiker as well as the wilderness expedition trekker. Design breakthroughs, new stitching techniques, and the use of lightweight, coated nylon has helped in making today's backpacks (and the smaller day-hiking packs) light and relatively inexpensive, yet strong enough to take years of hard use.

Good boots are the most important piece of basic equipment the backpacker must have. For the casual day-hiker, footwear is not so critical; some even prefer work boots or moccasins.

The main types of boots are: trail shoes (lightweight, ideal for gentle trails, and more shoe than boot); hiking boots (those in the three- to four-and-one-half-pound a pair range that are suitable for rocky trails); and the boots for climbing or mountaineering (large, heavy, stiff, designed for expeditionary use on ice, rock, and able to support heavy loads). The price range and availability of quality boots is as widespread as the sport of hiking itself. Hiking boots are tremendously popular even with nonhikers. They're fasionable, rugged looking and can be worn for years if resoled. Hikers and nonhikers alike are infatuated with the heavy, stiff boots with cleated soles. This is in part because most boots available in America today were actually developed for European mountaineering. The hikers in this country have gotten it in their heads that they are supposed to lug around a pair of six-pound boots even in the summertime. The fact is, climbing and mountaineering boots are not suited for hiking on trails because they were intended to be used in situations where insulation, protection, and performance are vital to success and survival—on high-altitude cross-country travel on rock and snow where the foot must be protected from extreme conditions. The heavier, stiff boots are hard to break in and can be downright uncomfortable. They are best suited for wintertime cross-country hiking.

Soles are fastened to the upper boots by cementing, inside stitching, welted construction, or injection moulding. Boot uppers are constructed of either top grain or split leather. Top grain leather is the outside or top layer of the cow hide. This layer is tough, flexible, and resistant to moisture because of its natural oiliness. Split leather, the layers of leather closer to the cow's meat, are not nearly as desirable for making uppers. The split leather stretches easily and is hard to waterproof. The thickness of cowhide allows for several layers of such split leather.

Most high-quality boots have several unmistakable attributes: toe and heel reinforcing, shanks to protect the instep, foam rubber padding throughout the ankle and a roll collar around the upper heel, reinforced eyelets and stitching, and lug soles made of high-carbon neoprene such as the Vibram® Montagna.

Sleeping bags, like packs, boots, and tents, are a major expense for the hiker, and thus should be thoughtfully chosen to suit one's specific needs. The design and the amount and type of fill are major considerations that dictate the bag's usefulness. Since the sleeping bags keep you warm by trapping tiny pockets of dead air that serve as insulation by keeping the body-generated heat in and the cold air out, the measure of a sleeping bag's efficiency is to what extremes in temperature it can protect the hiker—its "warmth rating."

The warmth of a sleeping bag depends on a number of factors: the kind and amount (loft, in inches) of fill used, be it waterfowl down or synthetic fiber; the shape of the bag, be it rectangular, mummy, or barrel type; the inner and outer shell construction; the methods by which the fill is compartmentalized; and the closures, zippers, and drawstrings. Perhaps the most important of these factors is the fill, and therein lies a controversy of which one is best. Each side is advocated by equipment manufacturers and users alike.

Down, which insulates waterfowl from extreme temperatures with millions of microscopic filaments of "fluff" that trap air between the skin and feathers, is the most efficient of the cold, dry-weather insulating fill for sleeping bags. Eider and duck down are commonly used, but goose down is best. Eider down is in too short supply and therefore is prohibitively expensive. Duck down isn't nearly as good an insulator per pound, and it will not stand up to wear (compression and expansion) as well as goose down. Goose down is light, very compressible, and lofts better than an equal weight of synthetics. The one major drawback of any down is that, when wet, it loses most of its insulating properties.

With the plastics age emerged synthetic fibers. Among the earliest used in sleeping bags were Dacron®, Fortrel®, and Kodel®. In the early 1970s, two chemical companies introduced "second-generation synthetic fillers, mainly Dupont's Fiberfill II®, and Celanese Corporation's

Polarguard®, which many claim are equal or better sleeping bag fillers than down. Two major arguments against synthetic-filled bags is that they don't compress into as small a package as do down bags of equal weight, and synthetic-filled bags weigh more than down bags of comparable loft. The overwhelming factors in favor of the new synthetics is that they absorb little, if any, moisture and don't lose their loft if soaked. The fillers are also nonallergenic. These bags can simply be wrung out and hung up to dry. Under similar adverse conditions (winter rainstorm, wet snow), a down bag would be virtually useless if it became soaked.

Wind Chill, Effective Temperature, and Insulation Thickness

U.S. Army research has established data to determine the thickness of insulation needed for comfort at various temperatures and levels of activity. Actual temperatures must be converted to "effective temperatures" by using the wind chill chart. To use the wind chill chart, find the estimated or actual wind speed in the left-hand column and the actual temperature in degrees Fahrenheit in the top row. The effective temperature is found where these two intersect. For example, with a wind speed of 10 mph and a temperature of $-10°F$, the effective temperature is $-33°F$.

WIND CHILL CHART

Wind Speed (mph)	Actual Temperature							
	40	30	20	10	0	−10	−20	−30
	Effective Temperature							
10	28	16	4	−9	−21	−33	−46	−58
20	18	4	−10	−25	−39	−53	−67	−82
30	13	−2	−18	−33	−48	−63	−79	−94
40	10	−6	−21	−37	−53	−69	−85	−100

Greater wind speeds have little added effect. Use the following chart for thickness and comfort values.

U.S. ARMY RESEARCH THICKNESS AND COMFORT VALUES

Effective Temperature	Thickness of insulation required for comfort (in inches)		
	Sleeping	Light Work	Heavy Work
40°F	1.5	0.8	0.20
20	2.0	1.0	0.27
0	2.5	1.3	0.35
−20	3.0	1.6	0.40
−40	3.5	1.9	0.48

(These figures are approximate but are a good base for an average healthy person.)

We're living in an era of campfireless cooking. More and more bac-kpackers are using single burner to boil water to reconstitute freeze-dried foods and to heat water for coffee, oatmeal, or cocoa. Trail cooking has been greatly simplified and now is much less time consuming. These stoves, which use a variety of fuels—white gas, propane, butane, kerosene, denatured alcohol, and solid fuel pellets—burn hot and can be relied on in even the most adverse climatic conditions. They range in price up to $50, but the average stove costs about $25. The availability of fuels, stove reliability, boiling speed, cold weather performance, starting, cleaning, the weight of the stove, ease of packing, durability, and safety are factors to consider when purchasing one.

Tests on each of approximately forty brands of backpacking stoves available today point out two startling conclusions: several brands are far superior, and firing up stoves in tents is dangerous because of the risks of asphyxiation and carbon monoxide poisoning. But stove safety extends beyond the fumes that they produce. Refueling, knocking over a stove, puncturing a canister, overheating a fuel tank, using defective cartridges, flare-ups, and filling hot stoves are the major causes of fires each year.

Backpacking stoves, while products of convenience, are far more dangerous than first supposed. Careful compliance with the manufacturer's directions is imperative to proper performance. Stoves should be lit only on level, solid ground. Overfilling and overpriming can cause excessive pres-sures and the possibility of a flare-up. Spilled fuel invites fire, as does refueling a hot stove. Stoves should be properly ventilated to ensure that heat is dissipated. A clean stove is more likely to function properly than a dirty one, much like a well-tuned automobile gets better gas mileage than one with fouled plugs.

Outdoor clothing has come a long way since the time of full-length wool coats, fur parkas, and the beaded "hunting shirts" of buckskin that Indians and rugged frontiersmen made famous. Outdoor garments—rain-gear, parkas, shirts, sweaters, knickers, wind shells and ski wear—have become increasingly lightweight, fashionable, and durable. High-quality clothing for the backpacker is now readily available through retail stores and has become a booming mail-order business.

The development of synthetic fabrics has been largely responsible for most of the new clothing, although old standbys of wool and cotton, as well as the new blends, remain very popular. Wool has remained a basic fabric for pants, socks, and sweaters because it offers the advantage of insulating even when wet. Air is trapped in its hollow fibers, and body heat isn't lost. Wool has a high "moisture regain," which means that body moisture is allowed to pass through and condense on the cooler, outer part of the fabric. Some of this condensation is absorbed by the fabric, while the rest is suspended as droplets that evaporate slowly while providing an excellent insulative layer. Raw wool contains lanolin, which gives the fabric a natural water repellency and shields the hiker from precipitation while not interfering with the transfer of body moisture.

Some types of fabrics currently being used extensively in outdoor clothing are:

Ventile Cloth   A very tightly woven, 100% cotton fabric which is water repellent yet provides ventiliation and minimizes condensation inside a garment. After cleaning, the fabric may be spray treated to restore water repellency.

Uncoated Cotton–Polyester   A rugged, breathable, cotton–polyester blend fabric with high abrasion resistance and tear strength and moderate water repellency.

Coated Cotton–Polyester   A rugged, coated cotton–polyester blend with high abrasion resistance and wind and water repellency.

"Ripstop" Nylon   A lightweight, breathable, uncoated nylon fabric that contains a reinforcing grid formed by a cross pattern of extra threads that increases its tear strength.

Nylon Taffeta   A dense, strong, uncoated nylon fabric that is down-proof, windproof, and slightly water repellent.

Coated Nylon Taffeta   A lightweight, coated nylon fabric that is water repellent and has a high tear strength.

Coated fabrics   These afford a greater measure of water repellency than uncoated fabrics, but condensation inside a garment made from a coated fabric must be expected. Coated fabrics cannot be considered completely waterproof since any seam is vulnerable to moisture and should be treated with a seam sealer.

Uncoated nylon   These fabrics provide good wind protection but are not water repellent for extended periods and should not be used for rain protection.

Gore-Tex® Treated Nylon   A radical technological breakthrough, a combination of breathable fabric and a microporous polymeric film. Parkas or wind shells treated with Gore-Tex® are windproof, waterproof, and breathable. The reason is nine billion pores per square inch. Each pore is twenty-thousand times smaller than a drop of water yet seven-hundred times larger than a molecule of water vapor. Thus, it allows body moisture to escape while raindrops are repelled.

The 60/40 blend of nylon and cotton is most often used in mountain parkas and provides excellent wind protection with slight precipitation repellency. The Chamois shirt, made of napped cotton, is soft and comfortable and long a favorite with hikers. Today, synthetic fills are used in both vests and jackets, as is down. The coated nylon fabrics used today in tent rainflys and packs is also a good material for ponchos and hip-length or full-length rain jackets.

Staying warm and dry is a backpacker's major concern. The proper selection of clothing and the tiresome but necessary chore of removing and adding layers are the only ways to ensure being comfortable on the trail under changing weather conditions. The advantage of the layering principle should be considered so that hikers choose items of clothing that will allow versatility when used in combination.

A tent is a backpacker's home away from home. It provides shelter from winter winds and freezing temperatures, downpours, bothersome insects, and "psychological" security from those unexplained rustlings in the bushes at night. Since Kentucky's climate is wet and humid and all camping is done in forests at elevations under five-thousand feet, the need for those specialized and expensive alpine tents is minimal. Gale force winds, sub-zero temperatures and deep snow are confined to December, January, and February (and rare at that). The A-frame "forest type" tents are preferred by many Kentucky hikers.

The emergence of nylon as the main fabric for backpacking tents has been applauded by hikers who are forever looking for ways to lighten the load without sacrificing the basic requirements of all-weather shelters. All tents were once made of cotton. Today cotton tents are largely restricted to family "car camping," and super-lightweight, compact nylon tents, equipped with rainflys, are favored for trail use. These new backpacking tents have seamless floors to keep out water, nylon screens to keep out insects and promote ventilation, sturdy stakes and aluminum poles, zippered vestibules (for storage of gear), and rainflys, which keep out precipitation. The "breathable" nylon allows moisture from a sleeping hiker to escape, while the coated polyurethene fly suspended above the tents keeps out rain and makes the tent cooler in the summer and warmer in the winter by trapping air as a layer of insulation. Good quality nylon tents range in price from $75 to $150.

While cotton tents are used by hikers, the disadvantages are that once the surface tension of a cotton tent is broken, water will seep in. Cotton is from two to four times heavier than nylon and all cotton tents require thorough airing out after each use to discourage mildew and rotting.

Tarps are an alternative to tents. Make sure you bring along plenty of rope, a ground cloth (a poncho will do in most cases), or make sure your sleeping bag has a bivouac cover and that you are lying on an Ensolite® pad. The obvious disadvantage of a tarp is that all precipitation isn't vertical and in a downpour you're likely to get soaked.

Equipment checklists are up to the individual. A good way to organize equipment, if you have the space to store it where each group is separated, is in the drawers of a big chest. The following is a typical list of equipment to have on hand, not necessarily used on every trip, but none-theless available when needed.

Backpack
Lightweight tent (tent, rainfly, poles, cord, and stakes in stuff sack)
Sleeping bag (in stuff sack)
Ensolite® foam pad (54'')
Straps to attach tent, sleeping bag, and foam pad to pack (2 sets)
Stuff sacks, 3 nylon or cotton (made from pants legs from cutoff jeans)
Backpacking stove
Fuel bottle (one pint)
Aluminum pail (one quart)
Sierra cup
Spoon
Matches (in waterproof container)
Pot lifter (tongs for removing pails of boiling water from the stove)
Ground cloth
Air mattress and pillow (inflatable)
First aid kit (antiseptic, bandaids, moleskin and small scissors, adhesive tape, gauze, lip balm, butterfly bandage, elastic bandage, aspirin, and salt tablets)

OPTIONAL EQUIPMENT
Ultralight fishing rod and reel
Spinners and other assorted ultralight lures
Split shot and hooks
Small spool of 4-pound-test line (monofilament)
35-mm camera body, and 24-mm, 55-mm macro, and 135-mm lenses
Lens cleaner and brush
Small lightweight tripod, both folding and C-clamp type
Color transparency film (36-exposure rolls)
Topographic maps
Orienteering compass
Small pad and pencil
Pocket knife
Water bottle and halazone tablets or iodine
Soap (liquid, biodegradable)
Small towel and washcloth
Small flashlight or candle lantern
Small folding toothbrush and toothpaste

Snakebite kit
Sunglasses

"Ragg" wool socks
Cotton long underwear
Wool pants
Hiking shorts
Camp shoes (boat shoes or sneakers)
Wool shirt
Chamois shirt
Rain gear
60/40 wind parka
Down or synthetic-filled vest
Down or synthetic-filled parka
T-shirt
Bandana
Wool sock cap
Wide-brimmed hat
Hiking boots
Blue jeans

Day pack

Squeeze tubes (for jelly, peanut butter, apple butter, etc.)
Salt and pepper
Chop sticks
Freeze-dried vegetables
Freeze-dried meat dinners
"Gorp"
Instant oatmeal
Instant tea
Instant cocoa
Beef jerky
Drink mix (fruit flavored)
Tea kettle
"Granola" bars
Freeze-dried soup mix

(A selected list of national and Kentucky outdoor equipment outlets is found in the Appendix.)

BACKPACKING FOODS

Trail weary hikers have been known to say that a good meal can be the high point of the day. Hiking burns up calories, no doubt about it, and fresh air seems to make everybody ravenously hungry. The backpacker's needs are specialized. Meals must be nutritious, appetizing, easy to pre-pare and provide enough calories to sustain the energy output level neces-sary for day after day of strenuous activity. Stoves, cooking utensils and foods alike must also be light in weight and easy to pack with a minumum of bulk.

The average person requires a diet of 2,700 to 3,100 calories a day. Under conditions of cold temperatures or especially strenuous hikes, an additional intake of 300 to 500 calories a day per person is necessary. The trick is to bring just enough food on a trip so that you'll never go hungry, and return with little, if any, surpluses. Once you've burned up all avail-able foods and surplus body fat, increased caloric intake is necessary.

The backpacker has a problem balancing meals, making sure that there's an adequate intake of fats, proteins, and carbohydrates (sugars and starches). They're all important to a proper diet; fats are used slowly, proteins provide a long-lasting energy source, and sugars are quick energy foods. Fats are most neglected in the backpacker's diet. Protein-rich foods such as nuts and jerky, candy and dried fruits, which are a good source of sugar and protein and are preferred by hikers, but they do not provide enough fat. Vitamins and water (in large quantities) are also important. Salt deficiency may cause headaches, fatigue, stomach cramps, and diarrhea; without proper fluid intake, the body becomes dehydrated.

The space program and research by the military have been responsi-ble for the development of dehydrated and freeze-dried foods that have helped enormously in cutting weight and bulk. There's virtually no chance of spoilage of foods in which all the moisture has been drawn out, and the packaging is minimal in weight when compared with tin cans and glass containers. The selection of these foods on the market today is astound-ing—vegetables, dinner entrees, juices, and breakfast foods.

Items that must be refrigerated have their place in the packer's diet as long as they're eaten quickly and not taken on long trips in hot weather. When repackaged in light polyethylene bags, they're well adapted for day-hiking or overnight trips. Whenever possible to cut costs, rely on these foods, but again, beware that under summer pack temperatures they may spoil or become a sticky mess. Fresh fruits, meats, chocolate, and pro-cessed cheeses have limitations in use. To cut cost, try to use as many products off the shelf as possible.

Here are some recipes that provide inexpensive, nutritious, nonper-ishable additions to meals.

PEMMICAN

First, you'll need 1 lb. of jerky or dried beef. You can buy this at a grocery or make you own by cutting 5 lbs. of lean beef (or venison) into ¼-inch thick strips and drying them in an oven.

Pound the jerky into fine bits with a steak hammer or cut it into thin flakes with a knife.

Next, take raw animal fat and render it to liquid by heating it over a low flame. Be careful not to burn the fat. Place the jerky bits into a square pan and mix in enough hot grease to thicken the ingredients to a sausage-like consistency. This is Indian-style pemmican. Since most people find the basic concoction a bit bland, you may want to stir in 2 or 3 Tbsp. of brown (or maple) sugar or molasses and a handful of raisins.

Let the mixture cool, slice into blocks, and store in plastic bags in a cool place.

In this form, pemmican will last for weeks without refrigeration. On the trail, you can eat it raw, fry it like sausage, or simmer it with water for a stew.

BANNOCK

Try this nutritious bread, which can be prepared in advance, on your next hike.

Mix the following ingredients in a plastic bag: 2 cups of all-purpose flour; ½ tsp. salt; 2 tsp. baking powder; 1 tbsp. sugar; and ¼ cup powdered milk.

When ready to use, simply add 1 cup of cold water and mix quickly and thoroughly in the bag. Spread dough in a hot skillet or baking pan greased with a spoon of shortening. Cook until brown on both sides. Bread can be turned in the skillet or pan or tilted to the coals to brown on top. Eat hot or cold.

BEEF JERKY

    1 flank steak (approximately 1½ pounds)
    1 teaspoon seasoned salt
   ⅓ teaspoon garlic powder
    1 teaspoon msg (monosodium glutamate)
    1 teaspoon onion powder
   ¼ cup Worcestershire sauce
   ¼ cup soy sauce

Trim off all fat. Semi-freeze meat. Cut with grain into ⅛ to ¼ inch thick slices. Combine seasonings. Combine sauces. Stir sauces into seasonings. Cover bottom of 9 × 15 × 2-inch Pyrex dish with sauce. Place one layer of flank strips in sauce. Brush on more sauce. Cover with more strips of meat. Brush on more sauce. Cover with more strips of meat. Brush on remaining sauce. Marinate overnight. Lay

strips of marinated meat in single layer on oven racks (place foil underneath to catch drips). Dry at 140° for 6 to 8 hours, till chewy as desired. Taste occasionally. This amount makes approximately ½ pound of jerky.
This recipe can be doubled or tripled if there is room in oven (pieces must not overlap). Seasonings given will be enough for one flank steak. If you wish, try one teaspoon liquid smoke, or cooking sherry.

You may find that eating less, when hiking, is a refreshing change. I have found that on long distance hikes, getting into a rhythm of mind and body, eating less and drinking lots of water gives me a feeling that I am cleansing myself of impurities. It is a fasting of sorts that is like slimming down and revving up, mentally and physically.

During cold weather or extremely demanding hikes, fasting, or greatly reducing food intake isn't wise because you may draw on body reserves too heavily and bring on exhaustion. Every long distance hiker has experienced the "body high" from taking in less calories than are being burnt up, but it isn't applicable to all hiking situations. Be careful!

BACKCOUNTRY PHOTOGRAPHY

Packing a camera into the backcountry is well worth the extra weight. During the backpacker's day in remote lands, many occasions will arise when time for photography can easily be set aside from the leisurely routine. Rambling hikes are actually conducive to photography. All around you are willing subjects—frost on multicolored ground plants, fog rising from an icy creek, a sunrise in the mountains, a snow-covered hemlock tree backlit in the sun, or summer wildflowers.

The 35-mm single lens reflex (SLR) cameras, and the even smaller pocket-size, full-frame 35-mm rangefinders are the most popular with trail travelers. Use the slowest ASA-rated transparency film. It will give you maximum color and enlargement. Kodachrome® 25 and 64 are excellent because they render lifelike color, and good prints can be made from the slides with the use of an internegative.

Lightweight folding tripods, tabletop tripods, and the C-clamp type tripods are all excellent choices. Camera bodies, lenses, film, lens cleaner, and paper should be protected by lightweight plastic or leather cases organized in a stuff bag for easy access. Take time at dawn or the end of the day, when the light is best, to set up some camp shots or portraits. You'll always be glad you took the time to remember a trip in pictures. Cumberland Gap National Historical Park, Red River Gorge Geological Area, and Beaver Creek Wilderness are excellent choices for a photography and hiking trip.

ORIENTEERING

Orienteering opens up a whole new world and enables hikers to embark on long, rambling treks through trackless woods far from the beaten path. The tools of cross-country navigation are the topographic map and the orienteering compass, which is different from conventional wristwatch or pin-on compasses as its needle is suspended in liquid and it has a clear protractorlike base and a revolving compass housing. Combining the vast store of information on topo maps and the newfound skill of navigation, the hiker can become free of crowded trails and explore remote areas visited by few. These areas are often the most beautiful and unspoiled backcountry.

Learning orienteering skills requires dedication, reading one of the excellent instructional texts on the market, and plenty of backyard practice. Once learned, the survival skill can become a hobby. Europeans have been intensely interested in orienteering ever since the invention of the orienteering compass in Sweden in the 1930s. A hotbed of competitive orienteering, that Scandanavian country has made orienteering a compulsory course in its public schools and boasts the largest number of orienteering hobbyists anywhere—an estimated five percent of Sweden's population. The largest competitive sporting event in the world is a five-day orienteering meet held outside Stockholm each summer.

The man responsible for introducing orienteering to Americans as a wilderness skill was Bjorn Kjellstrom, a Swedish orienteering champion who came to this country after World War II to market his compass, the Silva. One of the directors of the United States Orienteering Federation (USOF), Kjellstrom authored *Be Expert With Map and Compass,* the bible of orienteering in America.

I am not going to attempt to explain orienteering, space does not permit. Basically, orienteering skills entail determining exact locations according to longitude and latitude, understanding map symbols, contour lines expressing elevation, basic directions called cardinal lines, and map scales and distances. You must also know how to use a compass and how to differentiate between magnetic and "true" North Pole, understand the degrees of declination locally, know how to follow a degree reading (compass bearing) in the field, take degree readings from where you are to a point on the terrain, set a degree reading on a compass from the map, and most elementary of all, orient the map with the compass. All these skills must be mastered before one can travel by compass.

Topographic quadrangles (1/24,000 scale) can be obtained from the U.S. Geological Survey in Washington, D.C. or from outlets in Frankfort and Lexington. Address are in the Appendix.

TERRAIN AND WEATHER

Kentucky is divided geographically into five regions: the Cumberland Plateau, Knobs, Bluegrass, Pennyrile, and Jackson Purchase. Each region has distinct soils, plant communities, animal populations, and geologic formations. Kentucky is a state of varied landscapes—the ridges and narrow valleys in the Cumberland Plateau; distinctive pointed hills in the Knobs region; rolling carpetlike plains in the Bluegrass; and an uneven succession of hills, pastures, bottom lands and woodlots, and fields of row crops in the Pennyrile and Jackson Purchase regions.

The highest point in Kentucky is near Lynch, in Letcher County, where Black Mountain reaches 4,145 feet above sea level. The lowest point is near Hickman, in Fulton County along the Mississippi River where the land is just 237 feet above sea level.

According to the National Climatic Center, the climate of Kentucky, while continental in type, is of a variable nature because of the state's position in mid-latitudes. Kentucky is located on a belt of westerly winds and is subject to cyclonic and anticyclonic storms. Though located in the interior of the continent, Kentucky is not shut off from a great source of moisture—the Gulf of Mexico. Both high and low pressure systems pass through the area and the temperature generally varies with each passing system. Thus, in winter and summer there are occasional, brief, cold and hot spells that quickly moderate as the pressure ridge moves off. On the whole, the winters are moderately cold and the summers are quite warm. Temperatures of 100°F or more in summer and 0°F or less in winter are rare. Kentucky is geographically situated so that it receives rainfall from cyclonic storms particularly in the winter and spring as these storms move along a path extending from Texas to New England. It also receives rainfall from storms that move across the continent from west to east, cutting across the deep southern states.

Thunderstorms with lightning and heavy rainfall are common during the spring and summer months. As a result, precipitation is nonseasonal and varies from year to year and from month to month with the fall months usually being the driest. Generally, March is the month of the greatest monthly rainfall and October of the least. Snowfall, while seldom heavy, is common during the months of November through March. As with rainfall, amounts vary from year to year and month to month. Some snow has been recorded in October and April. Mean total amounts for the months of January, February, and March are about the same, with January showing a slight edge in total amount. Relative humidity remains rather high throughout the summer months.

Cloud cover is about equally distributed throughout the year, but the winter months are somewhat cloudier. The number of days with sunshine varies from month to month with the greatest amount during the summer months as a result of high pressure systems decreasing the sky cover. Heavy fog is unusual.

Mean temperatures in degrees Fahrenheit computed from the range of daily highs and lows are: January, 33.1; February, 35.8; March, 44.0; April, 55.9; May, 64.8; June, 73.3; July, 76.9; August, 75.9; September, 69.1; October, 58.1; November, 45.0; and December, 35.6. Temperatures below 32°F are rare after the middle of April, and the first hard frost after summer usually is around the first week in October. Winds are usually southwesterly with an average velocity of 10 mph. The strongest winds are usually associated with summer thunderstorms; tornadoes also occur, generally in the spring.

Average precipitation (in inches per month) is: January, 3.53; February, 3.47; March, 5.05; April, 4.10; May, 4.20; June, 4.05; July, 3.76; August, 2.99; September, 2.94; October, 2.35; November, 3.33; and December, 3.33. The average total for the year is 43.11 inches.

BEST HIKING SEASONS

Spring and fall are the seasons that veteran hikers seem to prefer in Kentucky, for a number of reasons. First of all, in spring (late March, April, May, and early June) the woodlands are brightened by a parade of wildflowers, a profusion of color amidst a sleeping forest. By the time the leaves are out and it begins to get real warm and humid, the insects become bothersome. Springtime is a good season for stream fishing too, and many a backpacker looks forward to a fried trout, or smallmouth bass fillet to liven up a steady diet of freeze-dried food.

Autumns in Kentucky are exhilarating. The clear, blue skies with scattered, fluffy clouds are a long-awaited relief from summer's swelter. The nights are cool, as in spring, and it's excellent sleeping weather. The leaves usually begin turning in early October and peak at the end of the month or in early November, depending on a number of factors—among them are rainfall and the onset of cool nights and warm days. A hiking trip through a forest of red, yellow, orange, and russet is a real treat.

ECOLOGICAL CONSIDERATIONS

Backcountry ethics for the hiker have been the subject of considerable debate in recent years as wilderness recreation has found its way into the mainstream of American outdoor life.

The problem we face today is that more and more people are visiting an ever-shrinking amount of remote land in this country. We are virtually loving our wild places to death. Many of the outdoor lessons taught to us by our fathers and grandfathers (burying trash, building open fires for cooking and cutting boughs to make a shelter) are simply not appropriate any longer.

The increasing number of backcountry visitors has prompted both the U.S. Forest Service and National Park Service to adopt ecological guidelines for backcountry users that basically say, "Pack out everything you pack in," and work to limit our impact on the land. Since the campsite is the first place that shows evidence of a hiker's presence, it is logical to adopt camping procedures that will leave things as undisturbed as possible. Never cut plants to make a smooth pad for your tent. Leave your campsite in better shape than you found it; erase all traces of ever having been there. Don't make a fire unless you have to, and if you do, make it at an established site, or camp by a watercourse and make your fire where highwater will erase all traces of it. Never cut live trees for firewood and make sure campfires are never left unattended; thoroughly drown out all campfires, scatter the ashes, and douse the ashes again. Fire scars and bits of noncombustible materials, mainly foil, are inconsiderate intrusions on someone else's wilderness experience. It is a point of courtesy to others who will pass where you have camped to work for minimum disturbance, to protect the backcountry that hikers seek out. Littering is also a shameful abuse of our wild lands. Respect and appreciation for the land are fundamental to the ecologically aware hiker.

RATING THE TRAILS

Rating systems that take into consideration a trail's difficulty and a hiker's physical condition simply haven't been formulated. The difficulty is in correlating walking pace, pack weight, distance between rest stops, and miles per day with the individual characteristics of each trail. It would have to be assumed that a hiker moves at the pace that is directly proportionate to his or her physical conditioning and stamina.

It all seems rather unimportant to me. Let's face it, hiking is walking. You just put one foot in front of the other, then in front of the other, etc . . . Hiking is not a highly technical sport like white-water canoeing. In my opinion, a rating system based on hiking trail difficulty and the hiker's ability, is a bit too much. It would reduce walking for sheer pleasure to a grueling, competitive sport since what would be strenuous for one person might be a cakewalk for another.

I don't think day-hiking and backpacking were meant to be like that. It wouldn't be much fun for me if I couldn't take my time and relax, with time set aside to photograph, fish, or just lazily sit on a rock and watch the riffles in a stream.

But there does need to be some way by which, at a glance, one trail's difficulty can be compared with another's. So I have provided a brief rating in the descriptive information for each trail.

Each trail is rated easy, moderate, or strenuous. In addition, the mileage, the type of surface of the trail, and the change in elevation of the trail are provided. In some cases a trail may deadend, peter out, or intersect another trail, so remember to double the distance to return to your starting point. (Distances on loop trails do not have to be doubled.) Similarly, a trail may descend to a creek bottom and then rise back up to the ridge top so that you must both descend and ascend. A + indicates that the trail ascends from its trailhead, and a − indicates that it descends.

NOTE: Trails included in this guide are only those trails that are officially designated by an organization that has a lasting interest in marking and maintaining the route. Trails that are temporary, poorly marked, or poorly maintained are not covered.

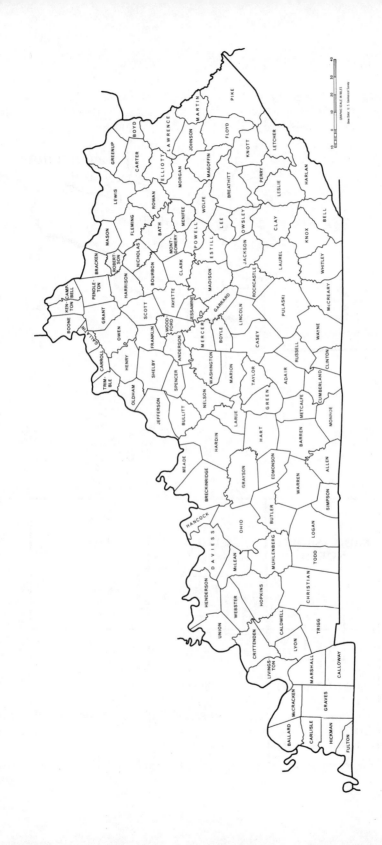

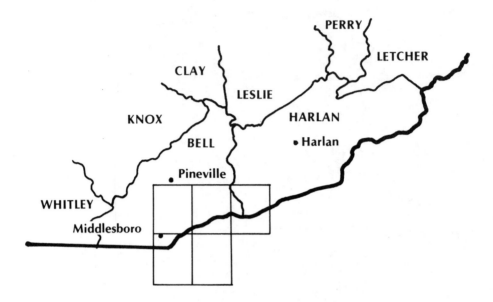

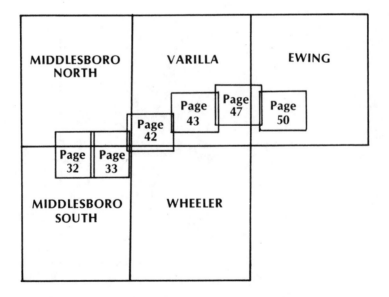

2
Cumberland Gap
National Historical Park

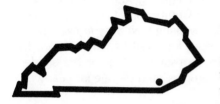

Cumberland Gap National Historical Park has always been my favorite place to hike in Kentucky because of the wonderful scenery, the feeling of truly being in the mountains, and the challenging trails. There is a total of 13 trails that cover more than 41 miles. Backcountry permits are required for all overnight stays on pack-in trips. Food and lodging accommodations aren't available in the park. The nearest soft bed and restaurant are in Middlesboro, Kentucky, Cumberland Gap, Tennessee, or Pine Mountain State Resort Park, 16 miles north on U.S. 25E in Pineville, Kentucky.

Cumberland Gap National Historical Park is the largest national historical park unit under the management of the National Park Service. The region's unique significance to the development of this country made it a candidate for public ownership.

On April 13, 1750, the land west of the Alleghenies was opened to extensive exploration and eventual settlement, which ultimately cleared the way for the establishment of America's fifteenth state—Kentucky. On that date, Dr. Thomas Walker, who had employed by the Loyal Land Company of Virginia to seek a site for future settlement beyond the mountains, discovered a great pass with an Indian road leading through it that later became the main artery of migration west. Walker named the pass in honor of the Duke of Cumberland.

Following the termination of the French and Indian War (1754–1760), which had temporarily postponed exploration, hunters passed through the gap in large numbers to venture deep into the fabulously rich land they had heard about from Walker and his men. Some established trade with the Shawnee and Cherokee Indians who visited Kentucky to hunt in the lowlands along Warrior's Path, the footpath that connected Cumberland Gap with the Ohio River.

Perhaps the most famous of these frontiersmen was Daniel Boone, who with his brother Squire, learned more about Kentucky than anyone else while hunting and exploring between 1769 and 1771. By 1773 he had convinced his family and four other families to move from their homes in Yadkin Valley, North Carolina, to Kentucky. But just before they reached the gap, Boone's son James and several others were killed during an Indian attack. As a result of this tragedy, they returned to North Carolina. But Boone was not discouraged easily. Two years later he returned with a party of axemen who met at the Holston River in what is now eastern Tennessee, and they began cutting the Wilderness Road. Moving north on what proved to be an arduous journey, the frontiersmen hacked their way through miles of thick canebrakes and brush. Fording both the Cumberland and Rockcastle rivers after passing through Cumberland Gap, they trudged for miles over hardpacked buffalo traces. Making their way in close proximity to the Warrior's Path, a north–south foot trail heavily traveled by Indians, Boone and his men had to be constantly alert for the sudden ambushes that plagued the expedition's progress and morale for nearly the entire trip.

The successful establishment of Fort Boonesborough at the trail's northern end was the realization of his lifelong dream. It was a personal victory for Boone, settling in an unspoiled land where game was plentiful and the soil was rich for farming.

In the years following the establishment of Fort Boonesborough and the American Revolution, the number of settlers passing through Cumberland Gap steadily increased. By 1800, it was estimated that of the approximately seventy-five percent of the 400,000 who had gone west had used the Cumberland Gap route. By that time the trail through the gap had been widened to a wagon road.

This floodtide of immigration soon brought cattle drives, stagecoaches and a new importance to Cumberland Gap. For as the storm clouds gathered for the greatest of America's internal challenges, the Civil War, the strategic value of the gap was quickly recognized, and the area figured prominently in the opening action on the western theatre of operations. Whoever occupied the great pass controlled Kentucky and the rebel states of Virginia and Tennessee. Even more important, they would control the railroad between Tennessee and Virginia.

During the course of the war, control of the gap changed hands four times. Initially it was occupied by the Confederates under the command of Brigadier General Felix K. Zollicoffer, who was later killed during an offensive campaign near Somerset that ended in defeat and the consequent loss of the gap to Union forces advancing southeastward through Kentucky to Tennessee.

After a series of captures and recaptures by both Union troops and the Confederates during the first two years of the war, the Cumberland Gap was finally controlled by Union forces from the fall of 1863 until the close of the war. By 1865, the once heavily wooded hillsides of the Gap and its adjacent mountains lay wasted, studded with stumps, pocked with entrenchments and scarred by deeply rutted supply roads. It was ravaged and deserted.

But interest in the gap again returned in the mid-1880s when geologists investigating the area found rich deposits of coal and iron. An industrial scheme was based on these discoveries; huge sums of money were invested by an English syndicate in railroads, coal mines, and iron furnaces. The resulting industrial boom gave birth to the city of Middlesboro, Kentucky, in the wide basin just north of the gap. During the Panic of 1893, however, financial reverses caused the boom to collapse although limited prosperity continued due to substantial investments made by northern capitalists.

Around the turn of the century, much of the scenic beauty had returned to the gap and the surrounding mountains by nature's regrowth. This encouraged many people to begin talking about the establishment of a park. Public recognition of these qualities at the 1922 Appalachian Logging Conference in Cincinnati that year led to the introduction of two bills in 1923 calling for the establishment of a park, but the final Congressional designation of the area as a park did not come until June 11, 1940, eighteen years later.

Cumberland Gap National Historical Park was formally dedicated on July 4, 1959, and it is the largest of the national historical units in the National Park System. The 20,194-acre park straddles the crest of Cumberland Mountain from a point of the Kentucky–Virginia boundary near Ewing, Virginia, southwestwardly for a distance of 17½ miles to the Tennessee–Kentucky corner, with an average width of only one and two-thirds miles.

Cumberland Gap National Historical Park is a park of precipitous mountains, clothed with dense deciduous hardwood forests. A 14½ mile section of the park along the crest of Cumberland and Brush Mountain is roadless, an area of rocky cliffs (shale, limestone, sandstone and coglomerate), high mountain valleys, and plateau land, with many commanding views of the valley and distant mountain ranges.

There are four major streams in the park. Martins Fork of the Cumberland River, one of six Kentucky Wild Rivers, is especially beautiful. A virgin stand of hemlocks guards its headwaters, and the stream rolls through narrow rock valleys canopied with heavy stands of rhododendron and mountain laurel, which bloom in the spring. Along the creek's moss covered banks thrive wildflowers and ferns. Access to all these streams requires long cross-country hikes.

Cumberland Gap National Historical Park is rich in plants and wildlife. The fifty-two species of mammals that have been identified by the park's biologist include the commonly encountered chipmunk, gray squirrel, raccoon, opossum, whitetail deer, and red fox.

From March to October, the moist mountainside valleys are carpeted with lush ferns and wildflowers that include the early blooming trailing arbutus, crested dwarf iris, and painted trillium. Warmer weather brings out May apples, the rare Turk's cap lily, Indian pipe, and yellow adder's-tongue. Because the altitude ranges from 1,300 to 3,513 feet above sea level, there is a diverse distribution of shrubs and evergreens, as well as herbaceous ground plants.

If you're a hiker who enjoys bird watching, you'll find the park has an abundance of birdlife, as has most of the Appalachian region. There are 115 species from thirty-one families known to be either residents or transient visitors. Seasonal visitors include the endangered bald eagle, the marsh hawk (a lesser-known bird of prey), and the blue-winged warbler (a meadow dweller). Perhaps the game bird most often sighted is the ruffed grouse. It is not uncommon to hear them "drumming" their wings during the annual spring mating season.

Cumberland Gap National Historical Park, P.O. Box 840, Middlesboro, Kentucky 40965. (606) 248-2817.

Cumberland Gap National Historical Park. Photograph courtesy of the Commonwealth of Kentucky, Department of Public Information.

32

N

Happy Hol

Dead Horse Hollow

Cemetery Hollow

BM 1235

Picnic Area

Hemlock Nature Trail

RIDGE

CU

Davis Branch

BM 1306

988

988

Sugar Run Trail

Dark Ridge

BM 1289

Continued on page 33

awn Gardens

25¢

elawn Mem Gardens

1200

Strip Mine

Radio Tower (WAFI)

Lynch Cem

1 MILE

1 KILOMETER

BM 1134

BM 1151

MIDDLESBORO

OLD   WILDERNESS

Visitor Center

Little Yellow Creek Trail

Yellow

Little Yellow Creek

UNION COLLEGE ENVIRONMENTAL EDUCATION CENTRE

BM 1288

ROAD

SKYLAND Road

Ridge Trail

The Pinn

Wilderness Road Trail

Cumberland Gap

Cudjo Cave

Iron Furnace

Tri-State Peak

Virginia Corner

Tri-State Trail

Cumbe

USGS QUADS: Middlesboro North, Middlesboro South   © Thomas Press

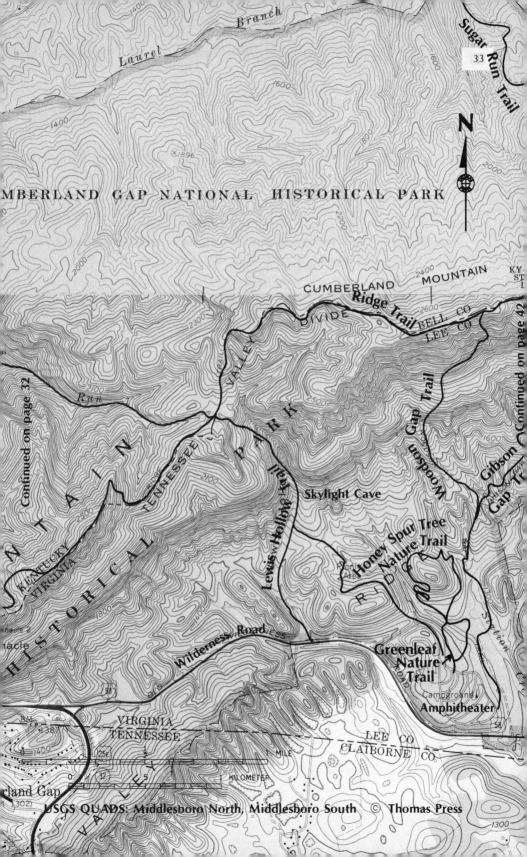

Laurel   Branch

1600

33

N

...MBERLAND GAP NATIONAL HISTORICAL PARK

CUMBERLAND   MOUNTAIN   KY
                                      ST
Ridge Trail   BELL CO
DIVIDE   LEE CO

Continued on page 32

Run

VALLEY   Woodson Gap Trail

Continued on page 42

Gibson
Gap Tr

Skylight Cave

Honey Spur Tree
Nature Trail

Lewis Hollow Trail

R I D G E

Greenleaf
Nature
Trail

Wilderness Road

Amphitheater

VIRGINIA
TENNESSEE

LEE   CO
CLAIBORNE   CO.

MILE

KILOMETER

VALLEY

...land Gap

USGS QUADS: Middlesboro North, Middlesboro South   © Thomas Press

NAME OF TRAIL: Little Yellow Creek Trail
MAP ON PAGE: 32
START: Visitor Center
END: Visitor Center
USGS QUADS: Middlesboro South
COUNTIES: Bell
TRAIL CONNECTIONS: None
RATING: Easy; 1.6 mi.; footpath; +30 ft.

The Little Yellow Creek Trail is a 1.6-mile loop for causal hiking that passes through mixed pine and hardwood forests behind the parking lot. It also goes by an old cemetery and railroad tracks. The woods openings along the trail are good bird watching spots.

NAME OF TRAIL: Hemlock Nature Trail
MAP ON PAGE: 32
START: Sugar Run Picnic Area
END: Sugar Run Picnic Area
TRAIL CONNECTIONS: None
USGS QUADS: Middlesboro North
COUNTIES: Bell
RATING: Easy; 0.2 mi.; paved trail; +20 ft.

The Hemlock Nature Trail is a two-tenths-mile paved loop designed to allow handicapped and blind visitors an opportunity to experience nature. By presenting a driver's license or other identification at the Visitor Center, it is possible to check out a cassette recorder for an audio interpretation of the trail.

NAME OF TRAIL: Wilderness Road Trail
MAP ON PAGE: 32
START: Iron Furnace at Cumberland Gap, Tennessee
END: Intersection with Tri-State Trail
TRAIL CONNECTIONS: Tri-State Trail
USGS QUADS: Middlesboro South
COUNTIES: Bell (KY) and Claiborne (TN)
RATING: Moderate; 0.5 mi.; paved trail; +300 ft.

The half-mile Wilderness Road Trail has a 300-foot gain in elevation. It begins at the iron furnace in Cumberland Gap, Tennessee. The 30-foot high rock furnace has been restored; a boardwalk encircles the furnace in which pig iron was smelted in the 1820s. It's possible to actually walk inside the chimney and closely inspect the remarkable masonry that was able to withstand temperatures in excess of 2800°F.

Wilderness Road Trail closely follows the original Wilderness Road that Daniel Boone cut in 1775. There are some remnants of the pioneer era along the trail—cultivated cherry trees and split rail fences. Gap Creek flows alongside the iron furnace; treatment of its water is advised before drinking. At the beginning of the hike, the rocky crest of Cumberland Gap looms in the backdrop.

NAME OF TRAIL: Tri-State Trail
MAP ON PAGE: 32
START: Parking area off U.S. 25E just below the saddle of the gap on the Kentucky side of Cumberland Mountain
END: Tri-State Shelter where Kentucky, Tennessee, and Virginia meet
TRAIL CONNECTIONS: Wilderness Road Trail
USGS QUADS: Middlesboro South
COUNTIES: Bell (KY), Claiborne (TN), and Lee (VA)
RATING: Moderate; 3.5 mi.; footpath, logging road, and gravel road; +400 ft.

Tri-State Trail is a 3.5-mile day-hiking trail that ascends 400 feet. It is a gravel-surfaced logging road through mixed hardwoods and pine trees.

Tri-State Trail intersects the Wilderness Road Trail about a tenth of a mile south (uphill) from the parking area off U.S. 25E.

From this intersection it is a steady climb with scattered patches of rhododendron at trailside. No water is available along the trail. When the leaves are off the trees there are several good views of Cumberland Gap, Tennessee, to the south. The first historic site the trail passes is George Morgan's commissary and magazine. All that's left of this former Civil War site is a huge hole in the ground. When the Confederates advanced on the gap, all usable articles of war that couldn't be carried away by the retreating soldiers were blown up. Historians speculate that the noise of the explosion may have convinced the Confederates that they were being shelled because they held up their advance for eighteen hours. An unmarked side trail to the right leads to the site of Fort Foote, a network of breastwork fortifications and cannons that guarded the western approach to the gap through Kentucky and Tennessee. The former site of the fort is approximately a tenth of a mile east of the Tri-State Trail. If you follow the unmarked trail past Fort Foote, it will eventually intersect with the Skyland Road, four-tenths of a mile from the Visitor Center off U.S. 25E.

The major point of interest on the Tri-State Trail is, of course, the point where Kentucky, Tennessee, and Virginia meet. Three interpretive markers (state seal, motto, flag, etc.), one for each state, are housed under a wooden shelter. Benches and a trail register are located at the shelter. There's an excellent view of Middlesboro, Kentucky. The state boundaries are inlaid copper in native stone.

Beyond the shelter (next ridgetop) is the site of Fort Farragut, which guarded the southern approach through the gap from Powell Valley. All that's left is a flat spot on the top of the ridge. Vandals have even destroyed the sign.

NAME OF TRAIL: Sugar Run Trail
MAP ON PAGE: 32–33
START: Sugar Run Picnic Area on KY 988, 1.7 miles
                         northeast of U.S. 25E
END: Intersection with Ridge Trail
TRAIL CONNECTIONS: Ridge Trail
USGS QUADS: Middlesboro North
COUNTIES: Bell
RATING: Strenuous; 2.25 mi.; footpath, woods road,
                         and gravel road; +800 ft.

Sugar Run Trail is a 2.25-mile paved and gravel and dirt footpath that ascends 800 feet. It begins at the Sugar Run Picnic Area on KY 988 (Sugar Run Road). Drinking water, grills, flush toilets, picnic shelter, and tables are available at the day-use site. The trail begins in hemlock and rhododendron thickets. It crosses the creek five times. Picnic tables are found in the woods at the beginning of the hike. There are three wooden footbridges. In the fall when the trail is covered with leaves, it is a bit difficult to follow when it ascends from the creek although it is wide and easily followed in most places even where it isn't blazed.

After leaving the creek bottom the trail enters open woods with some boulder fields. There are benches at the intersection of a logging road (a spur of Sugar Run Trail reached via KY 988, 1.0 mile southwest of picnic area). The trail becomes a well-maintained logging road paralleling the creek, a year-round source of water. There are several woods openings. Trail has numerous switchbacks near the intersection with Ridge Trail. Young Adult Conservation Corps (YACC) crews brushed out Sugar Run Trail in the summer of 1978. At the trailhead of the spur connector to Sugar Run Trail is a cable gate with a green post and a split-rail fence on right side of the road, driving towards Sugar Run Picnic Area (a tenth of a mile west of the overlook).

NAME OF TRAIL: Woodson Gap Trail
MAP ON PAGE: 33
START: 1.5 miles north of Wilderness Road Camp-
                       ground, off Gibson Gap Trail
END: Intersection with Ridge Trail
TRAIL CONNECTIONS: Gibson Gap Trail, Ridge Trail
USGS QUADS: Middlesboro North, Middlesboro South, and
                       Wheeler (VA)
COUNTIES: Lee (VA)
RATING: Strenuous; 3.0 mi.; footpath; +1000 ft.

The Woodson Gap Trail is a 3-mile spur off the Gibson Gap Trail. It is steep
and one of the most challenging trails in the park. It ascends 1000 feet before
it intersects with Ridge Trail. Climbing steadily from the beginning, it takes
hikers through deciduous forest with scattered pines. About three-quarters of
the way up, at an elevation of 2300 feet, the ridge levels off momentarily,
then the trail climbs steeply. The switchbacks become relentless and in the
last quarter mile the trail climbs 400 feet. Spring hikers get to see a wide
variety of wildflowers because of the rapidly changing elevation. Near the
top there are a few rock overhangs at trailside and scattered pockets of
hemlock and rhododendron. No water is available.

NAME OF TRAIL: Green Leaf Nature Trail
MAP ON PAGE: 33
START: Wilderness Road Campground Amphitheater
END: Wilderness Road Campground Amphitheater
TRAIL CONNECTIONS: Honey Tree Spur Trail
USGS QUADS: Middlesboro South
COUNTIES: Lee (VA)
RATING: Easy; 0.75 mi.; footpath; +60 ft.

The Green Leaf Nature Trail is a three-quarter-mile day-hiking trail for
casual after-dinner walks. It is used predominantly by campers at Wilderness Road Campground. The trail is practically level (60 foot rise). There
are several interpretive stations on the trail (self-guiding folders are available at the trailhead). Oak and beech woods and creek-bottom honeysuckle thickets are featured on this easy walk. Drinking water is available
at the campground.

NAME OF TRAIL: Honey Tree Spur Trail
MAP ON PAGE: 33
START: Intersection with Green Leaf Nature Trail,
                        Wilderness Road Campground on U.S. 58
END: Intersection with Green Leaf Nature Trail
TRAIL CONNECTIONS: Green Leaf Nature Trail, Gibson Gap Trail
USGS QUADS: Middlesboro South
COUNTIES: Lee (VA)
RATING: Easy; 1.1 mi.; footpath; +100 ft.

The Honey Tree Spur Trail is a 1.1-mile loop that rises 100-feet. It is an extension of the Green Leaf Nature Trail and begins at the log footbridge over a wet-weather tributary of Station Creek north of the Wilderness Road Campground Amphitheater. It ascends a small ridge in oak and beech woods, parallels the rocky creek bottoms, passes an old homesite, and follows a mowed path through honeysuckle thickets and pine woods.

    The Honey Tree Spur Trail is a favorite with bird watchers and nature enthusiasts. There are several interpretive stations along the trail that describe the relationships between plants and animals.

NAME OF TRAIL: Lewis Hollow Trail
MAP ON PAGE: 33
START: Wilderness Road Campground, park ranger
                      building where campers register
END: Intersection with Ridge Trail
TRAIL CONNECTIONS: Ridge Trail
USGS QUADS: Middlesboro South
COUNTIES: Lee (VA)
RATING: Strenuous; 1.68 mi.; footpath; +800 ft.

The Lewis Hollow Trail, commonly referred to as the Skylight Cave Trail, is a 1.68-mile footpath that ascends 800 feet. It begins as a moderate walk through mixed hardwoods, honeysuckle thickets, and woods openings between the campground and picnic area, but as soon as it starts climbing Cumberland Mountain, it takes on the character of almost all the hikes in the park—steep and challenging. The main point of interest on the hike is Skylight Cave, a 6-foot-high, 50-foot-wide opening in a rock outcropping, reached via an unmarked side trail. There's a 2-foot-wide hole in the ceiling from which it gets its name.

A network of connected underground passageways honeycombs the park—some are explorable, some are flooded year-round. The dry creek bed under the footbridge near Skylight Cave is part of the river system that is believed to drain into Cudjo Caverns at Cumberland Gap. The creek is dry most of the year, flowing only during periods of extreme precipitation when the underground chambers are completely full. Farther downstream, the river resurfaces to the dry creekbed. From the footbridge to the intersection with Ridge Trail, Lewis Hollow Trail steadily ascends through open woods of oak, hickory, pine, and poplar–hemlock associations. There are scattered boulder fields and mountain laurel and rhododendron thickets.

The trail has numerous switchbacks and is steep. If you were walking this stretch downhill it would be a real "toe pincher." The only reliable year-round water source on the trail is near the top. You'll notice a spur trail to the right. Follow it for fifty yards and you'll come to a spring pool. There's plenty of good water there.

NAME OF TRAIL:	Gibson Gap Trail
MAP ON PAGE:	33, 42
START:	Wilderness Road Campground on U.S. 58, two miles east of Cumberland Gap, Tennessee
END:	Intersection with Ridge Trail
TRAIL CONNECTIONS:	Honey Tree Spur Trail, Woodson Gap Trail, and Ridge Trail
USGS QUADS:	Middlesboro South, Wheeler (VA)
COUNTIES:	Lee (VA)
RATING:	Strenuous; 5.0 mi.; footpath and gravel road; +1500 ft.

The Gibson Gap Trail is a 5-mile trail that ascends 1500 feet. It begins at the Mischa Mokwa Trail sign in the Wilderness Road Campground. Beginning as a gravel road through bottom land with honeysuckle thickets, cedar, and oak woodlands, the trail crosses five footbridges over Station Creek, then begins a sharp ascent. It passes through much the same terrain as the Woodson Gap Trail on its way up Cumberland Mountain. Rhododendron, mountain laurel, stands of pine, hemlock, and oak–hickory woods flank the trail. No water is available after leaving Station Creek.

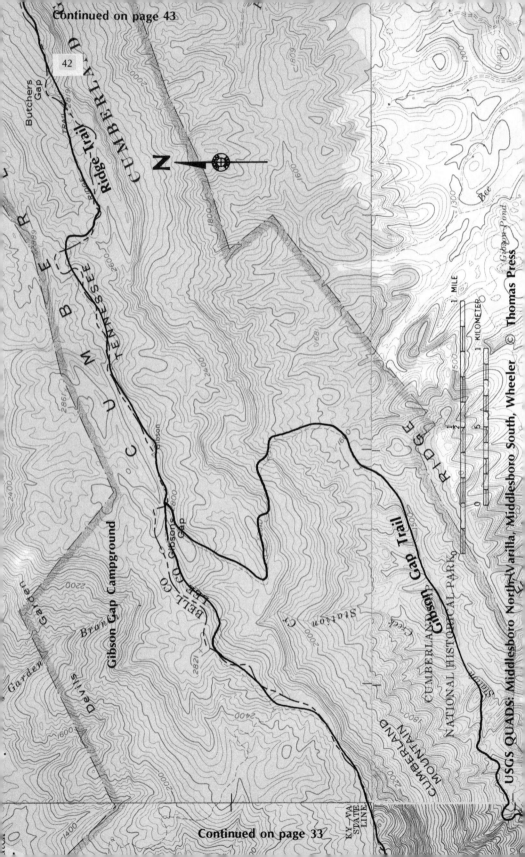

Continued on page 43

42

Butchers Gap

CUMBERLAND

Ridge Trail

TENNESSEE

CUMBER

N

Gibson Gap Campground

Garden

Garden

Devils Branch

Gibson

Gibson Gap

BELL CO.
HARLAN CO.

2821

Station Cr.

Creek

CUMBERLAND GAP
NATIONAL HISTORICAL PARK

Gibson Gap Trail

RIDGE

CUMBERLAND
MOUNTAIN

Sims

Bee

Gibson Pond

½ MILE
1 KILOMETER

USGS QUADS: Middlesboro North, Varilla, Middlesboro South, Wheeler © Thomas Press

KY–VA
STATE
LINE

Continued on page 33

43

Hensley Settlement

BELL CO.
LEE

Chadwell L

Ridge Trail

N

1 MILE

1 KILOMETER

Shillalah Creek Road

Hensley

3200

3334

B R U S H   M O U N T A I N

3153

2800

1626

1800

Creek

CUMBERLAND GAP NATIONAL HISTORICAL PARK

Butcher

3.56

KENTUCKY
VIRGINIA

Butchers
Gap

USGS QUADS: Varilla   © Thomas Press

NAME OF TRAIL:	Ridge Trail
MAP ON PAGE:	32–33, 42, 43, 47, 50
START:	Pinnacle Loop on Skyland Road
END:	White Rocks
TRAIL CONNECTIONS:	Sugar Run, Lewis Hollow, Woodson Gap, Gibson Gap, Chadwell Gap, and Ewing Trails
USGS QUADS:	Middlesboro South, Middlesboro North, Wheeler (VA), Varilla, and Ewing
COUNTIES:	Bell (KY) and Lee (VA)
RATING:	Strenuous; 16.0 mi.; logging road; +1000 ft.

Ridge Trail is a 16-mile trail with a change in elevation of approximately 1000 feet. It is the backbone of the trail system, a demanding trek atop Cumberland Mountain. While on the well-maintained logging road, hikers get commanding views of Powell Valley to the south (Virginia) and Brush Mountain to the north (Kentucky). Ridge Trail is a seemingly endless roller coaster of descents and steep climbs on or near the boundary dividing Kentucky and Virginia atop Cumberland Mountain. Oak–hickory woodlands, rock outcroppings and scattered stands of hemlock and rhododendron flank the trail.

Ridge Trail begins as a footpath (gravel) off the Pinnacle Loop. Take time at the beginning of the hike to follow the paved trail to the lookout point. Cherokee Indian chiefs were said to have consecrated treaties with their red brothers to the north, the Shawnee, at the overlook now called the Pinnacle. The trail is a gravel footpath when it begins, but after passing a wooden lookout shelter (no overnight camping allowed), it becomes a woods road. The first trail intersection is at Sugar Run Trail, which is followed by Lewis Hollow Trail, and then it intersects Woodson Gap Trail.

Between the intersection of the Woodson Gap and Gibson Gap trails is Table Rock, a 12-foot-high monolith. It is a favorite lunch stop on Ridge Trail. The balanced flat rock sits on the edge of a cliff, so be careful.

The next point of interest is the Gibson Gap Backcountry Camp, north of the Gibson Gap Trail and Ridge Trail intersection. The three small campsites (room for a total of six to eight tents) have several concrete and metal firepits. There's an intermittent spring at the campsite; water availability may be taxed in the late summer and fall. The pit toilet (a "one-holer") is a good three-quarters of a mile from the campground, a long walk if you're in a hurry.

Two miles east of the Gibson Gap Trail intersection is the Goose's Nest Sink, a deep sinkhole created by an underground stream that carved out a chamber whose sandstone roof eventually caved in.

Just before reaching Martins Fork Backcountry Camp there is a side trail to the left. It leads to Hensley Settlement, a 1930s mountaineer community of 508 acres on Brush Mountain. In its heyday during the Depression years, Hensley Settlement reached a population of 160 people, mostly from the Hensley and Gibbons families. The mountaineers grew all their own food, and raised livestock, poultry, and farm work animals. They had their own school, blacksmith, and midwives. The hill folk were very adept and self-sufficient. They produced sorghum molasses, kept bees, and distilled high-quality moonshine whiskey, which they often used to barter for manufactured goods they were unable to produce themselves.

In 1965, with the help of Jesse Gibbons, son of original Hensley Settlement resident, Lige Gibbons, the National Park Service began restoring and rebuilding the mountaineer community. Log cabins and split rail fencing were built in the old-time ways. There are permanent residents at the settlement now, which is a heritage demonstration area.

The largest of the three backcountry camps is at Martins Fork, where an overnight trail shelter is available.

The Martins Fork trail shelter is actually a restored log cabin originally built by Thomas Jefferson Culp in the 1920s. His creekside homestead is now the campground for hikers and horseback trail riders. The log cabin may be reserved by special arrangement with the National Park Service. The tent camping is first come, first served. Concrete and steel firepits, drinking water, pit toilets, and picnic tables are available.

The next point of interest on the Ridge Trail is Sand Cave. Take a left off Ridge Trail at the sign. This interesting geological phenomenon is not actually a cave but an undercut ledge. Over the years the action of water has eroded the weak sandstone bed, undercutting the stronger, more resistant sandstone above. The entrance arch has a span of 240 feet and rises more than 80 feet above the 1½ acre yellow, loose-sand floor, which inclines steeply toward the rear of the ledge. The product of 150 million years of geologic history, Sand Cave is 1½ miles west of White Rocks, on a three-quarter-mile side trail. The abundance of water at Sand Cave (a small waterfall) makes it an ideal spot for a lunch or snack stop. Be sure to sign the trail register at the beginning of the spur that leads to Sand Cave. The base of Sand Cave is a tangle of rhododendron and giant hemlocks that rise above the roof of the amphitheaterlike ledge.

At Sand Cave, as well as most of the way along Ridge Trail, there are vistas of mountains and valleys stretching off into the horizon. On a clear day it is possible to see the Great Smoky Mountains more than eighty miles to the south, from White Rocks at Ridge Trail's eastern terminus. To get to White Rocks from Sand Cave, continue to the left on Ridge Trail; there's a steady climb to the mountain top. A small spring crosses the trail about 300 yards east of the spur to Sand Cave. Oak, hemlock and rhododendron line the trail. The White Rocks Backcountry Camp is off to the left at the top of the climb. The campground is small and lacks water in the late summer and fall. Firepits and pit toilets are available. To get to White Rock, continue east (straight at the trail junction). Climb the steep footpath to the limestone bluff on top. What a magnificent view. In spring the mountaintop is abloom with rhododendron. There's plenty of room on the wide rock top to relax and eat a snack. Often it's too windy to light a stove, but I have enjoyed many a cup of tea from that lofty perch. Ewing, Virginia, lies in the wide valley below (south) and Alva, Kentucky, to the north. To continue on, descend from the rock and turn left at the sign; the trail descends steeply to Ewing Trail, which is the last link of the Mischa Mokwa Trail, a 22-mile Boy Scout Trail. The Mischa Mokwa is the Gibson Gap, Ridge and Ewing trails combined. Green markers with a bear inscription blaze the trail.

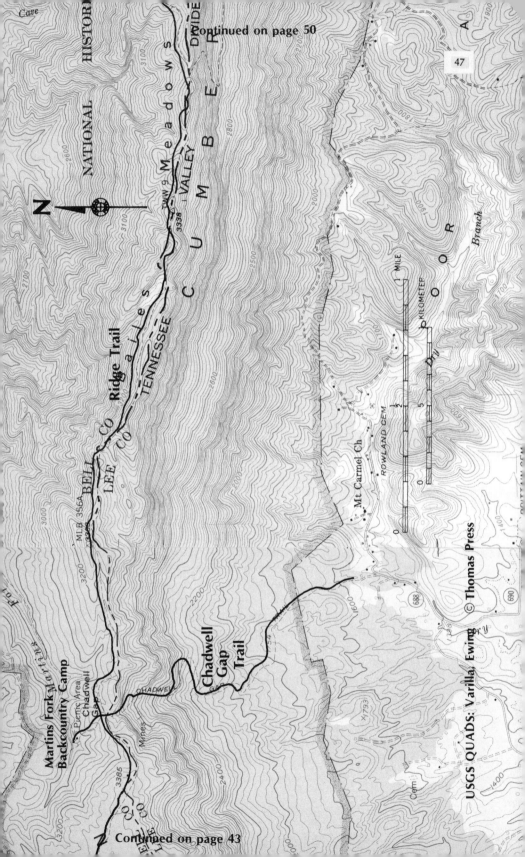

Continued on page 50

CAVE

NATIONAL HISTORIC

DIVIDE

Mt Meadows

TN 9

3100

3338

VALLEY

C U M B E R

N

Ridge Trail

ailles

TENNESSEE

BELL CO

LEE CO

MLB 356A

MLB 356

3000

3200

3100

Martins Fork

Martins Fk

Martins Fork Backcountry Camp

Picnic Area
Chadwell
Gap

CHADWELL

Mines

LEE CO
LEE CO

3386

3385

Chadwell Gap Trail

O O R

Branch

MILE

KILOMETER

Dry

ROWLAND CEM

Mt Carmel Ch

BOTTOM CEM

Cem

0

688

690

1400

1400

MILE

KILOMETER

Dry

USGS QUADS: Varilla, Ewing   © Thomas Press

Continued on page 43

NAME OF TRAIL:	Chadwell Gap Trail
MAP ON PAGE:	47
START:	VA 688, three miles north of Caylor, Virginia, off U.S. 58.
END:	Intersection with Ridge Trail, 0.2 miles southeast of Martins Fork Backcountry Camp
TRAIL CONNECTIONS:	Ridge Trail
USGS QUADS:	Varilla
COUNTIES:	Lee (VA)
RATING:	Strenuous; 2.3 mi.; footpath, logging road, and gravel road; +1600 ft.

The Chadwell Gap trailhead is at the home of Hubert Thomas, a former National Park Service employee. A trail marker on the left side of the road points the way up Cumberland Mountain. The trail begins in a barnyard with hog lots, a woodshed, and croplands fenced in split rails. The lower reaches of the trail are logging roads. Just after hiking into the woods, there's a gate at the park boundary. The logging road begins to ascend almost immediately, as Chadwell Gap Trail is the shortest, most direct route up the mountain, climbing 1600 feet in about 2.3 miles. The hike up Cumberland Mountain is not particularly beautiful although the higher you climb, the larger the trees are and the more diverse the plantlife seems to become. Near the beginning of the hike there is a clearing where deer are often seen in the mornings and late afternoon; the upper reaches of the trail contain some impressive boulder fields, cliffs, rhododendron thickets, and vistas of mountains and valleys through the trees. The last half mile of the trail is extremely steep. During wet weather the footing may be slightly difficult because some stretches of the trail periodically wash out although the YACC has worked hard to keep the trail in good shape. Water is scarce along the entire length of the trail. Sometimes during wet weather small springs can be found, but the water dripping from rocks dries up in the summer. On reaching the junction with Ridge Trail, White Rocks is to the right, five miles distant. Pinnacle Overlook is to the left, approximately 12 miles, and Martins Fork Backcountry Camp is 0.2 miles to the left. But before continuing, take a minute to catch your breath (you'll probably need to after that hard climb). Take off your pack and lean it up against the trail sign, 0.1 miles south of Martins Fork Backcountry Camp. Look through the peephole in the post facing south. Doesn't the rock formation look like a face? Take the footpath to your right (when you are facing east) off Ridge Trail. It leads to a spectacular overlook of the Powell Valley. It's a beautiful spot for relaxing, but be careful because there's no guard rail and it's a couple hundred feet down to the rocks. You've just climbed to Chadwell Gap, a mountain pass discovered by pioneers whose descendants still live in the tiny village of Caylor, 2,000 feet below you.

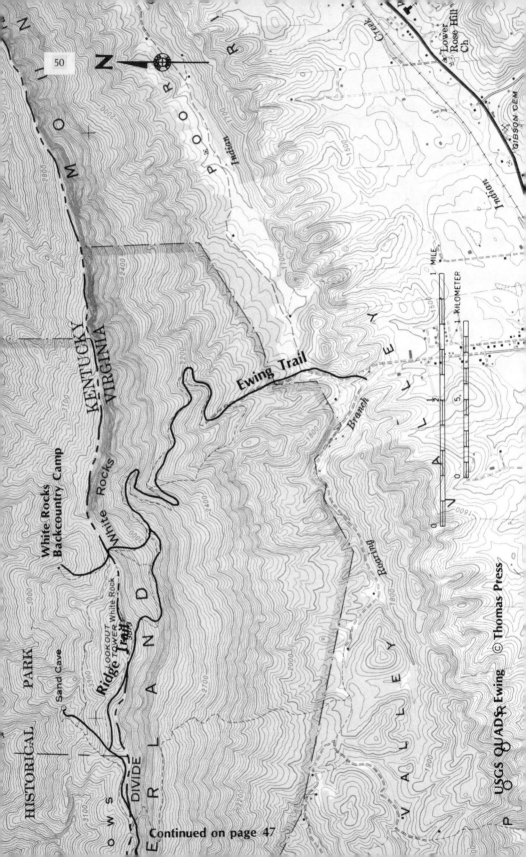

N

HISTORICAL PARK

KENTUCKY
VIRGINIA

CUMBERLAND MOUNTAIN

POOR

Indian

Creek

Lower
Rose Hill
Ch

GIBSON CEM

Indian

Indian

VALLEY

Ewing Trail

Branch

White Rocks
Backcountry Camp

White Rocks

Sand Cave

LOOKOUT White Rock
TOWER

Ridge Trail

White Rock
Trail

CUMBERLAND DIVIDE

Roaring

VALLEY

MEADOWS

MILE

KILOMETER

USGS QUAD: Ewing © Thomas Press

NAME OF TRAIL:	Ewing Trail
MAP ON PAGE:	50
START:	National Park Service boundary, two miles north of Ewing, Virginia, off U.S. 58. Driving from Cumberland Gap, turn left on the street between a barber shop and the People's Bank.
END:	Intersection with Ridge Trail
TRAIL CONNECTIONS:	Ridge Trail, White Rocks Trail
USGS QUADS:	Ewing
COUNTIES:	Lee (VA)
RATING:	Strenuous; 3.9 mi.; logging road and gravel road; +1600 ft.

Ewing Trail is the only hiking trail that provides access to the eastern reaches of the mountaintop park. Its trailhead is at a house east of the Civitan Picnic Area (take the gravel road to the right). White Rocks, a series of rock cliffs along the crest of Cumberland Mountain, looms in the distance. There's plenty of parking space off the graveled access road that leads to the trail. Ewing Trail is a gravel and dirt logging road; its entire length is 3.9 miles. While not as steep as the Chadwell Gap Trail, it nonetheless has some hard climbs and hairpin switchbacks. It ascends 1600 feet from its trailhead to intersection with Ridge Trail. Motorized vehicles of visitors aren't allowed on the trail although backcountry rangers often patrol the road in four-wheel-drive vehicles and sometimes on horseback. Near the trailhead there are two locked gates to prevent people from simply driving up the mountain.

Ewing Trail passes through open woods with some stands of big trees, but for the most part the scenery is nothing to compare with the view from the top. Numerous springs cross the trail and water is plentiful. About a mile from the top there's a narrow, steep footpath branching off to the right that leads to White Rocks. Ewing Trail is well maintained except for a few minor washouts on the steep, hairpin switchbacks.

52

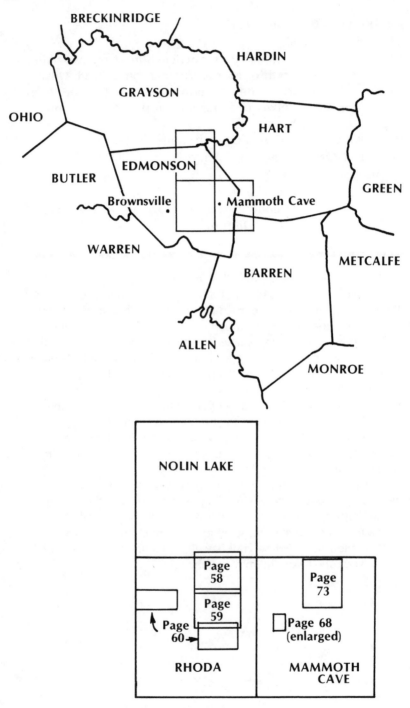

3
Mammoth Cave National Park

 The backpacking and day-hiking trails
in Mammoth Cave National Park,
Kentucky's largest national park, are
probably the most under-publicized
and under-used of all hiking trail systems in the Commonwealth.

For all practical purposes, Mammoth Cave National Park is a day-use
park. This assumption is graphically depicted by the example that during the
month of July, 1978, National Park Service visitor-use statistics indicate that
there were 342,327 visitor days and only 355 of them were spent on the trail
camping in the backcountry. That's clearly less than one percent of all
visitors using the backcountry.

Visitor use is extremely lopsided in the park. As anyone knows who
has ever visited Mammoth Cave in the summer, out-of-state tourists have a
virtual monopoly on the facilities. The rental cottages, motel rooms, campground, and cave tours are booked solid, and the visitors' center is
crowded all day. Mammoth Cave, the largest cave system known to man,
draws millions of visitors each year. The fascinating underground caves,
draped in flowstone and encrusted with stalagmites and stalactites, are a
major drawing card of Kentucky's tourism industry. Yet many people who
visit Mammoth Cave National Park, somehow overlook the fact that the
52,000 acres also contain some fantastic opportunities for hiking.

There are approximately 33 miles of backpacking and day-hiking
trails in Mammoth Cave National Park, 26 miles of which are north of the
Green River in an area that exceeds 20,000 acres and has no visitor developments, i.e., campgrounds, day-use historic points of interest, or picnic
grounds. There are seven hiking trails north of the Green River, and four
short, day-hiking trails near the Visitors' Center.

Backcountry camping is limited to three designated campsites on the
Good Springs Loop Trail and the Nolin and Green River bottoms. Thus, the
only trails in Mammoth Cave National Park that can't be camped overnight
on are the Collie Ridge Trail, Wet Prong of the Buffalo Trail, and the four
day-hiking trails south of the Green River.

As in all of our national parks, backcountry use permits are required for fires or overnight stays. These permits are issued by park rangers at the Visitors' Center (8:00 A.M. to 4:30 P.M. every day) at the main park campground, or at the Maple Springs Ranger Station after hours (if you can catch the ranger at home).

The following are some of the backcountry use rules as set forth by the National Park Service:

Litter—Pack out all nonburnable litter and refuse. **Never bury trash!** Campsites must be cleaned before departure.

Water—Most campsites are located near springs; however, for safety, water should be boiled or treated before drinking. To protect water sources from pollution, camping is prohibited within 50 feet of any well-defined water course or spring.

Fires—A Backcountry Use Permit is required. Fires are to be kindled only in existing fire rings at each campsite. Only down and dead wood may be cut for fire use. Be sure your fire is dead out before leaving it. Use of self-contained stoves is encouraged.

Horses—Horses are permitted only on trails or routes established for their use. Hitching horses within 100 feet of campsites, trails, or water sources is prohibited and hitching within 200 feet of any church, building, or cemetery is also prohibited. Horses must be slowed to walk when passing people on foot and pedestrians shall remain quiet when encountering stock.

Vehicles—All motor vehicles, including motorcycles and bicycles, are prohibited on all trails. All roads north of Green River are of gravel construction and require reduced speeds and extra caution. When parking vehicles, do not block churches, cemeteries, roads, gates, or trailheads.

Pets—Dogs, cats, and other pets must be on a leash or otherwise under physical restrictive control at all times.

Wildlife—All wildlife is protected within the park. Feeding, hunting, or otherwise disturbing wildlife is dangerous and prohibited. The possession or use of firearms or any device capable of discharing a projectile and the use of campsites as base camps for hunting are prohibited.

Caves—Entry into any cave within park boundaries, other than those specifically open for public use, is prohibited.

Insects—Flying insects, such as mosquitoes, are seldom a problem in the park; however, the area supports a high tick population. To minimize problems with ticks and chiggers:

1) Use a good insect repellent each day and reapply it several times a day.
2) Stay on trails. Tick concentrations are highest in brushy areas.

3) Check arms and legs frequently. The best time to remove a tick is **before** being bitten.

Snakes—Rattlesnakes and copperheads occur in the park. Stay
on trails, look before you step, use extra caution gathering firewood. Snakes are protected within park boundaries and are an
important part of the natural community—do not kill them!

Future plans call for the establishment of a 50-mile backpacking trail
that would incorporate some of the existing trails, but would, for the most
part, be a new trail. The proposed trail would circle the backcountry north
of the Green River. The few roadless areas in the park that are ideal for
cross-country hiking are the Bylew Creek and Robbins Branch drainages
on the Nolin Lake topographic quadrangle. Access is best from the Temple
Hill Cemetery on Houchins Ferry Road via the First Creek Lake Trail.

Backcountry visitors at Mammoth Cave National Park are reminded
to sign trail registers when they are encountered. This is so that the National Park Service may more accurately know just how many people are
using the trails. Future development will have to be justified by increased
use of backcountry areas, and trail registers are just about the only way to
keep track of day-use hiking that doesn't require a backcountry permit.
Trail registers are located at the trailheads of the following trails: Collie
Ridge, Wet Prong of the Buffalo, Good Spring Loop, First Creek Lake, and
Big Spring.

Indians of the pre-Columbian era were probably the first persons to
venture into Mammoth Cave. With reed torches as a light source, they
explored the main passageways of the vast underground world. These
prehistoric explorers left behind evidence that archeologists pieced into a
picture of primitive man—piles of ashes, wooden bowls, flint tools,
chipped gypsum deposits, blackened ceilings, and the mummified remains
of those who became lost or trapped and died, their clothing and bones
preserved by the constant temperature and humidity.

With the coming of the white man in the eighteenth century, the story
of Mammoth Cave began to unfold. A hunter trailing a wounded bear is
credited with finding the cave's main entrance, known today as the "historic entrance," in 1798. There is some reason to believe, however, that
passageways and sinks, later substantiated to be part of the Mammoth Cave
and Flint Ridge Cave systems, may have been superficially inspected by
earlier white "long hunters" in the 1770s.

The nineteenth century brought private ownership of the cave and
surrounding lands. The discovery of saltpeter, mixed with the fine, dry cave
dirt, was perhaps responsible for the initial interest in Mammoth Cave. The
embargo imposed by Britain during the War of 1812 made it necessary to
mine the nitrates needed in the manufacturing of gun powder in America

since foreign sources were shut off. If anything, the saltpeter mining operation in Mammoth Cave brought attention to the unique natural attraction
and fostered the idea of promoting it for profit. That possibility materialized
in 1816 when commercially guided tours began, although it was not until
1838 that a daring guide named Stephen Bishop, a black man, crossed
Bottomless Pit, opening the way to discovery of some points of interest that
would make Mammoth Cave a world-renowned tourist attraction.

Increased explorations spawned a period of scientific research in
Mammoth Cave. The first blind cave animal, the Mammoth Cave blindfish
(*Amblyopsis spelaea*), a small, colorless fish lacking pelvic fins, was captured from Echo River and described in literature by the ichtyologist De
Kay in 1838. Dr. John Locke of the Ohio Medical College published the
first description of gypsum cave formation, which opened discussions in
the scientific community about the other minerals found in the cave and
their possible uses. The stable environmental conditions inspired Dr. John
Croghan, master of Locust Grove Plantation in Louisville, to attempt to
establish the cave as a health spa and sanatorium for persons suffering from
consumption. The experiment failed, despite the fact that the air in Mammoth Cave was pure and highly oxygenated.

The grandeur of the cave awed visitors, and soon the word spread all
around the world. Dignitaries, performers, and evangelists flocked to see
the magnificent corridors, underground rivers, and crystalline formations.
Grand Duke Alexis of Russia dined in the banquet hall in 1872; the
"Swedish Nightingale," Jenny Lind, broke the silence, her voice ringing
like a golden chime through nature's greatest opera house. Billy Sunday,
moved by a visit to Mammoth Cave, wrote, "I felt smaller today than I ever
did in my life, there is only one word in the language to describe Mammoth Cave, and that is Mammoth."

Geologists tell us that the process that formed Mammoth Cave began
millions of years ago. As is the case in virtuallly all limestone caves,
subterranean water dissolving porous rock is responsible for the caverns
and the formations. Rainwater containing small amounts of carbonic acid
seeped through sinkholes and joints (fractures in rock layers) eventually
cutting passageways at multiple levels. The upper levels dried out. Then
the seepage, a drop at a time, deposited limestone to form travertine (cave
onyx), stalagmites, stalactites, draperies, and cascading flowstone, as in
Mammoth Cave's Frozen Niagara.

The trickles of underground water finally converged into underground rivers like Echo and Roaring River in Mammoth Cave. The main
passageways of Mammoth Cave were formed near the level of the water
table, therefore the caves do not go farther down than the deepest valley in
the vicinity cut by the Green River.

Mammoth Cave was the first known cave to contain gypsum, which is formed in the drier passageways of the upper levels by the slow leaching of calcium sulfate through porous limestone. The gypsum crystals, which form in beautiful patterns, crust the ceiling of the cave. In other areas, the roof has either collapsed forming sinks, or, in lower passageways, enlarging rooms with convex "domes," or deep pits between parallel passageways.

Unique formations that occur in Mammoth Cave include helictites, a form of stalactite that turns up at the tip; lily pads, an irregular deposit around a pool of standing water; and gypsum crusts of "flowers," as found in the Snowball Dining Room.

The years of private ownership of Mammoth Cave displeased many individuals who argued that property mismanagement and a complex trustee arrangement of ownership were responsible for decreased visitation after the turn of the century. As early as 1870, though, there had been public grumblings against private ownership of Kentucky's greatest natural resource. And about 1905, the matter was initially taken up with the Department of Interior through requests that the area become a national park. It was not until 1923 that a survey and discussion within the agency on the feasibility of such a park actually began. In July 1925 the park's spearhead group, the Mammoth Cave National Park Commission, was incorporated. By May 1934 the condemnation and purchase of lands for the park had begun, and two years later the park came under jurisdiction of the National Park Service. Mammoth Cave National Park was formally declared open to visitors on September 18, 1946 when it officially became the nation's twenty-sixth national park. Since almost half the land was either in cleared fields and eroded soil banks, a complete reforestation plan was initiated, with a major portion of the work done by the CCC (Civilian Conservation Corps).

Mammoth Cave National Park is located almost halfway between Elizabethtown and Bowling Green, Kentucky, off Interstate 65. Access is via U.S. 31W, KY 259, KY 70, KY 728, and KY 1827. Mailing address: Mammoth Cave National Park, Mammoth Cave, Kentucky 42259. (502) 758-2251.

58

Mammoth Cave Ferry Road

N

728

BM
850

Lincoln Sch

MAMMOTH CAVE NATIONAL PARK

Raymond

Collie Ridge Trail

RIDGE

Hollow

Connecting Trail

Blue Springs Branch

Boiling Spring

Big Spring

MAMMOTH CAVE NATIONAL PARK

NAT PARK

Ollie

Ollie

Blue Spring

Jaggers Cem

Houchins Ferry Road

Wet Prong of the

Buffalo Trail

Sand Spring Cem

Hollow

Continued on page 59

USGS QUADS: Nolin Lake, Rhoda   © Thomas Press

MILE
KILOMETER

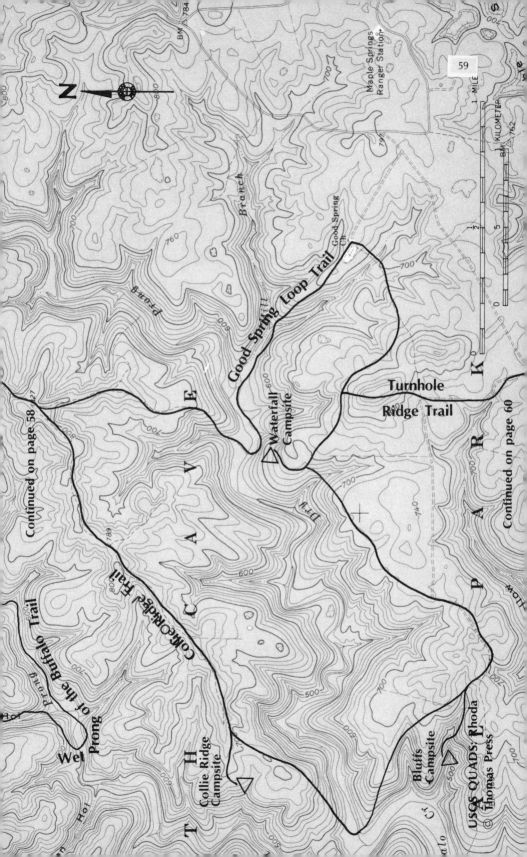

Maple Springs
Ranger Station

Good Spring
Ch

Good Spring Loop Trail

Turnhole
Ridge Trail

Waterfall
Campsite

Branch

Prong

Continued on page 58

Continued on page 60

Buffalo Trail

Wet Prong

Hol

Prong of the

Collie Ridge Trail

Collie Ridge
Campsite

Bluffs
Campsite

USGS QUADS: Rhoda
© Thomas Press

1 MILE

KILOMETER

Dry

C A V E   P A R K

T H

BM △ 784

N

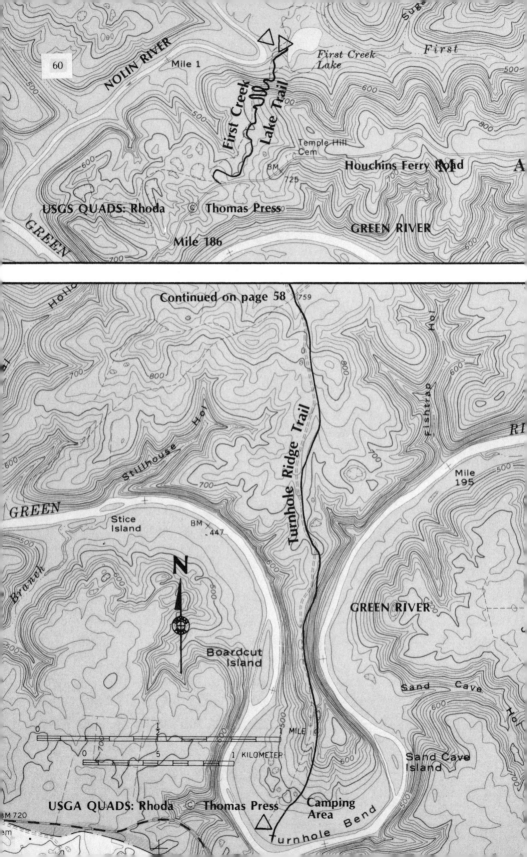

60

NOLIN RIVER

Mile 1

First Creek Lake Trail

First Creek Lake

First

Sug

500

600

800

Temple Hill Cem

Houchins Ferry Road

A

BM 725

GREEN

USGS QUADS: Rhoda   © Thomas Press

Mile 186

GREEN RIVER

600

700

Continued on page 58

759

700

800

Hol

800

Ho Ho

700

Stillhouse Hol

700

600

Turnhole Ridge Trail

700

Fishtrap Hol

600

RI

Mile 195

500

GREEN

Stice Island

BM X .447

N

600

GREEN RIVER

Branch

Boardcut Island

500

Sand Cave Hol

Sand Cave Island

MILE

0   1/2   1 MILE

0   .5   1 KILOMETER

600

500

USGA QUADS: Rhoda   © Thomas Press

Camping Area

BM 720

Turnhole Bend

NAME OF TRAIL: Collie Ridge Trail
MAP ON PAGE: 58–59
START: Lincoln School (now auto parts store) at
                      Ollie, 0.2 miles south of intersection of KY
                      728 and KY 1827 at the Mammoth Cave Na-
                      tional Park boundary
END: Intersection with Good Spring Loop Trail
TRAIL CONNECTIONS: Wet Prong of the Buffalo Trail and Good
                      Spring Loop Trail
USGS QUADS: Nolin Lake and Rhoda
COUNTIES: Edmonson
RATING: Easy; 5.0 mi.; logging road; +100 ft.

The oldest of the hiking trails in Mammoth Cave National Park, Collie
Ridge Trail is a five-mile-long ridgetop trace that has two distinct purposes
as part of the system of backpacking and day-hiking trails north of the
Green River. First of all, the Collie Ridge Trail connects the extreme northern boundary of the park with the internal trail system; and secondly, it ties
together the two most important trails—the Wet Prong of the Buffalo and
the Good Spring Loop Trail.

The Collie Ridge Trail is almost flat, and about ninety-five percent of
it is a logging road. There's no water available along the trail. The five
miles of old roadbed includes the 1.2-mile-long connecting trail described
in the section about the Wet Prong of the Buffalo Trail, and a 1.7-mile loop
of forest roads between Collie Ridge campsite (on the Good Spring Loop
Trail), and Good Spring Church. The Collie Ridge Trail is basically in the
shape of a "Y" with a circle at its base.

NAME OF TRAIL: Wet Prong of the Buffalo Trail
MAP ON PAGE: 58–59
START: Jaggers Cemetery on Houchins Ferry Road,
                        one mile south of Ollie, off KY 728
END: Jaggers Cemetery
TRAIL CONNECTIONS: Collie Ridge Trail
USGS QUADS: Rhoda
COUNTIES: Edmonson
RATING: Moderate; 3.0 mi.; footpath and logging
                        road; +200 ft.

Wet Prong of the Buffalo Trail is a 3-mile loop best hiked clockwise. The first 0.3 miles of the trail is a logging road that parallels Jaggers Cemetery, the trailhead. When you come to the split in the trail, bear to the left. The footpath (blazed with red tape) is relatively well maintained except for a few overgrown sections in the creek bottoms east of Blue Spring, which bubbles up from the ground at a rock ledge beside the trail. The spring is a year-round source of water and a welcome sight at the beginning of the hike, although it's soon evident that water availability is no problem on this trail.

The descent to the creek is easy and takes hikers through open woods of mixed deciduous trees. After crossing the creek, the trail ascends slightly and begins to parallel it amid rich beech woods with ferns as the understory. There's some damage to the trail from use by horses. Approximately 1.1 miles east of Jaggers Cemetery, the trail forks again. If you take the trail to the left, it is 1.2 miles to the junction with Collie Ridge Trail. This connecting trail parallels Blair Springs Branch on its left bank going upstream, then crosses at a shallow ford. There's a steep-to-moderate climb for several hundred yards; the trail eventually widens to a logging road as it levels off in open woods of pine and mixed hardwoods. At one point, to the right of the trail, there's a view through the trees of Collie Ridge. At the junction with Collie Ridge Trail, Lincoln is 1.7 miles to the left, and Good Spring Church is 2.6 miles to the right.

Continuing on the Wet Prong of the Buffalo Trail, Wildcat Hollow is 1.8 miles to the right (south). After crossing Blair Springs Branch at its confluence with the main creek (Wet Prong of the Buffalo), the trail snakes through the creek bottoms. Solomon's seal, cinnamon ferns, and mountain laurel are abundant. Crossing the creek numerous times, it is a beautiful walk. At times the trail is overgrown (poison ivy everywhere!) and there are numerous deadfalls that must be walked around. Ascending slightly, the trail follows the hillside overlooking the creek, then it passes numerous rock outcroppings.

The creek bottoms are lush with ferns, and it's easy to walk quietly. At one turn in the trail, three deer, feeding in the underbrush, bounded off ahead of me. The next stream crossing has an ideal swimming hole. At one point the trail skirts a clearing grown up in cedars and sumac, another good place to see deer in the morning or late afternoon.

At this point the trail leaves the creek and then descends back to it, finally ascending once again, this time through an overgrown field. Wildcat Hollow is a narrow gorge through which the creek flows. The last several hundred yards of the trail are logging road. From the creek bottoms to the Jaggers Cemetery you ascend 200 feet. Although there's plenty of room for camping along the Wet Prong of the Buffalo Trail, National Park Service backcountry rules forbid it. The closest designated backcountry camp is on the Good Spring Loop Trail at the Collie Ridge campsite. From the trailhead of the Wet Prong of the Buffalo Trail to Good Spring Church it's 4.9 miles. The Wet Prong of the Buffalo Trail is by far the most beautiful hike in the park.

NAME OF TRAIL:	Good Spring Loop Trail
MAP ON PAGE:	59
START:	Trailhead at Good Spring Baptist Church, west of Maple Springs Ranger Station off Mammoth Cave Ferry Road
END:	Good Spring Baptist Church
TRAIL CONNECTIONS:	Wet Prong of the Buffalo Trail and the Turnhole Ridge Trail
USGS QUADS:	Rhoda
COUNTIES:	Edmonson
RATING:	Moderate; 7.7 mi.; footpath and logging road; +400 ft.

At the present time the Good Spring Loop Trail is the only trail in the park well suited for weekend trips. The loop is 7.7 miles long and could easily be hiked in one day, but when I hiked it, I decided to spend the night on the trail so I could enjoy a leisurely pace.

The trailhead is at Good Spring Baptist Church, which was established in 1842. Many of the region's first settlers are buried in a small cemetery beside the church, which isn't used for services now. The hiking is relatively easy, and the loop is well marked and maintained. In the first 1.4 miles, the trail crosses two spring-fed creeks and follows ridgetop open woods until it descends along a cliffline to the Waterfall Campsite, the first of three backcountry overnight sites designated along the loop. During the summer there's not much of a waterfall, but there's plenty of cool spring water available. Space for tents is limited because there just isn't much flat ground, but the campsite is an excellent place for a lunch break. All of the three campsites are reached by short approach trails off the main loop.

The section of trail between Waterfall and Bluffs Campsite doesn't have water along it, so it's best to fill up your canteens before hitting the trail. This 1.6-mile section of the loop goes through ridgetop woods and fields that are grown up now but were once used for pasturing stock when the land was under private ownership. Part of this section of the trail is abandoned logging roads. The Bluffs Campsite is tucked away beside a cliffline near the mouth of Buffalo Creek amid a sizeable stand of beech trees. When you first walk on the campsite, there's a small waterfall, an ideal source of drinking water and just about perfect for showering in the buff. But if you value your privacy, it might not be a bad idea to post a sentry on the approach trail because there's no way you can see anybody hiking into the campsite. The water sputters off a fifteen-foot rock bluff and is icy cold, making it a perfect refresher for hot and sweaty hikers. There's room enough for four to five tents in the Bluffs Campsite farther back beyond the big boulder just past the waterfall.

The 1.5-mile section of trail between Bluffs and Collie Ridge Campsite is by far the most demanding on the loop. The trail follows ridgetops along numerous sandstone overhangs (ideal for quick refuge from thunderstorm) and then descends into the Dry Prong of the Buffalo Creek bottoms. The creek was appropriately named, too, because most of the year it's bone dry. There's no drinking water to be found anywhere along this section of the trail. After crossing the creek and snaking through heavy weeds, the trail sharply ascends to Collie Ridge, a wide, high ridge that divides the northern reaches of the park. Collie Ridge Campsite is by far the roomiest of the three backcountry camps. It sits atop a spur of the ridge, and has a fine little spring beside it that is an excellent water source.

The 3.2-mile hike back to Good Spring Church is enjoyable because a good bit of it is along the Mill Branch of Buffalo Creek, a picturesque stream that winds through canebreaks and dense woodlands. While hiking this trail, I saw several deer. Water is scarce along this section of the trail.

NAME OF TRAIL:	Turnhole Ridge Trail
MAP ON PAGE:	59, 60
START:	Trailhead 0.6 miles west of Good Spring Baptist Church on Good Spring Loop Trail
END:	Ends at Turnhole Bend of Green River
TRAIL CONNECTIONS:	Good Spring Loop Trail
USGS QUADS:	Rhoda
COUNTIES:	Edmonson
RATING:	Easy; 3.2 mi.; footpath and logging road; −300 ft.

The Turnhole Ridge Trail was built for horseback riding, but it is also used by backpackers. It is well maintained; trail crews of the Youth Conservation Corps (YCC) cleared the entire trail in the summer of 1978. More than half of the 3.2 miles is logging road that follows a ridge; there's no water along the trail. The entire trail is blazed with blue and red tape. The Turnhole Ridge Trail is relatively level and easy. It passes through a few stretches of open woods (some with big trees), but for the most part it parallels overgrown fields. Near the trail's end it descends into the river bottom, which is overgrown with weeds; camping space is limited to the sandy riverbank. The only water source is the river. High mud banks make access difficult.

NAME OF TRAIL: First Creek Lake Trail
MAP ON PAGE: 60
START: Temple Hill Cemetery on Houchins Ferry
                        Road, five miles south of Ollie, off KY 728
END: First Creek Lake
TRAIL CONNECTIONS: None
USGS QUADS: Rhoda
COUNTIES: Edmonson
RATING: Moderate; 2.3 mi.; footpath; −300 ft.

First Creek Lake Trail descends 300 feet 2.3 miles from the parking area at Temple Hill Cemetery to the Nolin River bottoms. It provides access to one of the most popular backcountry areas in Mammoth Cave National Park.

The Green River flows through the center of the park, and most of its tributaries, as well as those creeks draining into the lower end of the Nolin River, have good populations of muskellunge, bass, catfish, crappie, and panfish (bluegill, longear sunfish, warmouth, and green sunfish). Some of the best fishing is at First Creek Lake, a natural lake tucked away in the forested river bottoms in the northwestern tip of the park.

The ten-acre, spring-fed lake may be reached by boat from Houchins Ferry on the Green River by motoring two miles downstream, then turning right at the mouth of the Nolin River.

First Creek is approximately 1½ miles upstream to the right. To reach the lake, boaters must then run the narrow creek channel for a couple of hundred yards. There's usually enough water in the creek to run it in the spring. During the summer and fall, the creek and lake nearly dry up.

The hike into First Creek Lake is an enjoyable one. The footpath winds through ridgetop oak and hickory woods. Deer sign is everywhere, and the trail is lined with ferns and wildflowers. We identified seven or eight species of blooming wildflowers, including May apple, wild ginger, stonecrop, and bluets. After skirting the cliffline, the trail becomes a series of switchbacks and finally parallels the Nolin River along its high mud banks.

The lower reaches of the trail are lined with huge beech trees. There's a footbridge over First Creek, so fishers don't have to walk all the way around the lake to get to deep banks on the lower end of the lake where most of the good fishing is.

Backwater from the Nolin River naturally restocks the lake each spring, and it is an important spawning ground for rough fish and game fish alike. At high water, the lake extends back into the shoreline timber creating great cover for spawning bass and crappie.

The shallows where creek channels enter the lake seem alive with fish. The female bass we caught were full of eggs and just ready to go on the nest. It appeared that the carp were spawning because they were thrashing around in the heads of tiny creeks draining into the lake, muddying up the water as they always do.

As in all of our national parks, statewide fishing licenses are required, and fire permits (available at the Visitors' Center) must be issued to all overnight campers. Worms are the only form of live bait that may be legally used in the lake, but digging for them within the park boundary is prohibited. Trotlines and throwlines are legal as long as the hooks are spaced no closer than 30 inches apart.

Wading the flooded timber in hip boots, casting jigs and minnowlike surface lures among the drift, is an excellent way to pick up crappie and bass. Jigging artificial lures with a long cane pole from the bank could also be effective, although fishing from a boat is by far the best method for filling the stringer.

Take along plenty of mosquito dope as the shallow water is perfect breeding ground for those pesky little critters. The fringes of the lake are grown up in weeds; the best camping is on the east bank where spring water is available most of the year from First Creek. It's not shown on the topographic quadrangle (Rhoda), but there's a spring (year-round water source) on the west bank of the lake, but the area is too swampy for camping.

NAME OF TRAIL: Cave Island Nature Trail
MAP ON PAGE: 68
START: Historic Entrance of Mammoth Cave
END: Historic Entrance of Mammoth Cave
TRAIL CONNECTIONS: Green River Bluffs Trail and Echo River Trail
USGS QUADS: Mammoth Cave
COUNTIES: Edmonson
RATING: Easy; 0.9 mi.; footpath; −200 ft.

Cave Island Nature Trail is a nine-tenths-mile loop trail that descends 200 feet from the cliffs to the Green River. Along this trail day-hikers discover pockets of huge trees—towering beech, sycamore, and oak. The entrance to Dixon Cave is passed before the trail parallels the river. Dixon Cave is a winter hibernation roost for Indiana bats, an endangered species. There are numerous dirt side trails that provide access to the river for bank fishing. The river is drawn to a narrow chute between Cave Island and the southern bank of the Green River at the site of the first Mammoth Cave Ferry where small steamboats from Evansville once delivered passengers. One hundred-ninety-eight miles above the mouth of the river, and 172 miles from its source, the old Mammoth Cave Ferry was the farthest upstream that the packet boats could travel. A small footbridge must be crossed along the trail, although water availability is seasonal at best.

NAME OF TRAIL: Green River Bluffs Trail
MAP ON PAGE: 68
START: Picnic area across the parking lot from Visi-
                        tors' Center
END: Intersection with Cave Island Nature Trail
TRAIL CONNECTIONS: Cave Island Nature Trail
USGS QUADS: Mammoth Cave
COUNTIES: Edmonson
RATING: Easy; 0.9 mi.; paved trail; −100 ft.

The Green River Bluffs Trail is a nine-tenths-mile, paved day-hiking trail
that provides casual walkers with scenic views of the Green River and the
rolling forested hills in the distance. The easy, relatively flat trail follows
the ridgetop overlooking the river; there are numerous big beech, pignut
hickory, and oak trees along the trail. When I hiked it in late September,
the treetops were alive with squirrels cutting nuts. At the first of two scenic
overlooks there is a bench for resting. Other trail improvements include
guard rails, steps, and crossbars (erosion preventive devices). No water is
available along the trail. Stretches of the trail are quite charming. Rock
outcroppings and boulder fields are draped in ferns.

NAME OF TRAIL:	Echo River Trail
MAP ON PAGE:	68
START:	Parking area at Mammoth Cave Ferry on Green River Road
END:	Parking area at Mammoth Cave Ferry on Green River Road
TRAIL CONNECTIONS:	Cave Island Nature Trail and Sunset Point Trail
USGS QUADS:	Mammoth Cave
COUNTIES:	Edmonson
RATING:	Moderate; 2.25 mi.; footpath and gravel road; +200 ft.

The Echo River Trail is a 2.25-mile gravel and dirt loop trail that is the most interesting of the four day-hiking trails south of the Green River. The highlights of the trail are the River Styx Spring, Echo River Spring, Whites Cave, and Mammoth Dome Sink.

Hiking counterclockwise, the first point of interest is the Echo River Spring, where Echo River emerges from Mammoth Cave. Rainwater and melting snow from miles around drain into sinkholes to feed this watercourse. Access to the spring is difficult because of high mud banks. After paralleling the river through towering forests, the trail reaches River Styx Spring, which bubbles from the ground. A rock amphitheater surrounds the spring. River Styx Spring is one of several springs that flow from the honey-combed passageways beneath the ground. At highwater periods, backwater from the Green River is forced back into Mammoth Cave; at low water, the spring trickles to the river. The trail ascends to the next points of interest—two overlooks behind Sunset Lodge. Then the trail descends, skirting the cliffline through open woods of mixed deciduous trees. To the left of the trail is Mammoth Dome Sink through which water drains into the Mammoth Cave. Visitors on the Historic Cave Tour Trail pass the point where water falls 192 feet from the Mammoth Dome Sink into the Echo River.

After passing Mammoth Dome Sink, the trail continues through towering forests, then crosses a ridgetop clearing for a powerline right-of-way. The entrance to White's Cave is on the left. The cave is blocked to visitors by an iron gate, both to protect visitors from potential dangers (reptiles and mammals that seek the cool air), and to protect the cave from vandalism. White's Cave is a short (approximately 200 feet long), dead-end passageway. From White's Cave to the river, the trail descends through rock outcroppings and cedars mixed with hardwoods. A one-mile trail to the left connects the Echo River Trail with the park's campground adjacent to the Visitors' Center.

NAME OF TRAIL: Sunset Point Trail
MAP ON PAGE: 68
START: Mammoth Cave Hotel
END: Sunset Point
TRAIL CONNECTIONS: Echo River Trail
USGS QUADS: Mammoth Cave
COUNTIES: Edmonson
RATING: Easy; 0.3 mi.; paved trail; −100 ft.

The Sunset Point Trail is an easy three-tenths-mile paved trail whose only real point of interest is the Old Guide's Cemetery. Commercially guided tours began in 1816, but it wasn't until 1838 that a daring black guide named Stephen Bishop crossed Bottomless Pit, thus beginning the golden age of exploration in Mammoth Cave. Other slaves who gained fame as guides were Matt and Nick Bransford. Generations of famous guides are buried in this cemetery. For over a hundred years members of this "first family" of guides escorted visitors through Mammoth Cave.

The trail ends at Sunset Point, an overlook. No water is available along this ridgetop trail, which passes through mixed hardwoods and cedar thickets.

HARD CO.
EDMONSON CO.

Big Woods

Wilson Cave Hollo

Wilson Cave

Ugly Creek Road

Cem.

Cem

N

Little Jordan

Big Spring Hollow

Houchin Hol

Dennison Ferry Trail

BM
38

Big Spring Trail

800

GREEN

NORMAL POOL ELEV 421

Mile
205

Great Onyx
Cave

737

Great Onyx Cave
Pumphouse

Three Sisters
Island

Dennison Ferry

Three Sisters Hol

Pike Spring

Cave

Crystal
Cave

Flint Ridge
Ranger Station

Cave

Daniels Cem

0   ½   1 MILE

Collins
Spring

0
KILOMETER

Athletic
Field

Great Onyx Job Corps
Conservation Center

Cave

USGS QUADS: Mammoth Cave   © Thomas Press

Sewage Disposal
Ponds

ransford
mphouse

Bransford Spring   Blair Spring   Water Tank
                                                  ookout Tower

NAME OF TRAIL: Dennison Ferry Trail
MAP ON PAGE: 73
START: One mile east of Little Jordan Cemetery on
                        Ugly Creek Road, off Mammoth Cave Ferry
                        Road east of Stockholm
END: Green River, mile 205
TRAIL CONNECTIONS: None
USGS QUADS: Mammoth Cave
COUNTIES: Edmonson
RATING: Easy; 3.5 mi.; footpath and logging road;
                        −420 ft.

The Dennison Ferry Trail is similar to the Turnhole Ridge Trail in that it is a ridgetop logging road that descends to the Green River. Approximately 3.5 miles long and descending 420 feet, the Dennison Ferry Trail passes through mixed hardwoods, cedar thickets, and overgrown fields. There's no water along the trail. Near the river, the trail narrows to a footpath. Weeds along the river make camping less than ideal. There's no trail register at the trailhead, which can be easily driven past. The trailhead is distinguished by a small loop parking area off the Ugly Creek Road. A locked cable gate keeps motorists from simply driving to the river.

NAME OF TRAIL: Big Spring Trail
MAP ON PAGE: 73
START: Little Jordan Cemetery on Ugly Creek Road,
                      three miles east of Mammoth Cave Ferry
                      Road at Stockholm
END: Green River, mile 203
TRAIL CONNECTIONS: None
USGS QUADS: Mammoth Cave
COUNTIES: Edmonson
RATING: Moderate; 1.0 mi.; footpath; −280 ft.

Big Spring Trail is one mile long and descends 280 feet. It is difficult, if not impossible, at times to follow because of poor flagging and no trail improvement whatsoever. Big Spring Creek provides an adequate water source year-round, but camping is hampered by weeds. The trail passes through ridgetop woodlands (mixed hardwoods and cedar thickets), then plunges to the river bottom. It's difficult to follow the trail through rock outcroppings atop the ridge because one of the flagged trees has been blown over. It's easy to lose your way at that point. A hiking staff is useful on the steeper sections of the trail. Deer and squirrel sign are abundant. Striped pipsissewa is one of the summer wildflowers noted when hiking this trail.

76

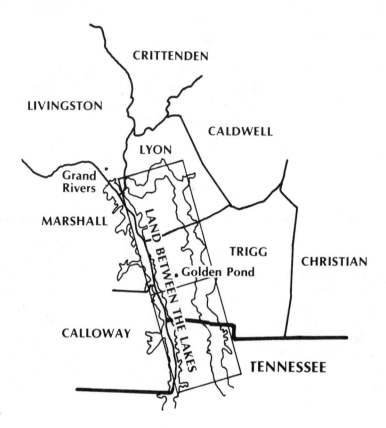

(A complete map of the Land Between the Lakes showing the North-South Trail is found on page 80.)

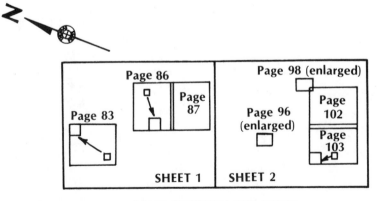

LAND BETWEEN THE LAKES

4
Land Between the Lakes

The Tennessee Valley Authority's 170,000-acre Land Between the Lakes (LBL), in western Kentucky and Tennessee, offers some excellent opportunities for day-hiking and backpacking although a surprising number of people think all you can do there is hunt, fish (in Lake Barkley and Kentucky Lake), and camp.

There really are some excellent trails in the vast outdoor demonstration area, which is a shining model of the wise use of natural resources for outdoor recreation. The management concept of LBL is not preservation, but rather revitalization and use of natural resources for outdoor recreation and environmental education. That concept covers a lot of ground and diverse recreational life-styles. Hiking is just a part of what's going on in LBL. The hard-core preservationists may be turned off by the fact that there's no scenery in LBL equal to our national forests and parks—no raging white-water rivers, natural rock arches, or towering waterfalls. The huge tracts of oak–hickory woodlands are interrupted by powerlines, pipelines, gravel roads, campgrounds, open lands, and agricultural and timber harvest lands. The hiker interested strictly in "wilderness experiences" in their truest sense probably wouldn't enjoy hiking in LBL, but the 151 miles of trail are quite impressive.

The LBL hiking experience is one that shouldn't be overlooked by the serious hiker. There are so many square miles of just nothing but woods and lakeshore that it would take a person a lifetime to explore it all on foot. The spaciousness of LBL can't be stressed enough. Also, with such an abundance of wildlife, the possibility of sighting waterfowl, eagles, deer, beaver, songbirds, birds of prey, mammals, and reptiles while hiking in LBL is so good that each hike is practically a field biology lesson.

The secret to having good hikes in LBL is to be there when you'll have the whole place to yourself—in late winter and early spring, before the April turkey-hunting season and the summer tourist season. Another advantage to hiking in the early spring is that the woods will be clear of worrisome vegetation. The hiking will be easier and visibility is much improved. And besides, spring is the season for wildflowers; and you won't have to worry about insects because it's still too cold.

The most pesky insects are of course ticks, and LBL has an incredible number of them. It's partly because of the high population of mammals there. TVA personnel have been working on ways to curtail the tick population so that summer hiking will be less of a hazard. Ticks cause .discomfort more than anything else, but in rare cases they can cause serious diseases (Rocky Mountain spotted fever).

All hikers in LBL are requested to check in at any one of the three information centers (two miles south of Barkley Canal on the Trace, at Golden Pond, or on the Trace north of U.S. 79 in Tennessee), to report their trip itinerary. Likewise, hikers are asked to check out so that all groups may be accounted for. Topographic maps of LBL and a trail brochure are available at all three information centers. The basic rules for hiking trails in LBL are: 1) pack out all garbage; 2) horses and motor vehicles are not allowed on trails; 3) hunting is allowed during legal seasons with proper state license and LBL permits; 4) sidearms are prohibited; 5) trailside water is not safe for human consumption without proper treatment; 6) plants and flowers should be left for others to enjoy; 7) campfires are permitted anytime except during periods of high fire danger; 8) overnight camping is allowed at informal use areas or at trailside only, but there is no camping at family or group campgrounds during hikes; 9) don't cut live trees or bushes for firewood; and 10) there is a limit of one night at any campsite along the trail.

In all, there are fourteen trail systems: 13 miles of trail in the 5,000-acre Environmental Education Center; 38 miles in the three family and two group camps; 14 miles in the Canal Loop Trail System; 26 miles in the Fort Henry Trail System, and the 60-mile North–South Trail, the longest trail in LBL.

Sun in plants. Photograph by Kalman Papp.

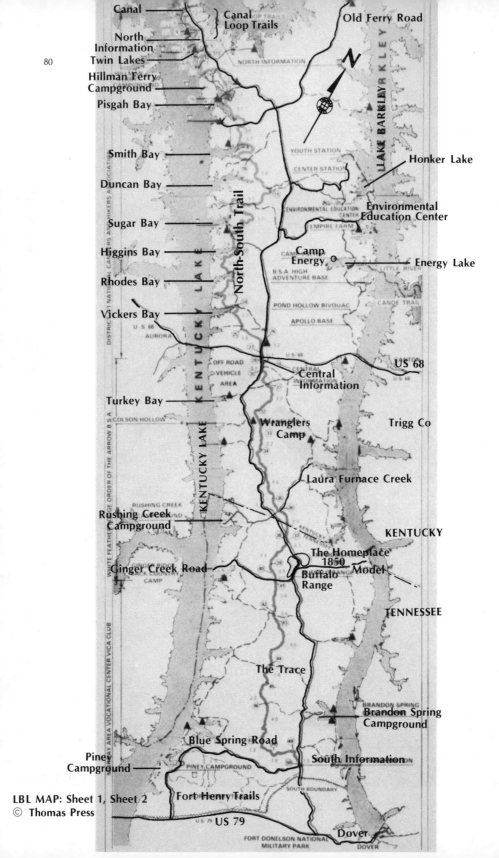

80

Canal

Canal Loop Trails

North Information

Twin Lakes

Hillman Ferry Campground

Pisgah Bay

Smith Bay

Duncan Bay

Sugar Bay

Higgins Bay

Rhodes Bay

Vickers Bay

Turkey Bay

Rushing Creek Campground

Ginger Creek Road

Piney Campground

Old Ferry Road

LAKE BARKLEY

Honker Lake

Environmental Education Center

Camp Energy

Energy Lake

US 68

Central Information

Trigg Co

Wranglers Camp

Laura Furnace Creek

KENTUCKY

The Homeplace 1850 Model

Buffalo Range

TENNESSEE

The Trace

Brandon Spring Campground

Blue Spring Road

South Information

Fort Henry Trails

Dover

US 79

North-South Trail

KENTUCKY LAKE

NAME OF TRAIL:	North–South Trail
MAP ON PAGE:	80
START:	Circular parking lot to the left of Kentucky Lake Drive at Kentucky Lake–Lake Barkley Canal
END:	South End Information Station
TRAIL CONNECTIONS:	Barkley Trial, Boy Scout Trail, and Fort Henry Trail System
USGS QUADS:	TVA Land Between the Lakes (Sheets 1 and 2)
COUNTIES:	Lyon, Trigg (KY) and Steward (TN)
RATING:	Strenuous; 60.0 mi.; footpath and logging road; +200 ft.

At this writing, the North–South Trail is the second longest continuous backpacking trail in Kentucky. The 60-mile (96.5-km) trail spans the entire length of the 170,000-acre national recreation area. The trail is blazed with a white Boy Scout symbol.

Dedicated in November 1977, the North–South Trail follows sections of an age-old route farmers took when they drove their stock to river ports on the Cumberland river in the 1800s. The trail was built with funds from CETA (Comprehensive Education and Training Act) and TVA at Land Between the Lakes. The actual flagging and cutting of the trail was done by TVA staff, members of Kentucky Lake Chapter of the National Campers and Hikers Association, Four-Rivers Boy Scout Council, and students from a vocational school in Murray. Trail maintenance is shared by the three groups that assisted TVA in the trail's construction.

The North–South Trail hasn't received as much attention by the hiking public as it deserves. Apparently only a handful of people have ever hiked the trail from beginning to end. When I went to the trailhead and examined the trail register, there was an active wasp nest under the eaves of the trail marker where the clipboard register was stashed. Perhaps that was why there was only one hiker's name and address listed.

The trail has two distinctive sections: the canal to U.S. 68, and U.S. 68 to the South End Information Station. The northern 34-mile (55.0-km) section of the trail is characterized by numerous lake views, rocky lakeshore, and hilly woods south of Sugar Bay. The trail passes through four lake access areas (Twin Lakes, Pisgah Bay, Smith Bay, and Sugar Bay) and one family campground (Hillman Ferry). An elaborate system of numbered signs along the trail pinpoints the hiker's location.

Treated drinking water is available on the northern section of the trail at trail sign locations 6, 14, 17, 21, and at the North End Information

Station. Water from the lake and feeder streams is considered unfit for human consumption without treatment. Points of interest on the first half of the trail include Pisgah and Smith bays, both waterfowl refuges, and Duncan Bay, an eagle santuary, that is closed to all activity from November 1 to March 31.

The 26-mile (41.5-km) section of the trail south of U.S. 68 practically follows the ridgetop divide between streams flowing east to Lake Barkley and west to Kentucky Lake. The North–South Trail parallels The Trace to the east until trail sign 37 at the Kentucky–Tennessee line where it crosses the paved highway. The North–South Trail remains west of The Trace all the way to its end at the South Information Station west of Dover, Tennessee, off U.S. 79. There are no sites where treated drinking water is available on the southern portion of the trail, and, during dry months, hikers are hard pressed to find natural water sources, springs, and creeks. Points of interest on the southern half of the trail include: Turkey Creek Off-Road Vehicle Area, a 2,500-acre area set aside for dirt bikes and four-wheel-drive vehicles; Wrangler's Camp, located in Lick Creek Valley with 25 miles of horse trail, barns, and camping facilities; The Homeplace 1850, a restored farm museum and center for primitive crafts study; the Buffalo Range, near the former site of Model, Tennessee, a center for iron making (Great Western Iron Furnace) and moonshine distribution; and the Fort Henry Trail System, a twenty-six-mile series of loop trails that connect with the North–South Trail. Probably the best way to beat the water shortage on the southern section of the trail is to stash plastic gallon jugs of water along the route before hiking it. This is an established method of solving water shortages, and is often used by long-distance backpackers. There are a few springs along the trail in the vicinity of Turkey and Laura Furnace creeks, but beyond Ginger Creek Road the trail is high and dry. The gain in elevation from north to south along the trail is approximately 200 feet; the lakeshore sections are about 400 feet above sea level.

Hikers on the North–South Trail experience the full diversity of land forms and forest types, recreational facilities, and historic sites of the LBL. Since all of LBL is divided into management units that are constantly in use, the trail passes through a series of open lands, agricultural lands, reverting fields, stands of hardwoods, and lakeshore (northern section of the trail).

Some general rules recommended by TVA for hiking the North–South Trail are as follows: (1) All hikers must register at either North, Central, or South Information Station; (2) Carry out all garbage; (3) Horses and motorized vehicles are prohibited; (4) Don't molest animals or plantlife; (5) Use only downed wood for campfires, don't cut live trees.

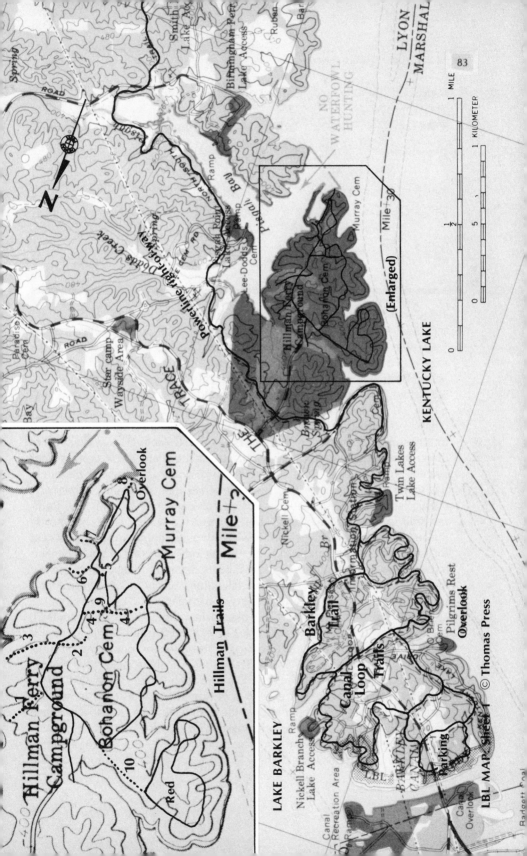

LYON
MARSHALL

83

Spring

ROAD

N

Powerline/Fishin' Way Dodds Creek

Paradise Cem

Bay

ROAD

THE TRACE

Smith

Lake Acc

Birmingham Ferry Lake Access

Ruben

Bar

NORTH Kuttawa

Camp

Outback

Ramp

Lee-Dodds
Cem

Piegali Bay

Murray Cem

Mile 30

(Enlarged)

KENTUCKY LAKE

NO WATERFOWL HUNTING

1   MILE

1   KILOMETER

½

5   1

0

Hillman Ferry Campground

Bohanon Cem

Bohanon Spring

Cem

Nickell Cem

Ramp

Twin Lakes
Lake Access

Star camp
Wayside Area

8 Overlook
7
6   5
9
4   4
2
10
Red
3

Murray Cem

Bohanon Cem

Hillman Ferry Campground

Hillman Trails

Mile 2

LAKE BARKLEY

Nickell Branch
Lake Access

Canal
Recreation Area

Ramp

Br

Information Station

Barkley

Br

Trail

Canal
Loop
Trails

Pilgrims Rest
Overlook

Parking

DRIVE

BARKLEY CANAL

LBL

Canal
Overlook

LBL MAP Sheet 1

© Thomas Press

Ramp

NAME OF TRAIL: Canal Loop Trail System
MAP ON PAGE: 83
START: Parking area on Kentucky Lake Drive (circular gravel lot)
END: North Information Station on the Trace (formerly KY 453)
TRAIL CONNECTIONS: North–South Trail
USGS QUADS: TVA Land Between the Lakes topographic map (Sheet 1)
COUNTIES: Lyon
RATING: Moderate; 14.2 mi.; footpath; −80 ft.

The Canal Loop Trail System is a 14.2-mile system that includes the Barkley Trail (9.9 miles), and four short connectors, all of which link Barkley Trail with the North–South Trail. **Barkley Trail** begins across Kentucky Lake Drive from the circular parking area, which is the trailhead of North–South Trail. The gravel lot overlooks the Lake Barkley–Kentucky Lake Canal, which links the sprawling twin impoundments. The trail is blazed with a blue "Y" and is practically level (no more than a 60-foot rise at any one climb). After paralleling the canal through woods edge and open fields, the trail passes through Nickell Branch Lake Access Area. (The availability of drinking water along this trail is not good. There are a few wet-weather streams that flow into the lake and the lake water itself, which definitely has to be chemically treated, but other than that, this trail is bone dry. Carry plenty of water in your water bottle or canteen.) Basically, the Barkley Trail follows the lakeshore, sometimes at the water's edge, but mostly in the woods above the water. The trail crosses numerous gravel access roads by which you could make the hike as long as desired if you have two automobiles for a shuttle from the trailhead. Sections of the trail are simply mowed strips through the weeds, so take along plenty of insect repellent if you're hiking during the warm months of the year.

The five connector trails, all blazed in yellow letters (A through E), are 0.8 miles, 0.8 miles, 1.0 miles, 1.3 miles, and 0.4 miles. The connector trails allow hikers to choose from progressively longer loops and, by turning north onto the North–South Trail, they can hike back to their car without backtracking. Connecting trails A, B, and C cross the paved Trace. Their crossing points are not easy to spot from the road as trees sometimes obscure them, but they're not impossible to find. Trails A, B, and C traverse slightly hilly terrain of hardwoods mixed with woods openings sometimes using old logging roads. Trail B intersects the North–South Trail at a microwave communications tower. Trails D and E are short connectors from the

North End Information Station to the North–South Trail. Drinking water is available at the information center.

NAME OF TRAIL:	Hillman Ferry Family Campground Trail System
MAP ON PAGE:	83
START:	Control gate, Hillman Ferry Family Campground
END:	Control gate, Hillman Ferry Family Campground
TRAIL CONNECTIONS:	None
USGS QUADS:	TVA Land Between the Lakes topographic map (Sheet 1)
COUNTIES:	Lyon
RATING:	Easy; 4.0 mi.; logging road and gravel road; −40 ft.

The Hillman Heritage Trail is a series of loops that was one of 72 trails across the United States designated a National Recreation Trail in 1975. In all there are 4 miles of trail, nine short sections of dirt and gravel roadbed, including connectors and cross-overs. Planned and built by the Kentucky Lake Chapter of the National Campers and Hikers Association, Hillman Heritage Trail passes through pine thickets, stands of mixed hardwoods, forest clearings, and by the lakeshore. One thing I remember about the trail when I hiked it in the fall was the abundance of persimmon trees ripe with their delicious, orange meaty fruit. Lip smacking good!

The nine numbered trails are south of the camping areas on the penninsula at the mouth of Pisgah Bay. **Trail 2** passes a connector to Bohanon Cemetery. There's a scenic overlook on **Trail 8.** No spring water is available on trail. All trails are easy; there is little, if any, gain in elevation.

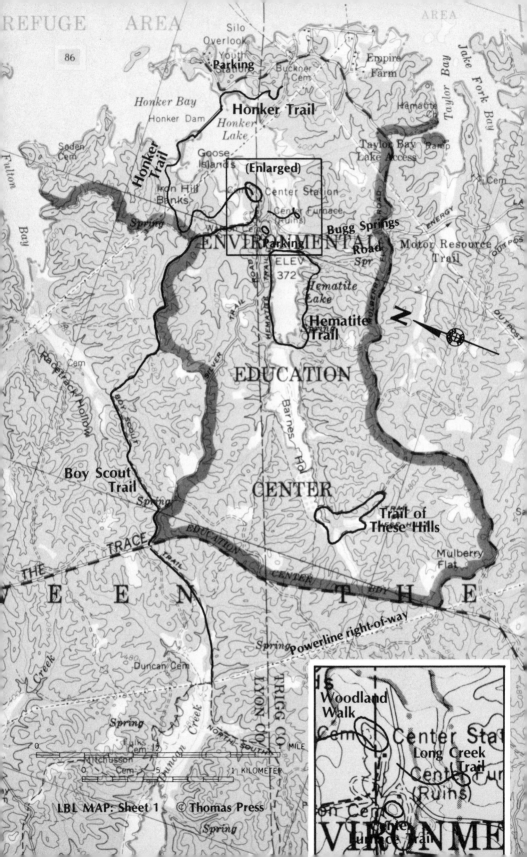

High Adventure
Base

Cumberland Cem
Wallace Cem 87

Crooked Creek Bay

Spring

Energy Dam

Spring

ENERGY

Apollo

OUTPOST ROAD

Energy Lake

Camp Energy
Group Camp

TRAIL

Shaw

Boardinghouse Branch

Bald Knob

Grace Cem

Pond Hollow
Bivouac

Hollow

Camporee Area

**Camp Energy
Trails**

OUTPOST

Ferguson
Spr
Cem

Spring

N

Ferguson Spring
(former site)

OUTPOST

Bald
Knob

Spring

Oakley Cem

Crooked Creek

OUTPOST

Underground

Little Creek

Pipeline

Franklin Creek

Energy
(former site)

Cem

Franklin
Cem

Pleasant Valley
Cem

JENNY

ROAD

Grace Cr

L A K E S

Cem

RIDGE

Newton Cem

Crooked Creek

Luton Cem

ROAD

520

THE   TRACE

IRONTON BRANCH

Cem

Springs

Erosion Control
Demonstration Station

Sanitary Land Field

Jenny Ridge

Sewage Lagoon

Spring

0   ½   1 MILE

Atmospheric Tread Station

0   .5   1 KILOMETER

Spring

Higgins Creek

Rhoades Creek

LBL MAP: Sheet L © Thomas Press

Rhoades Cem

Griff

NAME OF TRAIL: Boy Scout Trail
MAP ON PAGE: 86
START: Center Station, Environmental Education Center
END: Powerline right-of-way at Duncan Creek, intersection with North–South Trail
TRAIL CONNECTIONS: North–South Trail
USGS QUADS: TVA Land Between the Lakes topographic map (Sheet 1)
COUNTIES: Lyon
RATING: Easy; 6.0 mi.; footpath and logging road; −80 ft.

The Boy Scout Trail is a six-mile trail that follows old roadbeds along Silver Trail, so named because it was the route over which the payroll was shipped to Center Furnace during the boom years of pig iron production " 'tween the rivers." The trail passes through both the Racetrack Hollow and Duncan Creek bottoms, where the availability of water is seasonal at best. The trail is level and easy, and crosses the Trace (formerly KY 453). Points of interest along the Boy Scout Trail include old homesites.

NAME OF TRAIL: Trail of These Hills
MAP ON PAGE: 86
START: Mulberry Flat Road, one mile east of the Trace
END: Mulberry Flat Road, one mile east of the Trace
TRAIL CONNECTIONS: None
USGS QUADS: TVA Land Between the Lakes topographic map (Sheet 1)
COUNTIES: Trigg
RATING: Easy; 1.25 mi.; footpath; −20 ft.

Trail of These Hills is a 1.25-mile loop trail with twenty-five interpretive stations. Audio tracts explain the resource story of Land Between the Lakes, its timber, wildlife, and recreational potential with emphasis on management. There are wildlife observation benches located at wildlife food plots, a pond with an explanation of the aquatic ecosystem's role in food chains, and a deer enclosure with an explanation of the role of open lands in wildlife management.

NAME OF TRAIL:	Hematite Trail
MAP ON PAGE:	86
START:	Hematite Lake Dam, west of Center Furnace, off Bugg Springs Road
END:	Hematite Lake Dam, west of Center Furnace, off Bugg Springs Road
TRAIL CONNECTIONS:	None
USGS QUADS:	TVA Land Between the Lakes topographic map (Sheet 1)
COUNTIES:	Trigg
RATING:	Easy; 2.25 mi.; footpath and gravel road; −20 ft.

Hematite Trail is a 2.25-mile loop trail around Hematite Lake. The 100-acre impoundment of Long Creek was built in the 1930s by the CCC. Hematite Lake is allowed to fill up in the spring and is drawn down in the fall so that it becomes a quagmire of mudflat islands and potholes of water, preferred waterfowl habitat. Thousands of Canada geese and ducks use the lake as a feeding and rest stop staging area in the fall and winter. Diving ducks especially flock to Hematite Lake because of the rich beds of duckweed and aquatic plants.

During the summer the lake is abloom with water lilies. The level, easy trail around the lake is gravel and dirt with a wooden boardwalk at the lake's headwaters. There's a wildlife observation station on the north side of the lake and photography blind on the south bank. Mixed deciduous forest surrounds the lake, and it's not only a good place to observe muskrats, beaver, and eagles (during the winter migration), but also an excellent area for viewing fallow deer whose population is centered in the Environmental Education Center. On the south side of the lake there is a spring-fed creek that's a good water source.

NAME OF TRAIL: Center Furnace Trail
MAP ON PAGE: 86
START: Ruins of Center Furnace
END: Ruins of Center Furnace
TRAIL CONNECTIONS: None
USGS QUADS: TVA Land Between the Lakes topographic
                     map (Sheet 1)
COUNTIES: Trigg and Lyon
RATING: Easy; 0.3 mi.; footpath; +40 ft.

The Center Furnace Trail is a three-tenths-mile loop trail that is a tribute to the pioneer of the iron industry " 'tween the rivers," Thomas Tennessee (Doc) Watson (1805–1846). A 15-foot-high monolith marks the grave of the man who built the Empire Furnace on the Cumberland River in 1843. Two years later, in 1845, Watson built Fulton Furnace. His dream was to build a third furnace, named Center Furnace because it was geographically between the two others, but he died before construction was completed. Watson's partner, taking control of the company, renamed it the Hillman Land and Iron Company, and put Center Furnace into production in 1850. During a typical 48-week period of operation, the furnace could produce 2,140 tons of pig iron. The trail also passes abandoned charcoal and iron pits and the remains of the community of Hematite. The trail climbs 40 feet and is rated easy. No water is available, however.

NAME OF TRAIL: Long Creek Trail
MAP ON PAGE: 86
START: Parking area across from ruins of Center Fur-
                     nace on Bugg Springs Road
END: Wildlife observation station north of Long
                     Creek
TRAIL CONNECTIONS: None
USGS QUADS: TVA Land Between the Lakes topographic
                     map (Sheet 1)
COUNTIES: Trigg
RATING: Easy; 0.3 mi.; paved trail; −20 ft.

Long Creek Trail is a three-tenths-mile, paved trail for the physically handi-capped. It was designated a National Recreation Trail in 1971. There are nine interpretive stations along the trail that describe the surroundings in great detail and encourage observation through sight, sound, smell, taste, and touch.

NAME OF TRAIL:	Woodland Walk
MAP ON PAGE:	86
START:	Center Station, Environmental Education Center
END:	Center Station, Environmental Education Center
TRAIL CONNECTIONS:	None
USGS QUADS:	TVA Land Between the Lakes topographic map (Sheet 1)
COUNTIES:	Trigg and Lyon
RATING:	Easy; 0.75 mi.; footpath; −40 ft.

The Woodland Walk is a three-quarter-mile woodchip loop trail that descends the hill behind the Center Station to the bottoms at the head of Honker Lake. There are numerous benches along the trail so that visitors may sit to watch for wildlife; there are twelve interpretive stations.

Woodland Walk was once an old roadbed used in the nineteenth and early twentieth centuries to reach the large Negro slave cemetery to the left. The slaves were brought to this area to work at Center Furnace located in the valley below Center Station. It is also said that some of the first Chinese labor imported to this country worked at the furnace. The grave markers are crude, usually just a single limestone block or a pile of stones.

As the trail curves to the right, there is a small group of mature white oaks. Traditionally the oak is considered the king of trees, and the white oak is the king of kings, for these majestic trees possess mighty branches and long, deep roots. Well known for its sturdiness, the timber from the white oak carried New England sea captains around the world and served the pioneers well when they built their homes and bridges. A very American tree, it is the best all-around hardwood tree in the United States. The grayish-white bark and deeply lobed leaves distinguish it from its many oak cousins.

Farmers are not the only ones who make use of fields such as the small meadow dotted with trees that you come to next. Many animals are "creatures of the edge" who use these openings to fill their basic needs of food, shelter, and space. The plants of the field provide food and nesting sites while the wooded areas, fence rows, stream banks, and thickets offer protection from enemies and the elements. Deer, raccoons, skunks, and an occasional bobcat are only a few of the mammals that visit this opening. The field also provides homes for numerous rabbits, mice, and wood-chucks. Although the various inhabitants are not often seen, the tracks that they leave behind are evidence of their activities.

The trail now turns back into the wooded area beside a row of large loblolly and shortleaf pines. These trees were planted during the latter part of the 1930s to check erosion and provide food and cover for wildlife. Since the entire Environmental Education Center was once a part of the Kentucky Woodlands National Wildlife Refuge, this trail has been named after the old refuge.

Just across the trail from a large black cherry tree is an interesting partnership of two plants—poison ivy and sweet gum. Poison ivy does not restrict itself to the ground. Often it infests a tree so that the leaves appear to be the tree's own foliage. At first glance, this sweet gum tree seems to have the three-part leaf common to poison ivy. After looking more closely, however, the star-shaped leaves of the sweet gum can be seen near the top of the tree. Recognition of the three-leaflet combination of poison ivy is important to avoid the poisonous oil that is present in all parts of the plant.

Along the trail there are the skeletons of several dead and decaying trees. These are not cleared from the area because a dead tree in the forest is still useful. It may provide homes for squirrels, insects, bees, and rac-coons, or be a dinner table to woodpeckers and other birds that eat wood-boring insects. After falling to the ground, it returns its minerals to the soil, making it possible for new trees to take its place.

The trail soon passes one of the most valuable trees, the black wal-nut. This tree has been important since the times of the early settlers when pioneers used the hull of the nuts to make dye and the meat of the nuts to make candies and cakes. The black walnut is considered the finest cabinet wood in North America and is sought after by furniture manufacturers the world over.

In the field bordering the path, there is a tangle of briers and vines made up of blackberry and wild rose. This field is a good illustration of succession, what occurs when nature repairs itself. Blackberry vines and wild rose are examples of pioneer plants that will thrive in open sunlight. They pave the way for vegetation that needs some shade to grow. Eventu-ally, as one plant replaces another, the field will again give way to forest.

The trail enters the woods again and passes a pawpaw grove on the right. The pawpaw is often known as the "wild banana" because of its yellow bananalike fruits. Its large leaves indicate its tropical heritage. This curious tree prefers the moist, fertile soil of stream valleys and lower slopes and seldom grows to more than twenty feet high. There are few uses for the tree's wood, but the inner bark was woven into fiber by the Louisiana

Indians and used for fishing string by the pioneers. The fruit of the pawpaw is edible when its skin is nearly black and wrinkled. Most of the fruit is eaten fresh, but many people eat them baked and even serve pawpaw chiffon pie.

At the junction of the trail, the path at the left leads to a small limestone rock quarry. Millions of years ago this area was covered by shallow seas in which the mineral calcite was slowly deposited. As the seas receded, the calcium hardened to form the Great Limestone Plateau of Kentucky. This portion of Land Between the Lakes lies at the western end of the plateau. Limestone from this quarry was used in the construction of the original Center Furnace and in the iron blasting process that took place at the furnace. To reach the main trail again, return to the junction and follow the path that leads up the hill to the visitors' building.

NAME OF TRAIL:	Honker Trail
MAP ON PAGE:	86
START:	Center Station
END:	Honker Dam
TRAIL CONNECTIONS:	None
USGS QUADS:	TVA Land Between the Lakes topographic map (Sheet 1)
COUNTIES:	Trigg and Lyon
RATING:	Easy; 2.25 mi.; footpath and logging road; −70 ft.

Honker Trail is a 2.25-mile trail that crosses winter wheat fields, open lands, and bottomland woods encircling Honker Lake, a 190-acre sub-impoundment of Lake Barkley that was built in 1966. Honker Lake is a waterfowl refuge off limits to hunting and is the breeding grounds of LBL's resident flock of Canada geese. Biologists have installed special nesting islands (twenty-gallon washtubs filled with straw) that allow geese to nest without fluctuating water levels affecting the hatch. The washtubs are attached to rods anchored to the lake bottom, so that the "nesting platforms" remain stable and dry, rising and falling with the water level of the lake.

Honker Trail crosses Honker Dam and parallels the southern shore of the lake through stands of mixed hardwoods and open fields. In the mornings and evenings numerous species of wildlife can be observed from this trail: woodchucks, deer (fallow deer especially), hawks, squirrels, waterfowl, and eagles (during their seasonal migrations).

NAME OF TRAIL: Camp Energy Group Camp Trail System
MAP ON PAGE: 87
START: Control gate, Camp Energy Group Camp
END: Control gate, Camp Energy Group Camp
TRAIL CONNECTIONS: None
USGS QUADS: TVA Land Between the Lakes topographic
                        map (Sheet 1)
COUNTIES: Trigg
RATING: Easy; 12.0 mi.; footpath; −100 ft.

The Camp Energy Group Camp Trail System is a long, spurred loop, more than 12 miles of trail encircling Energy Lake, a 350-acre sub-impoundment of Lake Barkley, and the shoreline of Lake Barkley, northeast of the camp-ground. The 8-mile trail encircling Energy Lake is blazed in blue rectan-gles. A convenient starting point for this trail is Energy Dam, which sepa-rates the lake from the Crooked Creek embayment of Lake Barkley. Hiking clockwise from the dam, the trail parallels Energy Lake Road, then crosses it south of the control gate for the campground. This section passes through mixed hardwoods and is a gradual climb until it descends when crossing the road. On entering the campground, the trail again ascends slightly and passes near the archery range (via Trail 2). The trail parallels the lake to its headwaters at Ferguson Springs and crosses Crooked Creek by footbridge. The headwaters of Energy Lake are a wetland area with numerous pot-holes, a flooded creek (active beaver colonies), and an area surrounded by dense stands of willow and birch with scattered canebrakes. There are actually two fords across the Crooked Creek bottoms. After the second ford, the trail parallels a gravel road that ends at Ferguson Springs.

Now you are in the Little Creek bottoms. Off to the left there are two more footbridges to be crossed before reaching the south bank of Energy Lake. The trail crosses an open field, hugging the fenceline. The mouth of Little Creek at Energy Lake is a tangle of canebrakes and flooded timber. If you cut diagonally across the field to the head of the lake, after crossing the first footbridge, you'll find that the beavers have conveniently built a dam across the creek, allowing you to shortcut the trail, if you like. Once you've crossed the beaver dam, just continue up the ridge and you'll soon come up on the blazed trail again. The Little Creek bottoms are one of my favorite places in Land Between the Lakes. All of Energy Lake and its headwater tributaries is a waterfowl refuge, and, in the fall and winter, ducks and geese swarm in the area. Large flocks of wood ducks roost in the flooded timber and canebrakes virtually at the trail's edge. Biologists have known for years that there is more than one flock of wild turkeys in the area, and many deer hunters have found that, year after year, the Little Creek bottoms are a top area for large bucks.

On the south side of the lake the trail passes through overgrown creek bottoms, a few old homesteads, and pine woods, but mostly it follows the ridgetop through mixed hardwoods. The trail follows some old logging roads near its junction with the paved highway that crosses Energy Lake Dam (Bugg Springs Road).

The four numbered loop trails northeast of the campground are not nearly as scenic or interesting as the trail around the lake. But if you want to stretch your legs after dinner when you're camped at Energy Lake, the short, easy trails are just perfect.

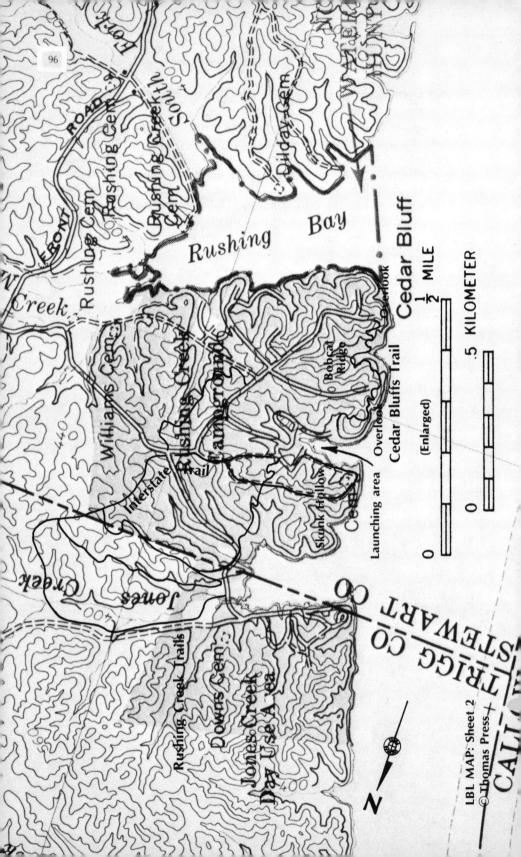

96

Fork

New

Creek

FRONT

ROAD

Rushing Creek North Cem

Rushing Cem

Rushing Creek South Cem

Dilday Cem

Rushing   Bay

Cedar Bluff

Williams Cem

Rushing Creek

Interstate Trail

Campground

Skunk Hollow

Cedar

Overlook

Bobcat Ridge

Cedar Bluffs Trail

Overlook

Launching area

Jones Creek

Rushing Creek Trails

Downs Cem

Jones Creek
Day Use Area

440

400

400

400

(Enlarged)

0   1/2   1   MILE

0   .5   KILOMETER

N

LBL MAP: Sheet 2
© Thomas Press

TRIGG CO
STEWART CO

CALLO

NAME OF TRAIL: Rushing Creek Family Campground Trail Sys-
                      tem
MAP ON PAGE: 96
START: Skunk Hollow
END: Bobcat Ridge
TRAIL CONNECTIONS: None
USGS QUADS: TVA Land Between the Lakes topographic
                      map (Sheet 2)
COUNTIES: Trigg (KY) and Stewart (TN)
RATING: Easy; 8.0 mi.; footpath and logging road;
                      +100 ft.

The Rushing Creek Family Campground Trail System consists of two short, easy day-hiking trails open to patrons of the campground only. The **Cedar Bluffs Trail** is a 1.5-mile trail (gravel and dirt) that begins at the tent camping area adjacent to the boat launching ramp at Skunk Hollow. The trail follows the bluffs atop the rocky shoreline of Kentucky Lake. Passing through mixed hardwoods and scrub cedar thickets, there are two scenic overlooks on the trail; one is at its end at the Bobcat Ridge camping area.

The **Interstate Trail** is five connected loops, 6.5 miles of old roadbed that crisscrosses the oak–hickory woodlands to the north of the Skunk Hollow camping area. The trails are marked by number, red numerals on a yellow background, or white rectangles. Trails 2, 4, and 5 cross the Jones Creek bottoms through croplands, woods openings, and mixed hardwoods. The short, easy network of trails gets its name because it is on the Kentucky–Tennessee border.

98

Fie

Dennis Cem
Murphey Cem
Williams Cem

Gatlin Cem

Gatlin Point
Lake Access

Stone Cem

360

N

Brandon Spring
Group Camp
(under const.)

Brandon Spring
Trails

Peripheral Trail

Ramp

Bards Lake

Commons

Dorm

Brandon Springs

Low Trail

Paw Paw Path

Bards Dam
Lake Access

Morrison Cem

Cross Trail

Hermon Cem

High Trail

1 MILE
Spring

.5 KILOMETER

0

0

THE

Jackso

520

440

400

400

Branch

Creek

Tharpe
(former)

Whitford Cem

WATER HO HUNTING

Barrett

380

Dunlap Cem

© Thomas Press

LBL MAP: Sheet 2

NAME OF TRAIL: Brandon Spring Group Camp Trail System
MAP ON PAGE: 98
START: Commons between the two dormitories
END: Commons between the two dormitories
TRAIL CONNECTIONS: None
USGS QUADS: TVA Land Between the Lakes topographic
                        map (Sheet 2)
COUNTIES: Stewart (TN)
RATING: Easy; 11.0 mi.; footpath and logging road;
                        +80 ft.

The Brandon Spring Group Camp Trail System is 11 miles of interconnected loops circling Bards Lake, a 320-acre sub-impoundment of Lake
Barkley, and crisscrossing the woodlands to the west of the dormitories,
commons building, boat dock, swimming pool, and play fields.
    The **Peripheral Trail,** which encircles the lake, is blazed in blue.
Hiked clockwise, the trail passes the recreational facilities of the unique
group camp for the disadvantaged, inner-city child and the physically handicapped, and crosses the Barrett Creek bottoms, which are annually
planted in crops. There's a wooden footbridge at the stream crossing.
Paralleling Tharpe Road for about 0.7 mile, the trail then turns south and
crosses the Bards Lake Dam, at the Gatlin Point Lake Access Area. It then
parallels the southern bank of Bards Lake through mixed deciduous forest,
crosses Brandon Spring Branch, and skirts the penninsula of land on which
the campground's facilities were built. Water is available year-round from
the Brandon Spring Branch, which flows through scattered canebrakes.
    The **Low Trail,** blazed in yellow, the **Cross Trail,** blazed in white, and
the **High Trail,** blazed in red, crisscross the woodlands to the west of the
dormitories and commons buildings. There was once a sprawling farm at
the springs, and for generations the Brandon family, who had a great love
of nature, protected some pockets of timber, allowing them to grow to
grand size. The trails of the system pass through some of the stands of
majestic trees, huge oaks and hickories. There are also numerous woods
openings created to enhance wildlife populations. There are a few old farm
buildings on the Cross Trail. The paved approach road to Brandon Spring
crosses all three of the short loop trails to the west of the group camp.
There is a total of 25 stations along the four trail systems, each with a
schematic map and location number so that hikers can tell at a glance
where they are on the trail. All trails are easy and practically flat. As at all
group camps and family campgrounds in Land Between the Lakes, the
day-hiking trail systems are open only to those staying at the facility.

There's no water at Gatlin Point Lake Access Area, so hikers who are on the Peripheral Trail should fill their canteens oefore departing. There's a group fire circle on Low Trail. The Mt. Zion Cemetery is passed when hiking the Peripheral Trail. At the intersection of the approach road to Brandon Spring and the Cross Trail is the Herndon Cemetery.

Another trail of importance at Brandon Spring Group Camp is the **Paw Paw Path,** 1500 feet of which is a paved trail for the physically handicapped. Paw Paw Path also serves as a demonstration trail for professional recreation planners, and students majoring in recreation. The trail has several different surfaces (sawdust, wood chips, and shredded bark) as a test of durability and comfort for hikers. Its design and progressive approach to interpretive stations have made the trail a model in the recreation field. There are twenty-five nature interpretive stations dealing with history, local plants and animals, their scientific names, and man's uses of natural resources.

Crooked Creek Embayment of Lake Barkley from Energy Lake Trail.
Photograph by the author.

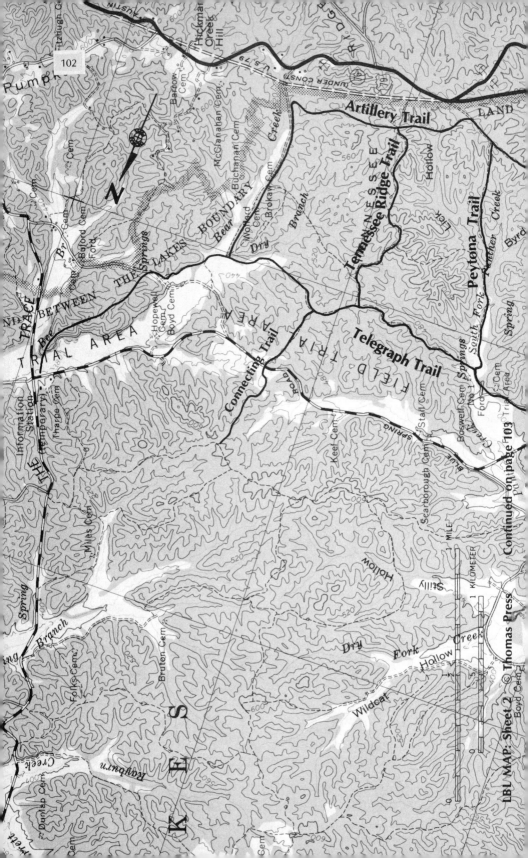

NAME OF TRAIL:	Fort Henry Trail System
MAP ON PAGE:	102–103
START:	Parking lot off Fort Henry–Blue Springs Road (clearly marked by highway signs)
END:	South Information Station
TRAIL CONNECTIONS:	North–South Trail
USGS QUADS:	TVA Land Between the Lakes topographic map (Sheet 2)
COUNTIES:	Stewart (TN)
RATING:	Strenuous; 26.0 mi.; footpath, logging road, and gravel road; +100 ft.

The Fort Henry Trail System is a series of loop trails, 26 miles and ten trails in all. Nine of the trails are color coded, each with their own distinctive blaze. Twenty-six trail signs, numbered consecutively, are located throughout the system so it's easier for hikers to orient themselves. The trails are **Picket Loop, Telegraph, Buckingham Hollow, Devils Backbone, Short Leaf Pine, Tennessee Ridge, Peytona, Artillery, Boswell,** and **Piney.** On the Telegraph Trail, at trail sign 10, there's a mile-long connector to the North–South Trail.

Another trail, which definitely has to be included in the system although it's strictly an interpretive trail, is the **Blue–Gray Trail,** a mile-long history lesson on the siege of Fort Henry, a Confederate outpost on the Tennessee River, which was taken by Union gunboats and troops under the command of Ulysses S. Grant during the Civil War. In early February of 1862, the Ohio-born, West Point-educated Grant led his troops from St. Louis in a bold move, and he both flanked the Confederate stronghold at Columbus, Kentucky, on the Mississippi River and captured two river fortresses that were the gateway to the mid-South. It was a key campaign for the Union early in the war. The Fort Henry Trail System traces the routes, as accurately as possible, used by both armies during the siege.

The Blue–Gray Trail passes through woods and fields on its way to the remaining breastworks on the shore of Kentucky Lake. The actual site of the fort is now underwater. The handsome woodchip trail, with plank footbridges over a wet-weather creek that winds through the trail, has eleven interpretive stations. Murals with text are located at all of the interpretive stations. The audio tracts, which portray the battle as it unfolded through sound effects and documented accounts of the action, are activated by walking onto a carpet buried under the woodchips.

The terrain encountered while hiking the Fort Henry Trail System is typical of Land Between the Lakes. To the south of the Fort Henry–Blue

Springs Road, the Panther Creek bottoms are extensively planted in corn, sunflowers and milo. Telegraph Trail winds through mowed strips along agricultural fields using old road beds and woodland footpaths. Springs are located in the Bear Creek bottoms and at the mouth of the South Fork of Panther Creek. These are the only water sources along the trail. The Buckingham Hollow and Short Leaf Pine trails are ridgetop footpaths through stands of mixed hardwood and short leaf pines, which are growing at the northern limit of their range. The extensive planting was done in the 1930s for erosion control and cover for wildlife. Devils Backbone is a footpath through an unnamed wet-weather stream. There's a footbridge at its junction with the Telegraph Trail. Don't expect to find any water on the Devils Backbone Trail. Artillery Trail parallels Telegraph Trail to the south along U.S. 79 (the southern boundary of Land Between the Lakes). The other two cross-over trails are the Tennessee Ridge and Peytona. The Tennessee Ridge Trail is a ridgetop footpath through stands of mixed hardwoods. The Peytona Trail parallels the South Fork of Panther Creek from head to mouth. The Piney Family Campground with the junction of Buckingham Hollow and Artillery Trails, passes through stands of mixed hardwoods and pines. Water is available year-round from a spring on the South Fork of Piney Creek.

NAME OF TRAIL: Piney Family Campground Trail System
MAP ON PAGE: 103
START: Control gate, Piney Family Campground
END: Control gate, Piney Family Campground
TRAIL CONNECTIONS: Fort Henry Trail System
USGS QUADS: TVA Land Between the Lakes topographic
                        map (Sheet 2)
COUNTIES: Stewart (TN)
RATING: Easy; 3.0 mi.; footpath, logging road, and
                        gravel road; +60 ft.

The trail system at Piney Family Campground consists of two separate footpaths, the **Songbird Walk** and the **Piney Hike 'n Bike Trail.** The total system is about 3 miles long.

Songbird Walk, adjacent to the main entrance of Piney Family Campground, is a quarter-mile loop trail planted with a variety of shrubs, trees, and annual plantings beneficial to wildlife. It is a place for visitors to enjoy wildlife, particularly songbirds, and a demonstration of wildlife management practices that can be duplicated in your backyard.

Several management practices have been employed in the vicinity of Songbird Walk. Black cherry, chokecherry, toringo crabapple, flowering dogwood, silky dogwood, autumn olive, barberry, beautyberry, Bessey cherry, bicolor lespedeza, blueberry, and Chinese chestnut trees have been planted to provide nesting cover, escape cover, and food (when they begin producing fruits and seeds). Through these plantings, along with natural plant species already in the area (such as staghorn sumac, sassafras, blackberries, and wild roses) a relatively large and diverse songbird population will be established for the enjoyment of all visitors.

An annual food plot was planted near the trail by TVA biologists. Millet, buckwheat, and sorghum have been seeded in the plot and all are relished by songbirds. TVA also installed numerous birdhouses. These houses provide nesting sites that may otherwise be in limited supply in natural settings. Bluebirds, for example, need cavities in which to nest; these are not abundant in this area so birdhouses are readily used.

Two feeding stations have also been placed in the area. These are filled with a variety of seeds, many of which are grown at Land Between the Lakes. The table indicates the variety, frequency of sighting, and seasons for observing the songbirds in the LBL.

SONGBIRD SIGHTINGS

	S	S	W	F		S	S	W	F
Turkey Vulture	c	c	c	r	Carolina Wren	c	c	c	c
Red-tailed Hawk	c	o	c	c	Catbird	c	c	c	r
Red-shouldered Hawk	c	o	c	c	Robin	c	c	c	c
Bobwhite Quail	a	a	a	a	Brown Thrasher	c	c	c	r
Killdeer	c	c	c	r	Eastern Bluebird	c	c	c	o
Common Snipe (Wilson's)	c	—	o	r	Starling	c	c	c	c
Mourning Dove	a	a	a	c	White-eyed Vireo	c	c	c	c
Whip-poor-will	r	c	r	—	Yellowthroat	a	a	a	—
Common Nighthawk	r	c	r	—	House Sparrow	a	a	a	a
Chimney Swift	c	c	c	—	Eastern Meadowlark	c	c	c	a
Ruby-throated					Red-winged Blackbird	c	c	c	a
Hummingbird	c	c	c	—	Common Grackle	c	c	c	o
Yellow-shafted Flicker	a	o	a	o	Brown-headed Cowbird	c	c	c	o
Red-bellied Woodpecker	a	a	a	a	Cardinal	a	a	a	a
Red-headed Woodpecker	c	o	c	c	Indigo Bunting	a	c	a	—
Yellow-bellied Sapsucker	c	—	c	c	Purple Finch	c	—	c	c
Downy Woodpecker	c	c	c	c	American Goldfinch	c	c	c	c
Eastern Kingbird	c	c	c	—	Dickcissel	—	c	—	r
Eastern Phoebe	c	c	c	r	Rufous-sided Towhee	a	a	a	a
Rough-winged Swallow	c	c	c	—	Slate-colored Junco	a	—	a	a
Barn Swallow	c	c	c	—	Myrtle Warbler	c	—	c	c
Cliff Swallow	c	c	c	—	Palm Warbler	c	o	c	o
Purple Martin	c	c	c	—	Chipping Sparrow	c	c	c	—
Blue Jay	a	c	a	a	Field Sparrow	a	a	a	c
Common Crow	c	c	c	c	White-throated Sparrow	a	—	a	a
Carolina Chickadee	c	c	c	c	Swamp Sparrow	c	—	c	r
Mockingbird	c	c	c	c	Song Sparrow	c	—	c	c

SEASON		STATUS	
S —	March–May	a —	abundant
S —	June–August	c —	common
F —	September–November	o —	occasional
W —	December–February	r —	rare

The Piney Hike 'n Bike Trail, open to foot travel and bicyclists only, is 2.75 miles long and is a series of loops around the shore of Kentucky Lake and throughout the campground. Gravel and paved trails connect the Chestnut and Black Oak camping areas with the play fields and crafts cabin. Along the Greenwood Way section of the trail there are footbridges and benches at two scenic overlooks. The Piney Hike 'n Bike Trail passes through open lands, stands of hardwoods and extensive plantings of short leaf pine, which was introduced into LBL by TVA for erosion control and wildlife cover. There are fourteen numbered schematic signs located throughout the trail system. A loop of the trail southwest of the Dogwood Loop camping area was taken out of the system by the construction of campsites in the summer of 1978. Bike racks are located at the Black Oak camping area and the activity fields. Trails that connect to the nearby Fort Henry Hiking Trail System (Buckingham Hollow Trail) originate at the "Y" in the approach road (Fort Henry Road) within sight of the control gate of the campground.

Pennyrile Forest. Photograph courtesy of the Commonwealth of Kentucky, Department of Public Information.

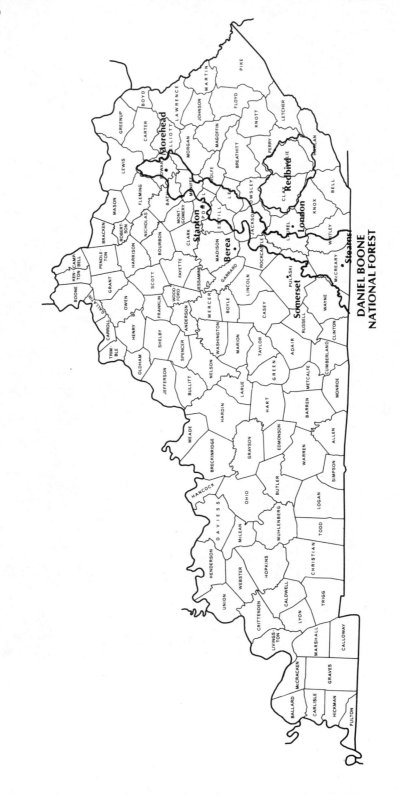

DANIEL BOONE
NATIONAL FOREST

5
Daniel Boone National Forest

 Stretching for more than 120 miles from the Kentucky–Tennessee border northward to Lewis County just south of the Ohio River, Daniel Boone National Forest appears on maps of Kentucky as a green corridor of land separating the Bluegrass Region from the Cumberland Mountains. More than 660,000 acres in twenty-two Kentucky counties are under public ownership, about thirty percent of approximately 2,043,584 acres within the forest's boundary.

In part because of its vastness, there are more miles of foot trail (165 miles, 66 separate trails) in Daniel Boone National Forest than anywhere else in Kentucky. The Commonwealth's most spectacular scenery and most remote lands are within the forest—raging white-water rivers, cascading waterfalls, rock arches, and trackless woodlands. Kentucky's only national wilderness area and national geological area, six Kentucky Wild Rivers and three sizeable roadless areas identified under the U.S. Forest Service's Roadless Area Review and Evaluation (RARE II) program, are within the boundaries of Daniel Boone National Forest. The diversity of recreational pastimes that are pursued in the forest in addition to hiking are white-water canoeing, stream and reservoir fishing, nature study, hunting, rock climbing, and family camping.

The Weeks Law, enacted by the U.S. Congress in 1911, enabled the Forest Service to purchase lands, which were first known as Cumberland National Forest. In the 1960s the forest's name was changed to honor frontiersman and settler, Daniel Boone, one of the first white men to extensively explore lands now under public ownership. Ranger District Headquarters, Daniel Boone National Forest, U.S. Forest Service, 100 Vaught Road, Winchester, Kentucky 40391. (606) 744-5656.

Administrative maps of the forest are available from the Daniel Boone National Forest Headquarters in Winchester. The three maps cover the north and south halves of the main body of the forest, and the Redbird Ranger District, which is located east of the southern half of the forest. The maps cost 50¢ each, and a $1.00 minimum order is required. Frequent references are made to the Forest Service roads (FS Road 000; rectangular symbol) and trails (FS #000; parallelogram symbol). Forest Service road numbers are indicated on the administrative maps, trails generally are not.

For management purposes, Daniel Boone National Forest is divided into seven separate ranger districts. From north to south, they are: Morehead, Stanton, Berea, Somerset, London, Stearns, and Redbird. The trails in this chapter will be described in their respective districts. The 300-mile Sheltowee Trace, which runs north to south through the Daniel Boone National Forest, is described in Chapter 6, "Trails of Special Mention."

Daniel Boone National Forest. Photograph courtesy of the Commonwealth of Kentucky, Department of Public Information.

MOREHEAD RANGER DISTRICT

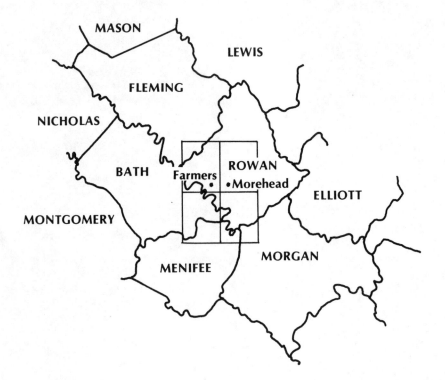

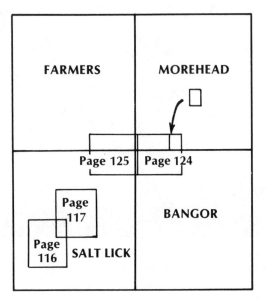

MOREHEAD RANGER DISTRICT

Morehead Ranger District, the northernmost of the Daniel Boone National Forest's seven ranger districts, is made up of 116,630 acres in Rowan, Menifee, Morgan, and Bath counties. The major recreational drawing card in the Morehead District is the Pioneer Weapons Hunting Area, a 7,300-acre tract of woodlands west of Cave Run Lake in Menifee and Bath Counties. It is reached via U.S. 60, KY 211, KY 801, and Forest Service roads 129 and 918.

There are eight hiking trails in the Morehead Ranger District. They total 21.25 miles. All but two of the trails are in the Pioneer Weapons Area. During the summer of 1978, construction on the Zilpo Road began. Unfortunately, the Cedar Cliffs Trail (FS #111) was used as the roadbed.

The ridgetop trail that previously connected Buck Branch Trail with Cross Over Trail was bulldozed, thus depriving the area of a complete footpath hookup between Clear Creek Recreation Area and the Cave Run Trail and Hog Pen Trail junction. Although the Cedar Cliffs Trail will be lost forever, the U.S. Forest Service plans to relocate trailheads along the Zilpo Road and continue their trail maintenance program for the system.

The new road will go from the junction of Forest Service roads 129 and 918 to Cave Run Lake at Zilpo, where construction on a campground and recreational complex will begin in 1979. Forest Service officials said drinking water, flush toilets, and showers will be available to campers at this recreational area due to be completed in the early 1980s.

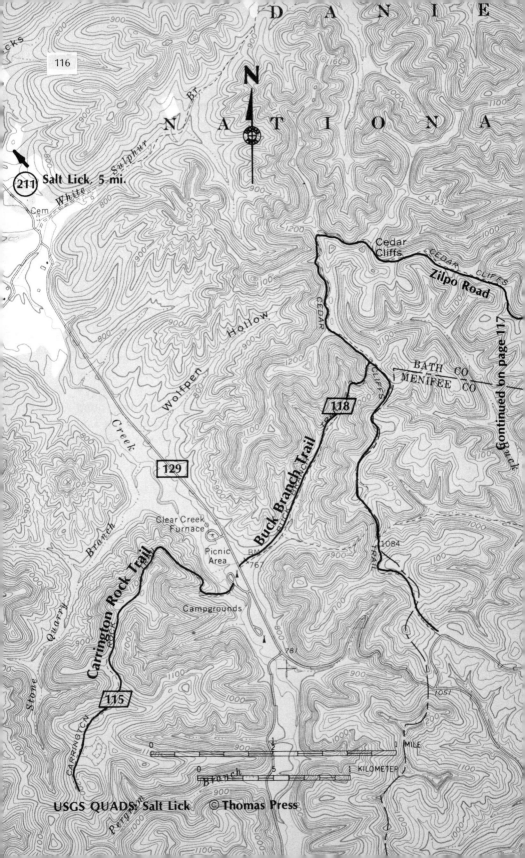

116

DANIE

NATIONA

N

Salt Lick, 5 mi.

211

White

Cem

Sulphur

Br.

Cedar
Cliffs

CEDAR
CLIFFS

Zilpo Road

X 1253

1100

1166

900

1200

CEDAR
CLIFFS

BATH CO.
MENIFEE CO.

Wolfpen

Hollow

118

Creek

129

Buck Branch Trail

1084

TRAIL

Branch

Clear Creek
Furnace

Picnic
Area

BM
767

1100

900

Campgrounds

781

1057

Carrington Rock Trail

Quarry

Stone

115

CARRINGTON

back to beginning on page 117

0   ½   MILE

0   .5   1   KILOMETER

Branch

Pergrm

USGS QUADS: Salt Lick   © Thomas Press

N

B O O N E

F O R E S T

Hog Pen Trail

106

Cross Over Trail 107

Cave Run Trail

112

PIONEER WEAPONS

Zilpo Road

918

HUNTING AREA

1388 Tater Knob
Lookout Tower

Continued on page 116

0   1 MILE
0   .5   1 KILOMETER

USGS QUADS: Salt Lick   ©Thomas Press

NAME OF TRAIL: Buck Branch Trail (FS #118)
MAP ON PAGE: 116
START: Clear Creek Furnace Campground on FS
                        Road 129, 5 miles south of Salt Lick, off KY
                        211
END: Zilpo Road
TRAIL CONNECTIONS: None
USGS QUADS: Salt Lick
COUNTIES: Bath
RATING: Easy; 1.25 mi.; footpath; +200 ft.

Buck Branch Trail was formerly the approach to the system of interconnected footpaths in the Pioneer Weapons Hunting Area. But with the construction of Zilpo Road, it is now best suited to day-hiking. Buck Branch
Trail is approximately 1.25 miles long and parallels Buck Branch of Clear
Creek, a wet-weather stream. Water is only available to hikers in the spring
or during rainy spells or from Clear Creek. Buck Branch Trail is an easy
trail, relatively flat, with only a few moderate-to-steep inclines (200-foot
rise) as it reaches its end atop Cedar Cliffs. It is well maintained and has
numerous switchbacks near the end.

NAME OF TRAIL: Carrington Rock Trail (FS #115)
MAP ON PAGE: 116
START: Clear Creek Furnace Campground on FS
                      Road 129, 5 miles south of Salt Lick, off KY
                      211
END: Carrington Rock
TRAIL CONNECTIONS: None
USGS QUADS: Salt Lick
COUNTIES: Bath
RATING: Moderate; 2.5 mi.; footpath; +400 ft.

The Carrington Rock Trail (FS #115) is 2.5 miles long and rises 400 feet. The trail steadily ascends from the Clear Creek Furnace Campground after crossing Clear Creek, the only water source on the trail. The ridgetop trail, blazed in white diamond, is part of the Sheltowee Trace. Carrington Rocks is a knoblike lookout point that was used by Indians, and soldiers, during the Civil War. The footpath passes through mixed pine and deciduous forest. A small natural arch and impressive rock outcropings highlight the walk.

NAME OF TRAIL: Cave Run Trail (FS #112)
MAP ON PAGE: 116
START: Trailhead at FS Road 918, one-half mile north
                      of Tater Knob Lookout Tower
END: Cave Run Lake
TRAIL CONNECTIONS: Hog Pen Trail (FS #106) and Cross Over Trail
                      (FS #107)
USGS QUADS: Salt Lick
COUNTIES: Bath
RATING: Moderate; 5.0 mi.; footpath and logging
                      road; +300 ft.

Cave Run Trail is the backbone of the trail system in the Pioneer Weapons Hunting Area. It is by far the best trail, and it offers hikers challenge enough to keep it interesting while running the gamut of forest types and scenery the region has to offer. The trail uses footpaths constructed especially for hiking and forest logging roads. Hiking northward from FS Road 918, Tater Knob Road, the trail follows a rocky ridgetop crowned in pine and mixed hardwoods; then it descends by numerous switchbacks to the Big Cave Run Creek bottoms. As the well-maintained trail descends, there is a noticeable change in forest types from communities of the higher elevation "dry sites" to the constituents of the slope forest. The bottom-land forest is predominantly beech with lush "gardens" of ferns and wild-flowers. Big Cave Run Creek was clear, cold, and running when I hiked the trail in July—an excellent water source for cooking, drinking, and bathing. A good trail for camping, it has numerous flat and soft sites along the creek that are canopied by hemlocks. Deer and raccoon are common in the area. Deer tracks were all along the trail and in soft mud along the creek. Hiking out, we saw two does run across the trail. A raccoon ambled into our camp after supper one night, so take care to protect your food from those "masked bandits" when sleeping. Much of the bottom land along the lake has been cleared as part of a wildlife management plan and is now in second growth timber and dense bushes.

Paralleling the creek and crossing it numerous times, the trail begins a steady ascent to its junction with Hog Pen and Cross Over trails. At the headwaters of the creek, in a narrow gorge, the trail makes a hairpin turn to the right and settles in along the contour of the hill through towering woodlands graced by crested dwarf iris, May apples and ferns. The trail ascends 300 feet in less than one mile, and has several leg warming stretches.

The 1.75-mile spur off the main trail descends from the ridge gradually (from the junction of Hog Pen and Cave Run trails) skirts a 253-foot-high knob, and finally ends at the lake.

NAME OF TRAIL:	Cross Over Trail (FS #107)
MAP ON PAGE:	117
START:	Zilpo Road one mile north of its junction with FS Road 918
END:	Junction with Hog Pen Trail (FS #106) and Cave Run Trail (FS #112)
TRAIL CONNECTIONS:	Hog Pen Trail (FS #106) and Cave Run Trail (FS #112)
USGS QUADS:	Salt Lick
COUNTIES:	Bath
RATING:	Easy; 1.5 mi.; footpath; −100 ft.

Cross Over Trail is an easy, ridgetop footpath with no water available to hikers. It is approximately 1.5 miles long and descends only slightly. It hasn't been maintained in years, and in some stretches hikers must fight the bushes. The trails pass through mixed deciduous and pine forest. With the construction of Zilpo Road, it appears that Cross Over Trail is destined to be what the Buck Branch Trail once was—an approach to the main hiking trails. The triangular brown Daniel Boone blaze is found at the trailhead.

NAME OF TRAIL: Hog Pen Trail (FS #106)
MAP ON PAGE: 117
START: Trough Lick Branch
END: Cave Run Lake
TRAIL CONNECTIONS: Cross Over Trail (FS #107) and Cave Run Trail
                        (FS #112)
USGS QUADS: Salt Lick
COUNTIES: Bath
RATING: Moderate; 3.0 mi.; footpath; −100 ft.

The Hog Pen Trail is a 3-mile trail that descends 100 feet from its beginning to its end. The trail has two distinct sections and each offers different scenery and hiking conditions. The eastern half of the trail, which connects the junction of Cross Over Trail and Cave Run Trail to Cave Run Lake, descends 300 feet from the ridgetops. There's no water along the trail as it passes through mixed pine and deciduous forest and second-growth timber near the lake. The trail ends at the water's edge within sight of a cove of flooded timber.

The western section of the trail descends 200 feet from the junction of Cross Over Trail and Cave Run Trail to Trough Lick Branch. There are scattered stands of mountain laurel, beech, and a few beautiful fern and wildflower gardens. Trough Lick Branch is an excellent water source year-round. This section of Hog Pen Trail is an excellent starting point for cross-country hikes along the lakeshore. The wide creek bottoms are ideal for camping.

NAME OF TRAIL:	Big Limestone Trail (FS #109)
MAP ON PAGE:	124, 125
START:	FS Road 16, 2 miles west of KY 519, south of Morehead
END:	KY 801, 2 miles south of Farmers
TRAIL CONNECTIONS:	Becky Branch Trail (FS #109)
USGS QUADS:	Morehead, Bangor, and Salt Lick
COUNTIES:	Rowan
RATING:	Easy; 6.0 mi.; logging road; −400 ft.

The Big Limestone Trail is a 6-mile-long trail that begins on Lockegee Road (FS Road 16) and ends on KY 801 east of Cave Run Dam. The trail is part of the Sheltowee Trace. It follows a ridgetop logging road most of the way. No water is available. Mixed stands of pine and hardwoods are passed, as are timber sale areas that are now in second growth timber and bushes. The Lockegee Rocks is the major point of interest on the trail.

Martins Branch

119

124

13

Rodburn Hollow Campsite

Martin Rodburn Hollow

Braney Branch

N

Mill Branch

109

TRAIL

Becky Branch

Becky Branch Trail

110

Big Limestone Trail

LIMESTONE

Limestone Knob

1435

Becky

MC-BRAYER

Branch

CHESAPEAKE

Triplett

Everett

Stillhouse Br

Biddle Hollow

Biddle Hol

Stillhouse

Creek

Scott

Lockegee Road

Lockegee Rock

BM 964

Claypit

1277

1263

BM

519

Hill Branch

USGS QUADS: Morehead, Bangor
© Thomas Press

MILE
KILOMETER

16

Continued on page 125

Continued on page 124

USGS QUADS: Morehead, Bangor, Farmers, Salt Lick

DANIEL BOONE NATIONAL FOREST

Big Limestone Trail

Cave Run Dam

Peter Everett Br

Phelps Branch

Thomas Press

Hungry Branch

Cline's Branch

Trailer Park

Farmers Ch

Moorehead-Rowan Co Airport

Filtration Plant

Caley Cem

109

PIPELINE

OHIO

AIRPORT RD

Hungry

1 MILE

1 KILOMETER

Carey Br

NAME OF TRAIL:	Becky Branch Trail (FS #110)
MAP ON PAGE:	124
START:	FS Road 16 (Lockegee Road)
END:	Becky Branch
TRAIL CONNECTIONS:	Big Limestone Trail (FS #109)
USGS QUADS:	Morehead
COUNTIES:	Rowan
RATING:	Easy; 1.0 mi.; footpath; −300 ft.

The one-mile-long Becky Branch Trail is a spur off the Big Limestone Trail. It can't be reached without first hiking 1.5 miles of the Big Limestone Trail from its trailhead on FS Road 16. Becky Branch Trail deadends on Becky Branch, a tributary to Triplett Creek. The trail descends 300 feet and water is available seasonally. Mixed pine and deciduous trees line the trail. In the pine woods off the trail there are some impressive wildflower gardens in the spring; pink lady's slippers abound. Across FS Road 16 from the trailhead of the Big Limestone Trail is an unmarked footpath that leads to Lockegee Rocks.

NAME OF TRAIL: Martins Branch Trail (FS #119)
MAP ON PAGE: 124
START: Rodburn Hollow Campground, FS Road 13,
                         1.3 miles east of Morehead
END: Rodburn Hollow Campground
TRAIL CONNECTIONS: None
USGS QUADS: Morehead
COUNTIES: Rowan
RATING: Easy; 1.0 mi.; footpath and logging road;
                         +200 ft.

The Martins Branch Trail is a one-mile, loop footpath used by casual day-hikers camped at Rodburn Hollow Campground. Drinking water is available at the campground from April 1 to November 1; the trail climbs the ridge 200 feet. Woods clearings, mixed pine and deciduous forest, a wildlife waterhole, and a walnut tree plantation are passed when hiking the trail.

STANTON RANGER DISTRICT

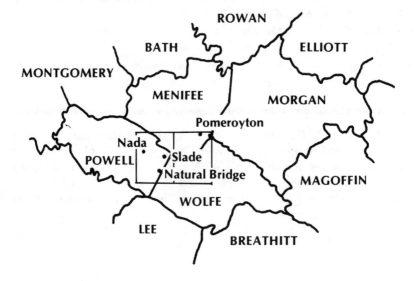

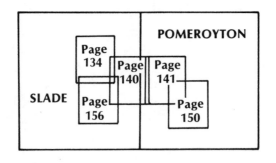

STANTON RANGER DISTRICT

The Stanton Ranger District of Daniel Boone National Forest encompasses 55,000 acres of forest lands under public ownership in parts of Menifee, Wolfe, Powell, Estill, and Lee Counties. The ranger district's major recreational attraction is the Red River Gorge Geological Area, 25,600 acres east of Stanton and reached via KY 15, KY 715, and KY 77.

In the late sixties and early seventies a controversy raged over a proposal by the U.S. Army Corps of Engineers to build a 5,000-acre impoundment on the North Fork of the Red River. Many residents of Clay City argued that the dam was needed for flood control; proponents of the project in nearby Lexington sought a new water supply for their growing metropolitan community. Environmentalists pointed out that rare communities of plants and animals, and the scenic, archeological, and geologic integrity of the region would be destroyed if the impoundment were built.

The price tag for the project was $34 million. The U.S. Army Corps of Engineers stated that the purposes of the dam were as follows: recreation, 43.5 percent; flood control, 41.0 percent; water supply, 7.5 percent; fish and wildlife recreation and redevelopment, 4.0 percent each. A benefit-cost ratio of 2:1 was challenged by environmentalists, and several groups sought to discredit the project because the money made from it would line the pockets of a few local landowners while costing taxpayers millions. Another major concern of environmentalists was the loss of habitat for such rare or uncommon animals and plants as the four-toed salamander, wood frog, soapwort gentian, and the yellow fringed orchid. Fifty-five families were to be displaced by the project.

Another concern was that the lake would shrink the land area open to recreation and concentrate use in the upper gorge, the section of the river valley between KY 746, north of Campton, and the KY 715 bridge in the heart of the gorge.

The Red River Gorge controversy was intense. There were marches on Kentucky's state capitol complete with speakers and folk singers, fund-raising drives, legal suits, and counter suits. The late Supreme Court Justice William O. Douglas, a noted environmentalist, even visited the gorge. It was a hot political issue that took media observers, concerned citizens, and politicians on a roller-coaster ride. One day it seemed the lake would finally go through; the next day it appeared the environmentalists would succeed in stopping it.

The project was killed in October 1975 when Julian Carroll, who became governor when Wendell Ford resigned to go to Washington as a newly elected senator, formally objected to the project after months of thorough investigation by appointed groups determined that the cost-benefit ratio didn't warrant the building of the dam.

The next important development for the unique area came in 1976 when 25,630 acres in the gorge were formally designated as a national geological area, giving the region a special, protective status and a place on the register of important scenic and natural areas in America. But the controversy and subsequent national designation that brought the area to the public's attention had a dramatic impact on the once-obscure region of Daniel Boone National Forest. Millions of people flocked to the gorge to hike its trails, canoe and kayak its boulder-strewn white water, and the area was nearly loved to death at the height of its popularity during the controversy. As a result, the area suffered from overuse—trampling of plant life, careless fire building, litter, and a general disregard of backcountry ethics by a many of the visitors, most of whom were novice outdoors enthusiasts.

In early 1979, two important developments affected the future use of the gorge. First, on January 4, the U.S. Forest Service proposed that 13,260 acres, the so-called Clifty Unit, become a national wilderness area. This was the result of an eighteen-month study, (RARE II) the Roadless Area Review and Evaluation, which was conducted nationwide in U.S. forests to solve land-use controversies. RARE II lands were categorized as either wilderness, lands designated for further study leading to classification, or lands set aside for nonwilderness uses such as campground or recreational development, tree culture, and wildlife management areas. Congressional approval is needed for the Clifty Unit to become part of the National Wilderness Preservation System. At this writing, the proposal for wilderness status of the unit in the Red River Gorge Geological Area has not been acted on.

The second important development was the nomination of the trails in the gorge to the National Trails System. By 1980, all of our national forests are to have at least two such trails. The other trail nominated in Daniel Boone National Forest was the Sheltowee Trace, which is under construction. A section of the Sheltowee Trace will pass through Red River Gorge Geological Area.

There are twenty-four designated day-hiking and backpacking trails in the Red River Gorge Geological Area. Their combined length is 37.4 miles. However, there are many short paths and logging roads that can be hiked as trails. Many lead to arches, rockhouses, and scenic overlooks. Some of these trails begin on private property and permission must be secured before hiking them. Thus, these trails have not been included in this unit. Perhaps in future editions of this book, there will be mention of them.

Known for its rugged topography, the Red River Gorge is character-ized by an abundance of rock arches and palisades, deep V-shaped valleys, cascading waterfalls, sandstone cliffs, and dramatic overlooks that provide sweeping vistas of heavily forested land.

Red River Gorge lies in the Pottsville Escarpment at the western edge of the Cumberland Plateau. It is the largest concentration of natural rock arches in the eastern United States. Over eighty are known to exist in the drainage of Red River, and eighteen major arches are in the drainage of the North Fork alone. (Arches National Park in Utah is the only area in the United States that has a larger number of these geologic phenomena.) In addition to the rock arches, other points of geologic interest include Tower Rock, Raven Rock, Hens Nest Rock, Angel Windows, Indian Staircase, and Chimney Top Rock (a palisade that affords visitors a spectacular overlook of the wooded river valley and bordering rock cliffs).

The geologic history of Red River Gorge began during Mississippian times, more than 340 million years ago. The major geologic formations are conglomerate sandstones, limestones, and siltstones, all overlaid by shale. Stream erosion and weathering processes formed the gorge on the North Fork of Red River in much the same way that Grand Canyon was cut by the Colorado River. Red River is a tributary to the Kentucky River, one of 11 major drainages in the state.

Rising in the southwest corner of Wolfe County, the Red River, a tributary to the Kentucky River, flows generally west for 95 miles. The serpentine path of the Red and its tributaries has sliced portions of the drainage into narrow, irregular valleys divided by steep ridges. Hilltop elevations range up to 1500 feet above sea level and may rise up to 500 feet above the valley floor. Today, layers of sandstone that have resisted the crumbling effects of the action of water and the weathering process stand out boldly as cliffs above the surrounding forests of the river valley.

As intensive examination of the flora of the Red River Gorge in 1970 revealed that 555 species of vascular plants from 100 families and 304 genera are found in the area. Forest types can be classified as those associated with ridge tops, slopes, and stream banks.

In general, the ridge tops of the Red River Gorge support an oak–pine community that consists of three species of pine and five species of oak. Other hardwoods associated with this community are pignut, sweet pignut hickory, and shagbark hickory.

Below the cliffs, the canopy layer of the forest consists of American beech, tulip poplar, American and white basswood, sweet birch, sugar and red maple, eastern hemlock, and yellow buckeye. The understory layer of plants in this community consists mainly of American holly and magnolia. Common shrubs in this forest type are rose bay rhododendron, spice bush, hazelnut, and mountain laurel—a shrub whose pinkish bloom flowers in profusion throughout eastern Kentucky in late May.

The stream bank forest includes American hornbeam, river birch, hazel alder, black willow, sycamore, and elm. In a short section of the Red River Valley below Copperas Creek there is an association of beech (a constituent of the slope forest), sycamore, and cottonwood—a grouping that is considered to be extremely rare. This section of the river is immediately below the KY 715 bridge.

The list of wildflowers in the region is extensive. Common species are trailing arbutus, bent trillium, rue anemone, rattlesnake plantain, partridge-berry, bloodroot, hepatica, scouring rush, yellow trout lily, squirrel-corn, violets, bluet, spring beauty, foam flower, Allegheny spurge, dwarf ginseng, and wild geranium.

Generally pollution-free, the Red River supports what is described as a high-quality stream fishery. Game fish include smallmouth bass, muskel-lunge, suckers, Kentucky (spotted) bass, rock bass, and other sunfishes. In some of the tributaries of Red River are populations of difficult-to-find chubs, minnows, and stream darters.

Wandering hunting parties of Shawnees were among the early visitors to the gorge. They came from the north to hunt the buffalo, elk, and deer that once inhabited the lowlands west of the gorge.

The most famous white hunter to explore the region was Daniel Boone. Historians say he probably visited the Red River Gorge area between 1769 and 1771. During that time, Boone roamed all over eastern Kentucky with his brother, Squire, and several other companions, living off the land. During the winter of 1769–1770, while his brother returned to North Carolina for supplies, Boone lived in the wilderness alone while dangerously low on powder, lead, and provisions. He slept in canebrakes and rock shelters to avoid capture by wandering bands of Shawnees.

Native wildlife in the Red River Gorge includes the gray fox, two species of squirrels, white-tailed deer, wild turkey, mink, beaver, muskrat, and, in all, 59 species of fish. Thirty-one species of amphibians, 105 species of resident birds, and 36 species of mammals are believed to have lived in the Red River Gorge area.

The 30-mile loop drive through the gorge begins at Nada, 1½ miles west of the Slade interchange of the Mountain Parkway on KY 15. At Nada you turn north (right) onto highway KY 77 and continue west on KY 715. Eight miles of paved highway parallels the river. KY 715 connects with KY 15 at Pine Ridge.

KY 77 passes through Nada Tunnel, which was cut by hand through a rocky ridge in 1877. Picks and shovels were used to excavate the 10-foot-wide, 13-foot-tall, and 800-foot-long tunnel that provided a narrow gauge railroad access to the giant timber of the area. Logging here was intense from the 1880s to the turn of the century.

In the summer of 1975 an information station was opened to assist visitors in learning more about the fascinating region and its recreational facilities. The information station is open April 1 to October 31 and it is located at the intersection of Rock Bridge (FS Road 24) and KY 715, just off the Pine Ridge exit of the Mountain Parkway.

Sky Bridge Picnic Area, Rock Bridge Picnic Area, Grays Arch Picnic Area, and Chimney Top Rock Overlook are open all year. There are three U.S. Forest Service–managed campgrounds in the Red River Gorge Geological Area. The Koomer Ridge Recreational Area, a fee area, is 3.5 miles southeast of the Slade exit of the Mountain Parkway on KY 15. Open August 1 to November 28, the campground, now under expansion, has 70 primitive campsites, pit toilets, drinking water, picnic tables, and grills. The Tunnel Ridge Road Group Camp and Chimney Top Rock Group Camp (primitive campsites, pit toilets), open year-round are available for church, civic, Scout, and other such groups through special arrangements with the U.S. Forest Service. Stanton District, Daniel Boone National Forest, KY 15, Stanton, Kentucky 40380. (606) 663-2852.

134

N

Courthouse
Rock

**Auxier
Branch
Trail**

203

Double
Arch

**Double
Arch
Trail** 201

Haystack Rock

**Auxier
Ridge
Trail**

202

204

**Courthouse
Rock
Trail**

Ravens
Rock

Ravens
Window

BM
707

Continued on page 140

L   B   O   O   N   E

221

Nada Tunnel

221

**Rough
Trail**

Grays Arch

**Grays
Arch
Trail**

205

0   ½   1 MILE

0   .293   .5   1 KILOMETER

TRAIL

Picnic
Area

1770

**D. Boon
Hut Trail**

TUNNEL

TUNNEL

RIDGE

39

R   I   D   G   E

USGS QUADS: Slade   © Thomas Press

Continued on page 156

NAME OF TRAIL: Auxier Branch Trail (FS #203)
MAP ON PAGE: 134
START: Courthouse Rock Trail (FS #202) 5.2 miles
                      north of KY 15 on Tunnel Ridge Road
END: Intersection of Courthouse Rock Trail (FS
                      #202)
TRAIL CONNECTIONS: Double Arch Trail (FS #201) and Courthouse
                      Rock Trail (FS #202)
USGS QUADS: Slade
COUNTIES: Powell
RATING: Easy; 0.8 mi.; footpath; −100 ft.

The Auxier Branch Trail is a eight-tenths-mile footpath that descends 100 feet from Tunnel Ridge to the Auxier Branch creek bottoms and then intersects the Courthouse Rock Trail. There are numerous areas suitable for camping along the trail. Extensive logging was done in the area during the early 1970s. Water is available year-round.

NAME OF TRAIL: Auxier Ridge Trail (FS #204)
MAP ON PAGE: 134
START: Trailhead parking area 3.9 miles north of KY
                      15 on Tunnel Ridge Trail
END: Haystack Road (overlook of Courthouse
                      Rock)
TRAIL CONNECTIONS: Courthouse Rock Trail (FS #202)
USGS QUADS: Slade
COUNTIES: Powell
RATING: Easy; 1.1 mi.; footpath; +200 ft.

The 1.1-mile Auxier Ridge Trail ascends 200 feet. The trail features many beautiful views; it's a ridgetop footpath through mixed deciduous and pine forests. Numerous red crossbill birds are often observed in November through March. A strip of bare rock known as the Judges Bench is encountered along the hike. Off to either side of the narrow rock walkway is a precipitous drop of several hundred feet. Double Arch, on the next ridge to the west, is easily seen from the vantage point. Ravens Rock is a prominent feature to the east. Blueberries are abundant on the ridge in August.

NAME OF TRAIL: Courthouse Rock Trail (FS #202)
MAP ON PAGE: 134
START: Auxier Ridge Trail trailhead, 3.9 miles north
                        of KY 15 on Tunnel Ridge Road
END: Courthouse Rock, approximately one-quarter
                        mile north of intersection of Auxier Branch
                        Trail (FS #203)
TRAIL CONNECTIONS: Auxier Ridge Trail (FS #204) and Auxier
                        Branch Trail (FS #203)
USGS QUADS: Slade
COUNTIES: Powell
RATING: Easy; 2.4 mi.; footpath; −300 ft.

The 2.4-mile Courthouse Rock Trail is a spur off the Auxier Ridge Trail. The trail descends 300 feet through scattered stands of hardwood and pine forest to the base of Courthouse Rock, a popular climbing spot. The beauty of this hike was severely limited by extensive logging in the early 1970s. There is no water along the trail. The trail ends a quarter-mile north of its intersection with the Auxier Branch Trail.

NAME OF TRAIL: Double Arch Trail (FS #201)
MAP ON PAGE: 134
START: Parking area 5.2 miles north of KY 15 on Tun-
                        nel Ridge Road
END: Double Arch
TRAIL CONNECTIONS: Auxier Branch Trail (FS #203)
USGS QUADS: Slade
COUNTIES: Powell
RATING: Easy to moderate; 1.0 mi.; footpath; +300 ft.

The 1.0-mile Double Arch Trail, which is easy to moderate in difficulty, ascends 300 feet through a forest of mixed hardwoods and pine and ends at a piggyback arch. Near the trailhead there is a series of wooden steps. The trail crosses several wet-weather streams and water availability is seasonal at best. After following the ridge and descending slightly, the trail ascends around an outcropping to a 12-foot-high, by 30-foot-wide arch topped with a 1.5-foot-high by 24-foot-wide span.

NAME OF TRAIL:	D. Boon Hut Trail (FS #1770)
MAP ON PAGE:	134
START:	Tunnel Ridge Road (FS Road #39), nine-tenths-miles north of KY 15 at the Grays Arch Picnic Area
END:	D. Boon Hut
TRAIL CONNECTIONS:	None
USGS QUADS:	Slade
COUNTIES:	Powell
RATING:	Easy; 0.7 mi.; footpath; −200 ft.

The D. Boon Hut Trail is a seven-tenths-mile trail that descends 200 feet to a rockhouse in which a crude hut of short split planks laid over a framework of poles was discovered in 1968. One of the planks bore the carved name: "D. boon." The hut is about the size of a pup tent, contains a small stone fireplace, and was definitely meant for no more than one person. There is some controversy over whether or not it was really built by the famous trapper, explorer, and settler. Remains of a potassium nitrate mine, possibly used during the War of 1812 or the Civil War, were also found in the cavernous overhang. The U.S. Forest Service has put a chain link fence around the relics to protect them from vandalism. The hike into the shelter has several switchbacks and is a maze of side trails and shortcuts, many of which promote serious washouts. When you reach the first rockhouse, the trail splits. They both lead to D. Boon Hut, but the one to the right is just as fascinating because it leads to a rockhouse with Indian petroglyphs. To get to D. Boon Hut requires some boulder hopping and negotiating wooden stairs. The base of the mammoth rockhouse has a sand floor. A few wet-weather streams are in the area; generally the water is scarce.

NAME OF TRAIL: Grays Arch Trail (FS #205)
MAP ON PAGE: 134
START: Picnic area nine-tenths miles north of KY 15
                        on Tunnel Ridge Road
END;   Intersection with Rough Trail (FS #221)
TRAIL CONNECTIONS: Rough Trail (FS #221)
USGS QUADS: Slade
COUNTIES: Powell
RATING: Easy; 0.3 mi.; footpath; +50 ft.

Grays Arch Trail is a three-tenths mile, easy walk connecting to Rough Trail. Grays Arch is one of the most spectacular of arches in the gorge. It is about 80 feet wide by 50 feet high and has trees growing atop it. No camping is allowed within 200 feet of the arch, although there is an excellent spring in the hollow adjacent to the base of the ridge from which the rock span was formed. About 300 yards north of the picnic area there's a wildlife opening. A small waterfall and some wooden steps are noted along this easy walk that ascends only 50 feet. No rock climbing or rappelling off the arch is allowed from April 1 to November 1 each year.

Sky Bridge, Red River Gorge Geological Area, Daniel Boone National Forest.
Photograph by the author.

Princess
Arch
233

235

Chimney Top
Rock Overlook
Trail

Pinch Em Tight
Gap

Rough Trail

Rush Ridge Trail
227

Continued on page 156 or 134

Pinch-Em
Tight Trail
223

39

T

Buck Trail
226

Koomer Ridge Trail

Continued on page 141

MILE

KILOMETER

220

Silvermine Arch Trail
225

Silvermine Arch

Hidden
Arch
Trail
208

Koomer Ridge
Camping and Picnic
Area

206 Tower Trail

PINE

Tower Rock

RIVER

Roadside Park

Roadside Park ×144

Hens Nest Rock

Roadside Park 715

BM 789

BM 750

214

Sky Bridge Loop Trail

Sky Bridge

×1158

D A N I E L   B O O

Castle Arch

Swift Camp

715

Laurel

Creek

Branch

Continued on page 150

Continued on page 140

CHIMNEY TOP

Whistling Arch Trail

234

N A T I O N A L   F O

×1181

Rough Trail

TRAIL

1231

221

Parched Corn

ROAD

Whites   Branch

219

SWIFT   CAMP

Swift Camp Creek Trail

Branch

Angel Windows

Angel Windows Trail

218

Sons

×1185

×1229

BM 1221

715

Wildcat Trail

WILDCAT

228

TRAIL

W

Cre

0   ½   1 MILE

0   5   1 KILOMETER

Reffes

USGS QUADS: Pomeroyton   **© Thomas Press**

Branch

Fork

NAME OF TRAIL:	Rough Trail (FS #221)
MAP ON PAGE:	134, 140–141
START:	KY 715, 4.2 miles north of intersection of KY 15 and KY 715
END:	KY 77, 1 mile north of Nada Tunnel
TRAIL CONNECTIONS:	Grays Arch Trail (FS #205), Swift Camp Creek Trail (FS #219), Koomer Ridge Trail (FS #220), Pinch-Em-Tight Trail (FS #223), and Rush Ridge Trail (FS #227)
USGS QUADS:	Slade, Pomeroyton
COUNTIES:	Wolfe and Powell
RATING:	Strenuous; 8.7 mi.; footpath; +600 ft.

Rough Trail is the longest and most strenuous hike in the Red River Gorge Geological Area. The 8.7-mile trail takes hikers through the heart of the gorge, passing the full range of forest types, rock formations (arches and rockhouses), and crossing several mountain streams, KY 15, and Chimney Top Road. From the first segment of the trail, the descent to the Parched Corn Creek bottoms, it is evident that the hike will be very scenic. Massive timber, boulder fields, sandstone cliffs, rhododendron "gardens," ferns, and wildflowers line the trail. Marked by the triangular brown and white "D.BooN" blaze, the trail is a footpath reinforced with water bars, although on some of the steep ascents, the trail is a bit washed out. The trail continually rises and falls from ridgetop to creek bottom, with a 600-foot change in elevation. Water is available year-round from Parched Corn and Chimney Top creeks, King Branch, and Martin Fork.

NAME OF TRAIL: Buck Trail (FS #226)
MAP ON PAGE: 140
START: Intersection with Pinch-Em-Tight Trail (FS #223)
END: Intersection with Koomer Ridge Trail (FS #220)
TRAIL CONNECTIONS: Pinch-Em-Tight Trail (FS #223) and Koomer Ridge Trail (FS #220)
USGS QUADS: Slade
COUNTIES: Wolfe
RATING: Easy; 1.5 mi.; footpath and woods road; +400 ft.

Buck Trail is a 1.5-mile connecting trail between Pinch-Em-Tight and Koomer ridges. The trail crosses the right fork of Chimney Top Creek amid thick stands of rhododendron. A narrow gauge railroad once paralleled the creek. All that is left is the bed for the tracks. Eventually there's a fork in the trail; one path continues along the creek, the other steeply ascends the hill. There are numerous switchbacks, and the trail rises approximately 400 feet. Water is available year-round from Chimney Top Creek.

NAME OF TRAIL: Chimney Top Rock Overlook Trail (FS #235)
MAP ON PAGE: 140
START: Parking area, Chimney Top Road
END: Chimney Top Rock
TRAIL CONNECTIONS: Princess Arch Trail (FS #233)
USGS QUADS: Pomeroyton
COUNTIES: Wolfe
RATING: Easy; 0.2 mi.; footpath; −50 ft.

The Chimney Top Rock Overlook Trail begins at the parking area at the end of Chimney Top Road off KY 715. The easy, two-tenths mile trail (no water available) leads to the most spectacular overlook in the Red River Gorge Geological Area. Along the wide footpath are numerous ledge overlooks of Raven Rock, Half Moon Arch, and the Chimney Top Creek bottoms. To the right of the trailhead, across the gravel parking area, is a short footpath leading to Princess Arch, a 32-foot-wide by 8-foot-high delicate rock span nestled in a rhododendron thicket. Pit toilets, garbage cans, and picnic tables are located at the parking area.

NAME OF TRAIL:	Hidden Arch Trail (FS #208)
MAP ON PAGE:	140
START	Left fork of gravel road in Koomer Ridge Campground
END:	Hidden Arch
TRAIL CONNECTIONS:	None
USGS QUADS:	Slade
COUNTIES:	Wolfe
RATING:	Easy; 1.0 mi.; footpath; −100 ft.

The Hidden Arch Trail is one of the newest trails in Red River Gorge Geological Area. It is one mile long and is practically level until the end, where it descends about 100 feet. At the end of the maintained section of the trail there's a view of the arch, which is tucked away in a cliffline. To get down to its base requires some scrambling.

NAME OF TRAIL:	Koomer Ridge Trail (FS #220)
MAP ON PAGE:	140
START:	Koomer Ridge Campground, 5.3 miles southeast of the Slade exit of the Mountain Parkway, off KY 15 (take the left fork of the campground road)
END:	Intersection of Rough Trail (FS #221)
TRAIL CONNECTIONS:	Rough Trail (FS #221) and Buck Trail (FS #226)
USGS QUADS:	Slade and Pomeroyton
COUNTIES:	Powell
RATING:	Easy; 5.3 mi.; footpath; −400 ft.

The Koomer Ridge Trail is a 2.3-mile trail that descends from Koomer Ridge to the Chimney Top Creek bottoms approximately 400 feet. The walk is easy on top of the ridge, although there are a few "toe-pinching" descents towards the end. Drinking water is available seasonally at the Koomer Ridge Campground and year-round from Chimney Top Creek. The trail passes through mixed hardwoods and pine atop the ridge and rhododendron, mountain laurel, and stands of towering tulip poplars in the creek bottom.

NAME OF TRAIL: Pinch-Em-Tight Trail (FS #223)
MAP ON PAGE: 140
START: Tunnel Ridge Road (FS Road 39), eight-tenths miles north of KY 15
END: Intersection with Rough Trail (FS #221)
TRAIL CONNECTIONS: Rough Trail (FS #221), Buck Trail (FS #226), and Rush Ridge Trail (FS #227)
USGS QUADS: Slade
COUNTIES: Powell and Wolfe
RATING: Easy; 1.8 mi.; footpath and woods road; −100 ft.

The Pinch-Em-Tight Trail is a 1.8-mile, easy walk atop Pinch-Em-Tight ridge. It passes through mixed hardwoods and pine along an old road bed. No water is available; the trail descends 100 feet.

NAME OF TRAIL: Princess Arch Trail (FS #233)
MAP ON PAGE: 140
START: Parking area at the end of Chimney Top Road, approximately 3.8 miles north of KY 715
END: Princess Arch
TRAIL CONNECTIONS: Chimney Top Rock Overlook Trail (FS #235)
USGS QUADS: Pomeroyton
COUNTIES: Wolfe
RATING: Easy; 0.2 mi.; footpath; −100 ft.

Princess Arch Trail is an easy, two-tenths-mile trail that descends 100 feet. It leads to a beautiful bare span of rock approximately 8 feet high and 32 feet wide—one of the most delicate and spectacular of arches in the Red River Gorge Geological Area. It is easily reached and, although the trail leads to the top of the arch, it is not difficult to get to the base. The arch is especially beautiful when the rhododendron is in bloom. If you're going to photograph the arch, take the widest lens you have and shoot from the base out towards the spur of the ridge. No water is available on this hike.

NAME OF TRAIL:	Rush Ridge Trail (FS #227)
MAP ON PAGE:	140
START:	Tunnel Ridge Road, eight-tenths miles north of KY 15 (just south of the Grays Arch Picnic Area)
END:	Intersection with Rough Trail (FS #221)
TRAIL CONNECTIONS:	Rough Trail (FS #221) and Pinch-Em-Tight Trail (FS #223)
USGS QUADS:	Slade
COUNTIES:	Powell
RATING:	Easy; 1.0 mi.; footpath; −50 ft.

The Rush Ridge Trail is a 1-mile ridgetop (practically level) approach hike to Rough Trail. The easy walk through mixed hardwoods and pine is rather uneventful. No water is available along the trail.

NAME OF TRAIL:	Silvermine Arch Trail (FS #225)
MAP ON PAGE:	140
START:	Koomer Ridge Campground (right fork of gravel road, first loop)
END:	Silvermine Arch
TRAIL CONNECTIONS:	None
USGS QUADS:	Slade and Pomeroyton
COUNTIES:	Wolfe
RATING:	Easy; 1.0 mi.; footpath; −150 ft.

Silvermine Arch Trail is a 1-mile trail that leads hikers to a 30-foot-high, by 60-foot-wide rock arch. It is an easy walk atop Koomer Ridge through forests of mixed hardwoods and pine. The last two-tenths mile of the trail descends approximately 150 feet to a series of steps at the base of the arch. There are some unusually large hemlock trees in the creek valley below the ridge.

NAME OF TRAIL: Tower Trail (FS #206)
MAP ON PAGE: 140
START: Fee deposit sign at entrance to Koomer Ridge Campground on KY 15, 5.3 miles east of Slade exit on the Mountain Parkway
END: Koomer Ridge Tower
TRAIL CONNECTIONS: None
USGS QUADS: Slade
COUNTIES: Wolfe
RATING: Easy; 0.4 mi.; footpath; +60 ft.

The Tower Trail is an easy, four-tenths-mile walk from the Koomer Ridge Campground to the last lookout tower remaining in the gorge area. Fire surveillance is done by airplane now, and the tower was left so that visitors could get an eagle's eye view of the surrounding countryside. Since the gorge is plateau land, though, you're really not high enough to look down into many valleys. The main section of the gorge can't be seen from the top of the 60-foot tower, but it's an excellent vantage point at sunrise and sunset, if you've got the nerve to negotiate the steps in the dark.

NAME OF TRAIL: Angel Windows Trail (FS #218)
MAP ON PAGE: 141
START: KY 715, 3 miles south of Sky Bridge at the Parched Corn Creek Overlook
END: Angel Windows
TRAIL CONNECTIONS: Swift Camp Creek Trail (FS #219)
USGS QUADS: Pomeroyton
COUNTIES: Wolfe
RATING: Easy; 0.3 mi.; woods road; +100 ft.

The Angel Windows Trail is three-tenths miles long. It simply leads through ridgetop woods to a rock formation on the adjacent cliffline. Angel Windows is a small arch with two "windows," holes through the sandstone cliffline. Both are about 5 feet high. No water is available; the trail is easy. The walk back to the parking area ascends 100 feet.

NAME OF TRAIL:	Sky Bridge Loop Trail (FS #214)
MAP ON PAGE:	141
START:	Picnic area at the end of Sky Bridge Road off KY 715
END:	Sky Bridge
TRAIL CONNECTIONS:	None
USGS QUADS:	Pomeroyton
COUNTIES:	Wolfe
RATING:	Easy; 0.9 mi.; footpath; +100 ft.

The Sky Bridge Loop Trail is a nine-tenths-mile loop trail beginning atop the ridge from which Sky Bridge was formed. One of the most hiked trails in Red River Gorge Geological Area, the paved footpath is popular with casual day-hikers and those who picnic at Sky Bridge. The loop simply circles the natural rock arch, ending at its base. Hikers walk atop Sky Bridge and then descend along the contour of the cliffline. A series of steps leads to the base of the arch. It's all downhill to the base of the arch; the return hike climbs 100 feet. The trail is rated easy; there is no water available. Sky Bridge is approximately 75 feet wide and 25 feet high. A second arch at its base measures 6 feet high and 9 feet wide. An alternative to retracing your steps is to follow the trail on the east side of the ridge. It leads up some wooden steps to the parking lot.

NAME OF TRAIL:	Whistling Arch Trail (FS #234)
MAP ON PAGE:	141
START:	KY 715, three miles south of Sky Bridge Parking Area
END:	Whistling Arch
TRAIL CONNECTIONS:	None
USGS QUADS:	Pomeroyton
COUNTIES:	Wolfe
RATING:	Easy; 0.2 mi.; footpath; −50 ft.

Whistling Arch is an easy, level, two-tenths mile footpath that begins on KY 715 at its junction with Sky Bridge Road. The trail leads to a 5-foot-high, 8-foot-wide arch in the cliffline. It affords a magnificent view of Parch Corn Creek bottoms. The trail is easy, but there is no water available along it.

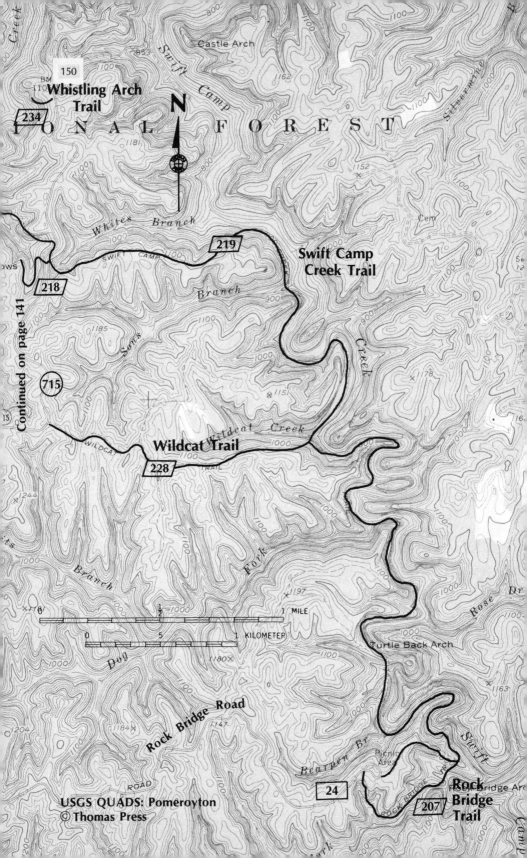

Castle Arch

853

150
BM

Whistling Arch Trail

234

ONAL FOREST

N

Whites Branch

Swift Camp

219

Swift Camp Creek Trail

218

SWIFT CAMP

Branch

Sons Branch

1185

715

WILDCAT **Wildcat Trail**

228

TRAIL

Wildcat Creek

Creek

1178

Fork

1197

Continued on page 141

Branch

1181

½ 1000 1 MILE

0 5 1 KILOMETER

Dog

1180

1000

1244

Turtle Back Arch

1163

Rose Dr

1100

Rock Bridge Road

1184

1147

ROAD

Bearpen Br

Swift

Picnic Area

24

ROCK BRIDGE

207

Rock Bridge Trail

USGS QUADS: Pomeroyton
© Thomas Press

NAME OF TRAIL:	Wildcat Trail (FS #228)
MAP ON PAGE:	150
START:	KY 715, 1.5 miles south of Angel Windows trailhead
END:	Intersection with Swift Camp Creek Trail (FS #219)
TRAIL CONNECTIONS:	Swift Camp Creek Trail (FS #219)
USGS QUADS:	Pomeroyton
COUNTIES:	Wolfe
RATING:	Easy; 2.0 mi.; footpath and logging road; −200 ft.

Wildcat Trail is a 2-mile long trail that intersects with Swift Camp Creek Trail approximately 4.5 miles north (downstream) of Rock Bridge. The Wildcat Creek bottoms are extensively used for backcountry camping, and the trail is well suited for short hike-in overnight trips or as a shortcut to KY 715 for those who don't wish to hike the entire Swift Camp Creek Trail. Wildcat Trail is fairly flat above the cliffline where it meanders through pine woods and mixed deciduous forest along an old logging road. As it descends the cliffs (200 feet), it goes through a grove of hemlocks and rhododendron thickets. Near its intersection with Swift Camp Creek Trail, there are numerous rockhouses. Water is available only below the cliffline. The trail is an easy to moderate hike. During fall of 1978, the trail was maintained by Young Adults Conservation Corps (YACC) crews. Near the intersection of Swift Camp Creek Trail there are two large holly trees.

NAME OF TRAIL: Rock Bridge Trail (FS #207)
MAP ON PAGE: 150
START: Parking area at end of Rock Bridge Road (FS
                      Road 24), off KY 715
END: Parking area at end of FS Road 24
TRAIL CONNECTIONS: Swift Camp Creek Trail (FS #219)
USGS QUADS: Pomeroyton
Counties: Wolfe
RATING: Easy; 1.3 mi.; footpath; +200 ft.

Rock Bridge Trail is a 1.3-mile loop trail beginning and ending in the picnic area at the end of Rock Bridge Road. Hiking counterclockwise, the trail sharply descends along the cliffline amid towering hemlocks and lush undergrowth of rhododendron and mountain laurel. Ferns, numerous species of wildflowers, and mosses line the trail. The trail parallels the Rockbridge Fork of Swift Camp Creek, one of the most beautiful streams in the red River Gorge Geological Area. Rock Bridge, a 50-foot-wide by 15-foot-high span of rock, is the only natural arch in the region that has a stream flowing beneath it. Rock Bridge is a beautiful spot for a pack-in, pack-out day-hiking picnic. The hike back to the picnic grounds climbs about 200 feet and ends in a pine thicket. The trail is rated easy to moderate and is exceptionally beautiful. Water is available year-round on the self-guided nature interpretive trail.

NAME OF TRAIL: Swift Camp Creek Trail (FS #219)
MAP ON PAGE: 141, 150
START: Rock Bridge Trail (FS #207)
END: KY 715, 4.1 miles north of KY 15 at the Pine
                      Ridge exit of the Mountain Parkway
TRAIL CONNECTIONS: Rock Bridge Trail (FS #207) and Wildcat Trail
                      (FS #228)
USGS QUADS: Pomeroyton
COUNTIES: Wolfe
RATING: Moderate; 6.7 mi.; footpath; +200 ft.

Swift Camp Creek Trail is one of the most scenic and popular hiking trails in the Red River Gorge Geological Area. It is also historically interesting. White settlers who came to this secluded creek valley in the late 1800s were awed by the magnificent stands of timber and began an era of extensive timbering.

During the early logging operations, a series of splash dams was built at intervals along Swift Camp Creek to increase the stream volume. These dams were made of long tree trunks staked to one another and sealed with rock and mud. Each dam backed up water to a depth of six to eight feet. Cut timber was then piled in the stream bed between dams, and when spring rains filled the river, the dams were opened either with explosives or, if of the revolving type, by pulling a pin. This unleashed a flood and the logs in the channel were picked up by the current and floated down to the next dam. This dam, too, was blasted and the process continued in this manner until all the logs reached the Red River.

Stationary dams were used in the smaller feeder streams such as Silver Mine Branch where logging was done in a short time. The revolving splash dams were used over and over and were usually built on the larger streams such as Swift Camp Creek or Gladie Creek. There were also several revolving dams in the Red River. The remains of one of the revolving dams is still visible in Swift Camp Creek about a quarter mile below Rock Bridge. Logs that were floated down Swift Camp Creek and the Red River to Clay City were sawed into lumber at the Broadhead and Garrett Mill, one of the largest band mills to operate in eastern Kentucky. Settlers paid for land by simply selling the timber off it.

The 6.7-mile Swift Camp Creek Trail parallels the creek on its western bank, basically following the cliffline. From the trail's beginning at the intersection of Rock Bridge Trail to its end at KY 715, it ascends roughly 200 feet. There are numerous rhododendron thickets, giant hemlock trees, rock outcroppings, and wildflowers (in the spring) to highlight the walk.

For most of the hike, the creek is in sight of the trail. Numerous spring-fed branches cross the trail, providing year-round water sources. Before Dog Fork Creek is Turtle Back Arch, off the trail to the left, up the cliffline. The arch is 6 feet wide and 15 feet high.

About 1.5 miles below Rock Bridge on Swift Camp Creek is an area known as Hells Kitchen. This was the site of one of the early logging camps in the gorge area. The logging crews would assemble at this area while they waited for the spring rains to float the logs downstream. The spot received its name because of the rugged terrain, the long wait, and the logging camp cooking. From the trail can be seen stunning rock cliffs across the gorge as the trail tops a narrow ridge.

Camping is best in the Wildcat Creek bottoms, although space is limited and hiker impact is much in evidence. The Swift Camp Creek Trail is often combined with Rough Trail for a strenuous 16-mile hike.

Daniel Boone National Forest. Photograph courtesy of the Commonwealth of Kentucky, Department of Public Information.

Continued on page 134

156

Grays
Arch
Trail

221

Rough
Trail

205

Rush
Ridge
Trail

227

D. Boon
Hut Trail

1770

223

Pinch-Em
Tight Trail

R   I   D   G   E

39

F   O   R   E   S   T

TUNNEL

Branch

15

15

Oil Wells

216

Whittleton Branch Trail

217

Whittleton
Arch Trail

Whittleton Arch

R   I   D   G   E

Whittleton
Branch
Campground

Owls
Window

BM Granny
732

Leap
Meship
Rock

S   T   A   T   E   P   A   R   K

Natural Bridge
Balanced Rock

Bridge

0   1 MILE

0   5
KILOMETER

USGS QUADS: Slade   © Thomas Press

NAME OF TRAIL: Whittleton Branch Trail (FS #216)
MAP ON PAGE: 156
START: Whittleton Branch Campground in Natural Bridge State Resort Park
END: KY 15 and Tunnel Ridge Road intersection, 3.5 miles east of Slade exit of Mountain Parkway
TRAIL CONNECTIONS: Whittleton Arch Trail (FS #217)
USGS QUADS: Slade
COUNTIES: Powell
RATING: Easy; 1.9 mi.; footpath and logging road; +500 ft.

The Whittleton Branch Trail is a gradual climb, a 500-foot ascent in 1.9 miles. It parallels the creek bottom upstream and then uses the old bed of the narrow gauge rails of the Mountain Central Railroad that went out of business in 1928. Old ties (some of which are used as water bars), rails, and spikes can still be found along the trail. Near the end of the trail there is a bend in the road bed on which a train wreck once occurred; according to local historians, three men were killed. Water is available seasonally; the forest is predominantly pine.

NAME OF TRAIL: Whittleton Arch Trail (FS #217)
MAP ON PAGE: 156
START: Intersection with Whittleton Branch Trail (FS #216), 1 mile east of Whittleton Branch Campground
END: Whittleton Arch
TRAIL CONNECTIONS: Whittleton Branch Trail (FS #216)
USGS QUADS: Slade
COUNTIES: Powell
RATING: Easy; 0.2 mi.; footpath; +300 ft.

The two-tenths mile Whittleton Arch Trail is a spur off the Whittleton Branch Trail that ascends 300 feet. A popular cross-country hike is to continue across Whittleton Ridge and descend Double Cave Branch to Mill Creek Lake at Hemlock Lodge. The trail passes through stands of hardwoods, hemlock, and tulip poplar. There is no water available.

BEREA RANGER DISTRICT

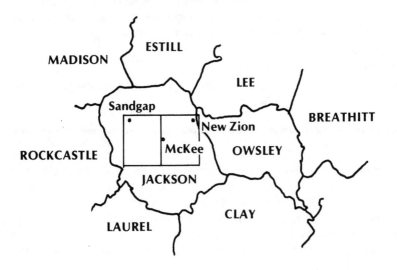

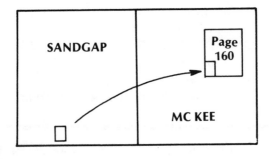

BEREA RANGER DISTRICT

The Berea Ranger District encompasses 73,000 acres of federally owned lands in Lee, Estill, Owsley, Jackson, and Rockcastle counties. There are only two trails in the ranger district, 2-mile Hughes Fork Trail (FS #302) and the 2.2-mile Renfro Trail, FS #302. There are only two trails in the district because the federally owned lands are scattered in small tracts. There are vast private landholdings in the area. The only area suitable for cross-country "bushwacking" is the War Fork Creek area north of the Turkey Foot Recreation Area.

Berea Ranger District, Daniel Boone National Forest, Berea, Kentucky 40403. (606) 986-8434.

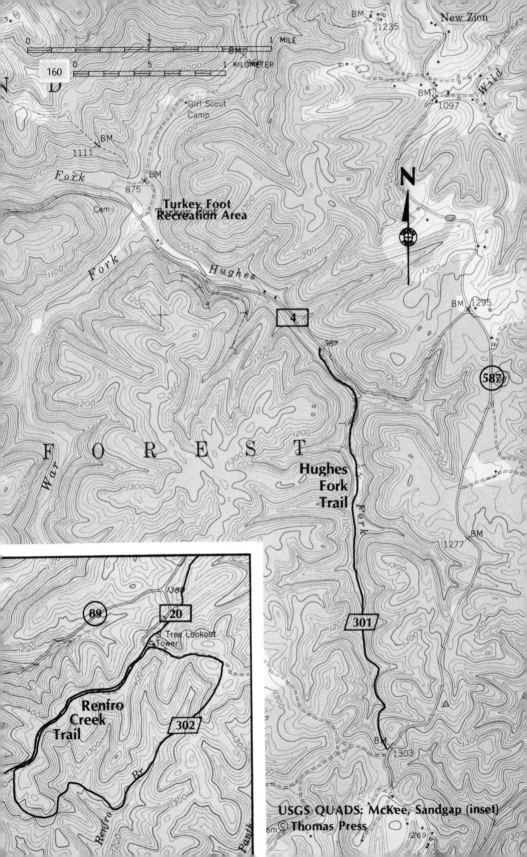

New Zion

BM 1235

BM 1097

Wild

N

BM 1295

587

Girl Scout Camp

BM 1111

Fork

BM 875

Cem

Turkey Foot
Recreation Area

Fork

Hughes

4

967

F O R E S T

Hughes
Fork
Trail

War

Fork

BM 1277

301

1386

89

20

Tree Lookout Tower

Renfro
Creek
Trail

302

1303

Renfro Br

Panth

USGS QUADS: McKee, Sandgap (inset)
© Thomas Press

160

NAME OF TRAIL: Hughes Fork Trail (FS #301)
MAP ON PAGE: 160
START: KY 587, one mile south of Turkey Foot Recreation Area
END: FS Road 4
TRAIL CONNECTIONS: None
USGS QUADS: McKee
COUNTIES: Jackson
RATING: Easy; 2.0 mi.; footpath; −300 ft.

The two-mile Hughes Fork Trail, built by the Civilian Conservation Corps (CCC) in the 1930s, parallels Hughes Fork Creek from its headwaters to its junction with FS Road 4. Hughes Fork Trail descends about 300 feet from the ridgetop to the creek bottoms, which are suitable for overnight camping. The availability of water is seasonal. During dry spells, many of the spring-fed branches dry up. The trail crosses the creek many times and meanders through rich stands of cove hardwoods containing beech, sugar maple, and hemlock, with scattered pockets of rhododendron.

There has been some stream improvement work done (installation of rock gabions) to enhance habitat for rainbow trout, which are stocked in War Fork Creek and swim up Hughes Fork Creek. Wildflowers are abundant.

NAME OF TRAIL: Renfro Trail (FS #302)
MAP ON PAGE: 160
START: S Tree Recreation Area, end of FS Road 20,
                        off KY 89 west of McKee
END: S Tree Recreation Area
TRAIL CONNECTIONS: None
USGS QUADS: Sandgap
COUNTIES: Jackson
RATING: Easy; 2.2 mi.; footpath and logging road;
                        −300 ft.

The Renfro Trail is a 2.2-mile loop trail beginning and ending at the look-out tower at the S Tree Recreation Area. The trail is best hiked counterclockwise. The first mile is a logging road through ridgetop woods of mixed pine and deciduous trees. Then the trail descends, by numerous switchbacks, 300 feet to Renfro Branch and parallels it on its west bank until reaching the headwaters. In 1970 the woodlands on the east bank of the creek were cut by selective harvest and a pond was constructed so that wildlife would have a year-round water source since the creek dries up in the summer. After leaving the creek, the trail ascends the cliffline to a logging road atop the ridge about one-quarter mile east of the S Tree Lookout Tower. The trail is an easy to moderate hike.

Hiker resting by Beaver Creek in the Beaver Creek Wilderness, Daniel Boone National Forest. Photograph by the author.

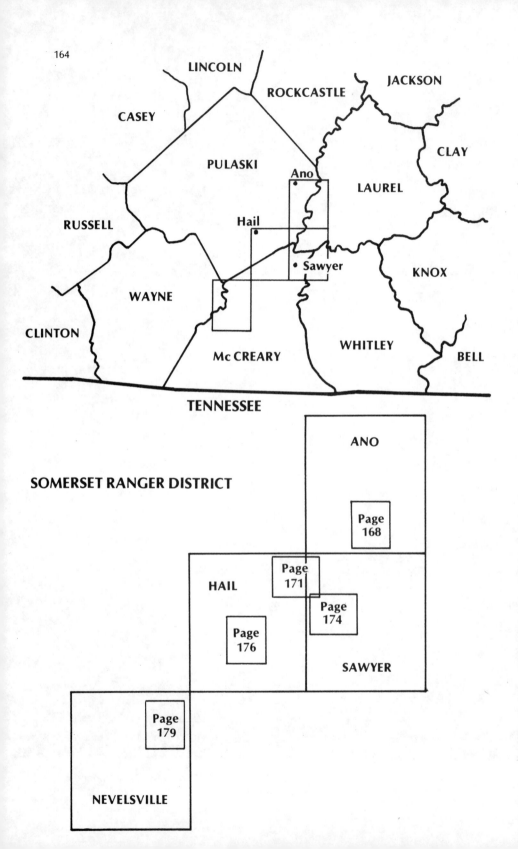

LINCOLN

ROCKCASTLE

JACKSON

CASEY

PULASKI

Ano

LAUREL

CLAY

RUSSELL

Hail

Sawyer

KNOX

WAYNE

CLINTON

McCREARY

WHITLEY

BELL

TENNESSEE

ANO

SOMERSET RANGER DISTRICT

Page
168

Page
171

HAIL

Page
174

Page
176

SAWYER

Page
179

NEVELSVILLE

SOMERSET RANGER DISTRICT

The Somerset Ranger District contains 64,000 acres of land under federal ownership in McCreary and Pulaski counties. This district of Daniel Boone National Forest has some of the finest hiking areas in all of eastern Kentucky—e.g., Beaver Creek Wilderness, The Narrows of the Rockcastle, and Natural Arch Scenic Area.

There are ten trails in the ranger district that cover a total distance of 18.7 miles. Although there are only two short trails (1.2 miles total length) in Beaver Creek Wilderness, the 5,500-acre area is very popular with hikers. This nearly roadless area is east of Alpine on FS Road 50, off U.S. 27.

The Eastern Wilderness Areas Act of 1975, which designated sixteen "instant" wilderness areas and seventeen study tracts in some of the thirty-six states under its authority, evolved through a combination of the provisions of two earlier proposed bills: Senate Bill 22, The National Forest Wild Areas Act 2, and Senate Bill 316, The Eastern Omnibus Wilderness Bill.

The third smallest of the eighteen wilderness areas established, Beaver Creek represents 1.91 percent of the total of all the wilderness acres combined. Cohutta Wilderness in Georgia and Tennessee is the largest of the eastern wilderness areas (37,300 acres) and Gee Creek Wilderness in Tennessee is the smallest (2,570 acres). Wildernesses were established in Alabama, Arkansas, Florida, Michigan, Missouri, New Hampshire, North Carolina, South Carolina, Vermont, Virginia, West Virginia, and Wisconsin.

Forest types in Beaver Creek Wilderness can be classified as those associated with slopes and stream banks. Below the cliffs, the canopy layer includes American beech, yellow poplar, ash, American and white basswood, sweet birch, several varieties of oak and hickory, red maple, elm and eastern hemlock—all constituents of the mixed mesophytic forest, the oldest and most diverse forest type in the eastern United States.

Big leaf magnolia, dogwood, and American Holly are generally prevalent in the understory of the slope forests of Beaver Creek, and common shrubs include rose bay rhododendron, spice bush, hazelnut, and mountain laurel.

Before the white man settled the land, bands of Choctaw, Cherokee, and Shawnee Indians roamed over this part of southeastern Kentucky living off the game-rich land and sometimes growing crops by a crude form of agriculture that was later adopted by mountaineers. The Indians left pottery, flint pieces (arrowheads, scrapers, and spear points) and mussel-shell beads as evidence of their living in the area. The Indians came in the spring and usually stayed on through into the warm fall days the settlers later called Indian Summer.

Settlers first came to Beaver Creek in the early 1800s—most by flatboat down the nearby Cumberland River. In the following hundred years, the land was settled, farmed, and timbered. Mud-chinked cabins were built on the main creek, garden patches and stock lots were cleared for use below the cliffline. Some of the mountaineers grew corn on the ridgetops; often surplus was made into "moonshine." Almost all activity around Beaver Creek ended rather abruptly in the early 1900s when commercial timber operations ceased. Only scattered pockets of timber remained. These stands were found in the steep, narrow side hollows where loggers found access difficult. Abandonment of the land by the loggers and subsistence farmers gave way to several decades of undisturbed forest renewal. Federal ownership of Beaver Creek came in 1937 when Cumberland National Forest was established.

There has not been much human use of the Beaver Creek area for about seventy years. Some sections of the creek drainage haven't been substantially altered since the times of the first settlers. Only four gravel access roads and a number of wildlife openings, which were maintained to promote huntable populations of whitetail deer under a state game management plan, are evidence of man's presence in the Beaver Creek region.

In secluded hollows, where sandstone cliffs border steep, narrow valleys, the land is remarkably wild and fresh. It is in these hard-to-reach backcountry sections of Beaver Creek that the character of the land comes forth; where sparkling waterfalls tumble into clear, pebble-bottomed pools amid fern-draped boulders shaded by stands of eastern hemlock and rose bay rhododendron.

Spring comes to this Appalachian plateau with a parade of wildflowers that continues until October, when the cold nights and warm days help set the valleys ablaze with autumn color. Wildflowers are abundant everywhere in the woodlands of Beaver Creek. In late March and early April, trailing arbutus, rue anemone, spring beauties, bluets, and hepatica add color to the damp mat of leaves on the forest floor. Soon crested dwarf iris, large-flowered trillium, bent trillium, and violets appear on sunny hillsides. May brings warmer, longer days and such wildflowers as jack-in-the-pulpit; pink lady's slipper; false Solomon's seal; stone crop, with its fleshy leaves and white blossoms, matted on ledges and boulders in the woods; wild geranium; partridgeberry; wild pink; and May apple, with its large umbrellalike leaves.

The surrounding cliffline was formed over 300 million years ago during the Pennsylvanian period of geologic history; major geologic formations of the area are sandstones and siltstones overlaid by shale. Weathering processes have eaten away at the softer layers of rock and exposed iron deposits and strata of colored gravel called conglomerate. In the evening light, these cliffs sometimes take on an orange or golden cast.

The scraggly, weather-beaten pines that grow from these rugged cliffs cling to life precariously.

Beaver Creek Wilderness is a favorite area for backpack-in stream fishing. The lower five miles of Beaver Creek have many big, deep pools that support some braggin' size smallmouth bass. A series of riffles and pools, Beaver Creek is lined with boulders, and hemlock trees and rhododendron shade the banks.

Access roads above the cliffline lead into the upper reaches of Beaver Creek Wilderness—FS Road 130 to Hurricane Fork, FS Road 839 to Middle Fork, and FS Road 128 to Freeman Fork. Pull-offs along U.S. 27 make good drop-off points for cross-country hikes.

The Narrows of the Rockcastle River is another popular cross-country hiking area. On the western bank of the river there are two hiking trails, (FS #409) Bee Rock Nature Trail, and (FS #503) Rockcastle Narrows Trail. Hiking cross-country though, it is possible to walk all the way upriver to the KY 80 bridge, a 17-mile riverside walk through boulder fields draped with vegetation, open stands of hardwoods and views of awesome Class-III and Class-IV rapids like Stair Step and Beech Narrows. (Class VI rapids are the most dangerous.) House-sized rocks litter the channel, and sandstone bluffs tower over the valley.

The Natural Arch Scenic Area has a network of 7.4 miles of trail in the vicinity of the 50-foot by 90-foot Natural Arch rock span and the Gulf Bottoms to the west. KY 927 cuts through the area on the ridgetop; the system of loop trails encircle the creek bottoms, which are flanked by sweeping forests that lead up to sheer cliffs.

Somerset Ranger District, Daniel Boone National Forest, Route #2, Box 507, Somerset, Kentucky 42501. (606) 679-2018.

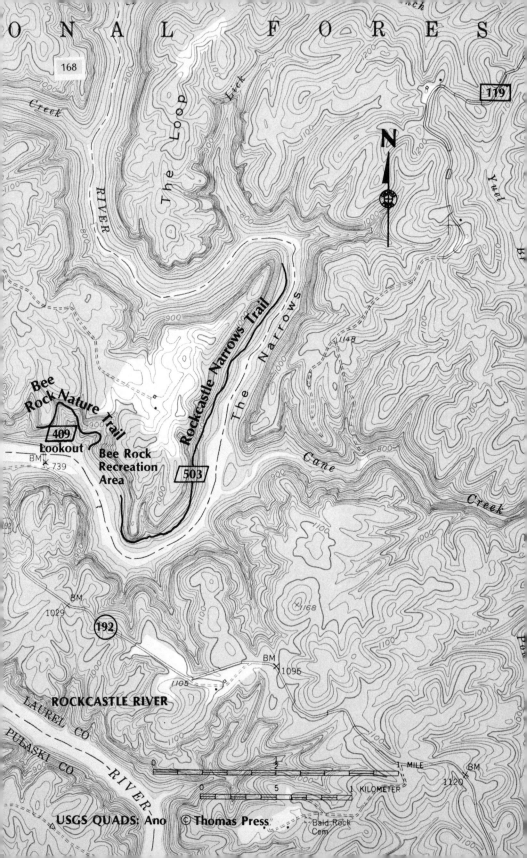

ONAL FOREST

168

119

Creek

RIVER

The Loop Lick

Creek

N

Rockcastle Narrows Trail

The Narrows

1148

Bee
Rock Nature Trail

409
Lookout
BM
739

Bee Rock
Recreation
Area

503

Cane

800

Creek

900

BM
1029

192

x 1168

1100

1100

BM
1096

1105

ROCKCASTLE RIVER

LAUREL CO

PULASKI CO

RIVER

0   1 MILE
0   5   1 KILOMETER

BM
1120

Bald Rock
Cem

NAME OF TRAIL: Bee Rock Nature Trail (FS #409)
MAP ON PAGE: 168
START: Bee Rock Recreation Area
END: Bee Rock Overlook
TRAIL CONNECTIONS: None
USGS QUADS: Ano
COUNTIES: Pulaski
RATING: Moderate; 0.5 mi.; footpath; +200 ft.

The Bee Rock Nature Trail is a half-mile footpath that climbs to a bluff overlooking the Rockcastle River. It climbs at least 200 feet and so is a challenging hike. But it's well worth it because, when you get to the top, there's a magnificent view. The trail, which was upgraded by YACC crews in the summer of 1978, crosses a footbridge, passes through stands of mixed hardwoods, and has some trailside rockhouses. No water is available. At the end of the trail, the U.S. Forest Service has built a rock lookout point with guard rails.

NAME OF TRAIL:	Rockcastle Narrows Trail (FS #503)
MAP ON PAGE:	168
START:	Bee Rock Recreation Area
END:	Lower narrows of Rockcastle River
TRAIL CONNECTIONS:	None
USGS QUADS:	Ano
COUNTIES:	Pulaski
RATING:	Easy; 1.4 mi.; footpath and logging road; −60 ft.

The 1.4-mile Rockcastle Narrows Trail parallels the western bank of the Rockcastle River near its lower narrows. The well-used trail, which begins (no trail sign) at the far end of the campground, is a combination of a logging road and footpath. The trail isn't well maintained since it is plagued by high water. Floods have swept a lot of trash into the floodplain, and this detracts from the beauty of the hike. At first the trail is easy to follow, then a maze of side trails head off towards the river, confusing hikers. This series of interconnected paths leads to the jumble of boulders (called the lower narrows) just upstream from the big pool. At low water, the narrows are especially beautiful; the white-water river is drawn to a tight chute. The river valley is flanked by sandstone bluffs, and huge boulders litter the channel of the watercourse. Much of the beauty of the lower narrows was lost, though, when the summer pool of Lake Cumberland was raised to near normal level in the summer of 1978 after six years of low water while repair work was done on Wolf Creek Dam. Backwater from the lake now covers much of the lower narrows.

Up the ridge from the narrows the trail turns into a logging road again. Keep to the left or else you'll end at the river's edge fighting for your life in thick bushes.

When you get to Beech Narrows, there's a campsite overlooking the river. The woods along the river are rather nondescript, with only a few big trees in scattered hemlock groves.

There's a great deal of camper evidence along the creek because the area is used by both hikers and canoe campers. Also, there's a private inholding of land just outside the Wild River right-of-way, and four-wheelers have cut a muddy road along the river that begins where the trail ends.

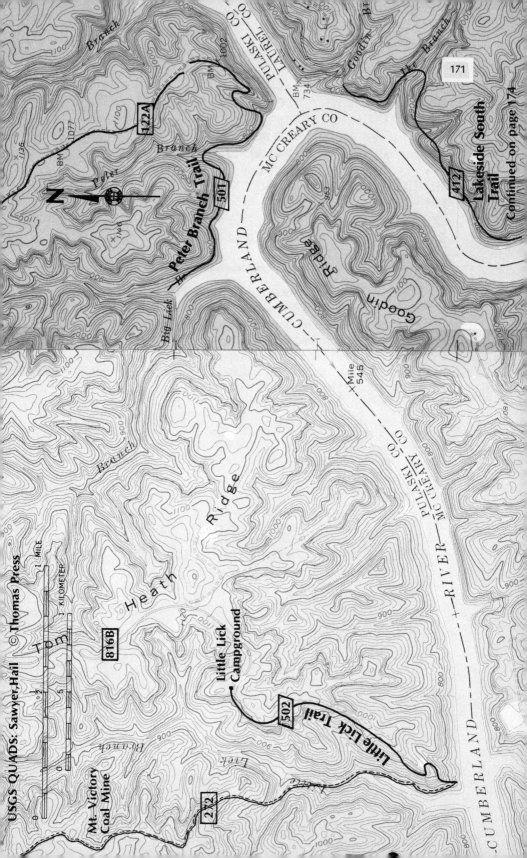

USGS QUADs: Sawyer, Hail © Thomas Press

Tom Branch

Heath

Ridge

816B

Little Lick
Campground

Little Lick Trail
502

2X2

Mt. Victory
Coal Mine

Branch

Lick Branch

CUMBERLAND

RIVER — MC CREARY

PULASKI CO

MC CREARY

Mile
545

1 MILE

1 KILOMETER

Branch

Peter Branch Trail

122A

501

Peter

Branch

N

Big Lick

CUMBERLAND

PULASKI CO
LAUREL CO

BM 1002

BM 734

MC CREARY CO

Goodin Branch

Lke Branch

171

412

Lakeside South
Trail

Continued on page 174

Goodin Ridge

NAME OF TRAIL:	Little Lick Trail (FS #502)
MAP ON PAGE:	171
START:	FS Road 816B at Little Lick Campground
END:	FS Road 122, two miles south of Mt. Victory coal mine
TRAIL CONNECTIONS:	None
USGS QUADS:	Hail
COUNTIES:	Pulaski
RATING:	Easy; 4.0 mi.; footpath; −300 ft.

The 4-mile Little Lick Trail begins on Heath Ridge at the Little Lick Campground, wanders atop rocky clifflines, and then descends 300 feet to Lake Cumberland through pine and mixed hardwoods. There are many views along the trail of both the lake and hills in the distance. The mouth of Little Lick Branch is a jumble of boulders with overhanging trees. Several rockhouses line the path. Water is available year-round. In the summer of 1978 the trail was linked to FS Road 122 by YACC crews.

NAME OF TRAIL: Peter Branch Trail (FS #501)
MAP ON PAGE: 171
START: Parking area at end of FS Road 122A
END: Big Lick Creek on FS Road 272
TRAIL CONNECTIONS: None
USGS QUADS: Sawyer
COUNTIES: Pulaski
RATING: Easy; 1.7 mi.; footpath, and logging road;
                      −200 ft.

The 1.7-mile Peter Branch Trail begins atop a ridge and descends 200 feet to Cumberland River bottoms. Several species of pine are noted along trail, as well as a small natural arch. There is a bench mark (geographic marker) set in limestone on the trail. It is an easy descent into the bottoms around the mouth of Peter Branch. There are many lake views and water is available year-round from Peter Branch and Big Lick Creek. The trail was brushed out by YACC crews in the summer of 1978 and was extended to hook up with FS Road 272, which was built as access to a timber sales tract.

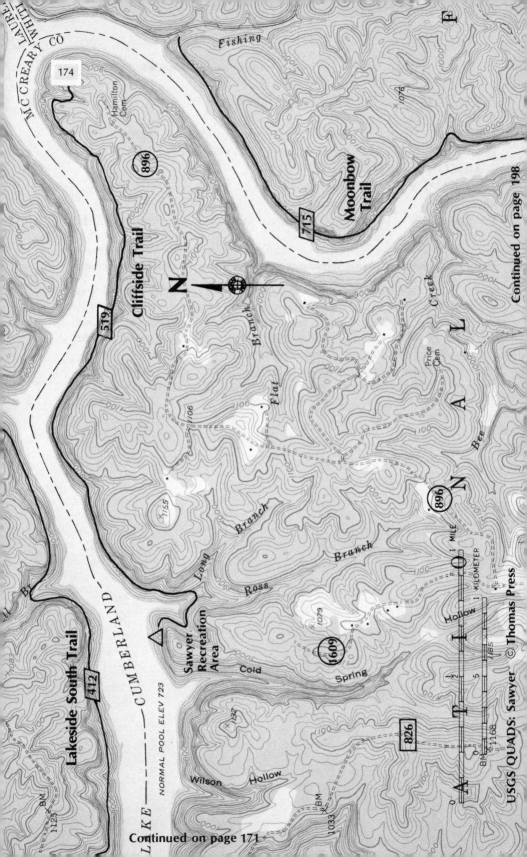

Lakeside South Trail

412

Cliffside Trail

519

Moonbow Trail

174

896

715

896

1609

826

CUMBERLAND LAKE

NORMAL POOL ELEV 723

Sawyer Recreation Area

Hamilton Cem

Fishing

Branch

Flat

Long Branch

Ross Branch

Branch

Cold

Spring

Hollow

Wilson Hollow

Price Cem

Bee Creek

Hollow

MC CREARY CO
WHITLEY CO
LAUREL CO

N

N

USGS QUADS: Sawyer © Thomas Press

MILE

KILOMETER

Continued on page 198

Continued on page 171

NAME OF TRAIL: Cliffside Trail (FS #519)
MAP IN PAGE: 174
START: Sawyer Recreation Area on KY 1609
END: KY 896
TRAIL CONNECTIONS: None
USGS QUADS: Sawyer
COUNTIES: McCreary
RATING: Easy; 2.5 mi.; footpath; +100 ft.

This 2.5-mile trail parallels the Cumberland River along its southern bank where it makes a sweeping bend between the mouth of the Rockcastle and Laurel Rivers.

Sawyer Recreation Area was closed the entire summer of 1978 for extensive renovation. Gravel pads for tents, lantern poles, picnic tables, and concrete grills were installed.

The Cliffside Trail was also renovated. A bridge was built across Long Branch Creek, and the brush and deadfalls were removed along the trail. During the summer months, the cliffs that border the trail to the right are for the most part hidden by foliage. The trail is gently rolling and easy. There are a few points along the trail from which hikers get a view of the lake. Brier patches are a nuisance to hikers although the trail is generally clear. Landslides along the shore of lake inlets are responsible for the thick annual growth of bushes that overtake the trail. A few impressive stands of hardwoods (mammoth oaks, hemlocks, maples, and birch) line the trail. Water is available seasonally at both ends of the trail. A second bridge was also constructed at the trail's end on KY 896. Treated drinking water is available at Sawyer Recreation Area.

USGS QUADS: Hail   © Thomas Press

176

USGS QUADS: Hail   © Thomas Press

N   A   L   F   O   R

Three
Forks of
Beaver
Creek
Overlook
Trail

Beaver Creek Loop Trail

518

512

Three Forks of Beaver
Overlook

Bauer Road

50

50

Bauer Road

Rams Horn Branch

Martin

Ridge

RIDGE

Baby Stocking Ridge

Bauer

Hurricane Fork

Middle Fork

NAME OF TRAIL:	Three Forks of Beaver Creek Overlook Trail (FS #512)
MAP ON PAGE:	176
START:	FS Road 50 (Bauer Road), 5.7 miles southeast of Alpine off U.S. 27
END:	Overlook
TRAIL CONNECTIONS:	Unmarked footpath along Beaver Creek
USGS QUADS:	Hail
COUNTIES:	McCreary
RATING:	Easy; 1.0 mi.; footpath; +100 ft.

The 1-mile Three Forks of Beaver Creek Overlook Trail begins at the gravel parking lot on the gravel road (right, south) off Bauer Road (parking facilities for approximately 100 feet and ends at the overlook, a rock bluff 300 feet above the conjunction of the Freeman, Middle, and Hurricane forks of Beaver Creek. Pine trees shading the overlook were knocked down by a tornado that ripped through southern Daniel Boone National Forest in April of 1974.

The trail begins in a pine woods parallel to an abandoned logging road, then descends along cliffline through mountain laurel and hemlock groves. The ridgetop trail provides impressive vistas of wooded creek bottoms. There are excellent opportunities for rappelling from cliffs to the left of the trail. The trail crosses a wet-weather creek, so water is seasonal at best. After a series of switchbacks along the contour of the ridge, the trail ascends to the overlook. Blueberries are abundant at the overlook in late summer. To descend to the creek, hikers must walk down the logging road up in the weeds and small trees. The trail to the overlook is well maintained and heavily traveled. A flagged but unnumbered trail parallels the creek downstream from Three Forks.

NAME OF TRAIL: Beaver Creek Loop Trail (FS #518)
MAP ON PAGE: 176
START: FS Road 50 (Bauer Road) at bridge over
                      Beaver Creek
END: Bridge over Beaver Creek
TRAIL CONNECTIONS: Unmarked footpaths upstream from bridge
USGS QUADS: Hail
COUNTIES: McCreary
RATING: Easy; 0.2 mi.; footpath; −20 ft.

The two-tenths-mile Beaver Creek Loop Trail begins and ends at the concrete bridge over Beaver Creek approximately 2.5 miles northeast of gravel parking lot for Three Forks of Beaver Creek Overlook Trail. With the establishment of Beaver Creek Wilderness, the gravel road was blocked off with a gate to prohibit vehicle use in the area. Thus, those who wish to hike the Beaver Creek Loop Trail must walk the gravel road from the parking area before reaching the trailhead. The gravel road is a steep, winding road that descends to the creek bottom with numerous hairpin turns.

The Beaver Creek Loop Trail parallels Beaver Creek downstream from the bridge, passing through creek bottom stands of hemlocks and lush vegetation of rhododendron and many species of wildflowers. Allegheny spurge *(Pachysandra procembens)* is especially abundant. The trail crosses a footbridge of stones in the creek and returns to the concrete bridge. Water is available from feeder branches, some of which may be crossed by footlogs when the creek is high. The trail is rated easy, with little, if any, ascent. For those who wish to camp overnight, there are plenty of level campsites up Rams Horn Branch, east of the trailhead.

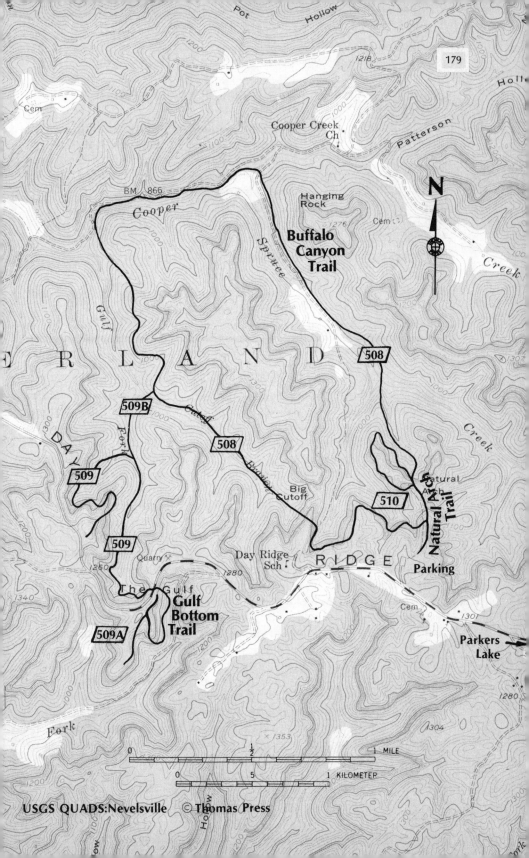

NAME OF TRAIL:	Buffalo Canyon Trail (FS #508)
MAP ON PAGE:	179
START:	Two-tenths miles north of parking area of Natural Arch Scenic Area off Natural Arch Trail (FS #510). The Natural Arch Scenic Area is two miles west of the town of Parkers Lake, off U.S. 27 on KY 927.
END:	Natural Arch
TRAIL CONNECTIONS:	Natural Arch Trail (FS #510) and Gulf Bottom Trail (FS #509)
USGS QUADS:	Nevelsville
COUNTIES:	McCreary
RATING:	Moderate; 5.0 mi.; footpath, logging road, and gravel road; +200 ft.

This 5-mile loop trail is best hiked clockwise from its junction with Natural Arch Trail. The Buffalo Canyon Trail is well maintained and marked with a white diamond blaze. The first and last mile of the trail are gravel and dirt footpaths, although once you've descended into the Cooper Creek bottoms the trail becomes a logging road. For the first several hundred yards the trail hugs the cliffline and passes through dense stands of rhododendron canopied by towering hemlocks; ferns, partridgeberry, and mosses grace the trail. Water is plentiful along most of the way. There are numerous rockhouses along the first mile of the trail.

At one point early in the hike there's a footbridge across a cascading brook that flows through an absolutely beautiful hollow littered with huge boulders that have fallen from the steep cliffs. After crossing the footbridge, the trail follows the hillside, crosses another small stream, and descends through open woods to yet another small stream. When you get to the trail sign, continue uphill by a series of steep switchbacks to Chimney Arch, which was formed out of a steep cliffline. The arch is approximately 30 feet high and 25 feet wide. The forces of nature not only carved out the arch, but also sliced a deep crevice between the parallel monoliths and created a skylight effect when you stand directly under the formation. Chimney Arch is approximately one mile west of Buffalo Canyon trailhead by trail.

After leaving the arch the trail follows the cliffs through a dense pine woods. Chipmunks, squirrels and birdlife seemed particularly abundant along this section of the trail. When I hiked it after a thunderstorm, mushrooms were just beginning to pop up through the moist ground cover of pine needles.

Once the trail passes Cutoff Branch and finally descends into the Gulf Fork Branch of Cooper Creek, the logging road begins. The creek bottoms are ideal for camping and water is abundant. The moist bottoms are filled with plantlife. Crested dwarf iris, Indian pipe, and rattlesnake plantain were observed along this section of the trail, which is canopied by pine and hemlock trees. As I was crossing one of the many small feeder streams that intersect the trail, a grouse flushed from the rhododendron along the creek.

The trail signs at the junction of the Gulf Bottom Trail have been vandalized so, if you want to continue the buffalo Canyon Loop, hike straight ahead. The middle two miles of the loop are always within earshot of Cooper Creek and cross numerous feeder streams along the way. Cooper Creek is itself actually crossed twice. There's a convenient bridge of stepping stones at the first crossing; the second crossing has a foot log. At the mouth of Spruce Creek I found some litter and fire scars left by careless campers. This area appears to support a small herd of whitetail deer as there were hoof prints all along sandy trail. The area has apparently been logged some years back because it is now in second growth saplings and thick bushes. The last mile of the trail ascends through open woods along Spruce Creek—the last water source before reaching Natural Arch. There's a small waterfall at the left of the trail. Overall, the trail is easy, although it does climb about 200 feet in the last half-mile, the most difficult stretch in the 5-mile loop. The Buffalo Canyon Trail is an excellent choice for an afternoon day hike, but it could also be adapted to a leisurely overnight backpacking trip.

NAME OF TRAIL:	Gulf Bottom Trail (FS #509)
MAP ON PAGE:	179
START:	Three miles west of Parkers Lake, on KY 927; across the road from the first of two parking lots for scenic overlooks of Gulf Bottoms
END:	0.2 miles west on unmarked logging road off KY 927
TRAIL CONNECTIONS:	Buffalo Canyon Trail (FS #508)
USGS QUADS:	Nevelsville
COUNTIES:	McCreary
RATING:	Easy; 1.2 mi.; footpath; +200 ft.

This 1.2-mile loop is one of the most fascinating of the area's footpaths. The trailhead is on KY 927 (left side of the road) just after crossing an iron bridge approximately one mile west of the entrance to the Natural Arch Scenic Area. A small sign marks the beginning of the trail.

Gulf Bottom Trail parallels KY 927 atop a steep ridge for about a tenth of a mile then sharply descends the cliffline by flights of metal steps. It hugs the bluffs passing through numerous rockhouses; a wooden rail guards hikers from the precipitous dropoff to the right. The trail then goes under the KY 927 bridge through a narrow, 30-foot-deep gorge. It's an imaginative way to explore the rock cliffs, but the potentially beautiful spot is spoiled by litter (beer cans, animal skeletons, and paper) that has been thrown off the highway bridge to the trail below.

Once you've crossed under the highway, there's another set of stairs that leads even farther below the rocks. The trail then follows the base of simply magnificent cliffs that shelter huge hemlock and poplar trees and gigantic boulders draped in ferns and stonecrop. After crossing a small stream, the trail gradually climbs (by a series of switchbacks) until it comes to the sign that indicates the turnoff to the Buffalo Canyon Trail.

Gulf Bottom Trail is connected to the Buffalo Canyon Trail by a 1-mile footpath (to the hiker's right) that parallels the Gulf Fork of Cooper Creek. This flat, easy segment of the trail passes through beech woods and then an overgrown bottom (lots of poison ivy and weeds). It crosses the creek (foot stones) near its junction with Buffalo Canyon Trail.

To complete the hike back to KY 927, proceed straight ahead when you get to the Buffalo Canyon turnoff. The half-mile section has numerous switchbacks and stairs that help hikers climb the cliff. The last two-tenths miles are steep (200-foot rise) and are the most strenuous climb in the entire trail system.

NAME OF TRAIL:	Natural Arch Trail (FS #510)
MAP ON PAGE:	179
START:	Parking lot of Natural Arch Scenic Area off U.S. 27, on KY 927, two miles west of Parkers Lake
END:	Natural Arch
TRAIL CONNECTIONS:	Buffalo Canyon Trail (FS #508)
USGS QUADS:	Nevelsville
COUNTIES:	McCreary
RATING:	Easy; 1.2 mi.; paved trail; +100 ft.

Natural Arch Trail is the most used footpath of the four in the Natural Arch Scenic Area. It is asphalt and 1.2 miles in length, including the half-mile Shawnee Nature Trail that circles Natural Arch. The imposing 50-foot-high and 90-foot-long sandstone arch was once a favorite camping area for wandering bands of Shawnee Indians who lived north of the Ohio River and came to Kentucky in the summer.

The facilities at Natural Arch Scenic Area, open year-round, include parking space for about thirty automobiles, picnic tables, grills, and pit toilets. There are no trash receptacles for picnickers as the day-use area is managed under pack-in, pack out regulations. The first tenth of a mile of the trail is suitable for the handicapped in wheelchairs, but several flights of steep steps limit their use of the entire trail. The two scenic overlooks near the trailhead can be reached by wheelchair, though.

Natural Arch is one of the most spectacular of the rock arches in Daniel Boone National Forest. It was formed from a ridge line and has trees growing atop it. There are a loose dirt floor and numerous boulders under the arch.

The Shawnee Nature Trail, a gravel footpath marked by a white diamond blaze, follows the cliffline from which Natural Arch was formed. At some stretches of the trail there is access to the top of the rock formation, which appears to have excellent potential for rappelling or top rope climbing. The Shawnee Nature Trail is self-guided and has many rock-houses and interpretive stations along the trail that describe the plantlife and geology of the area.

The trail ascends about 100 feet and is easy except for the flights of stairs, which may seem formidable to some of the tourists who seem to dominate the use of the day-hiking trail.

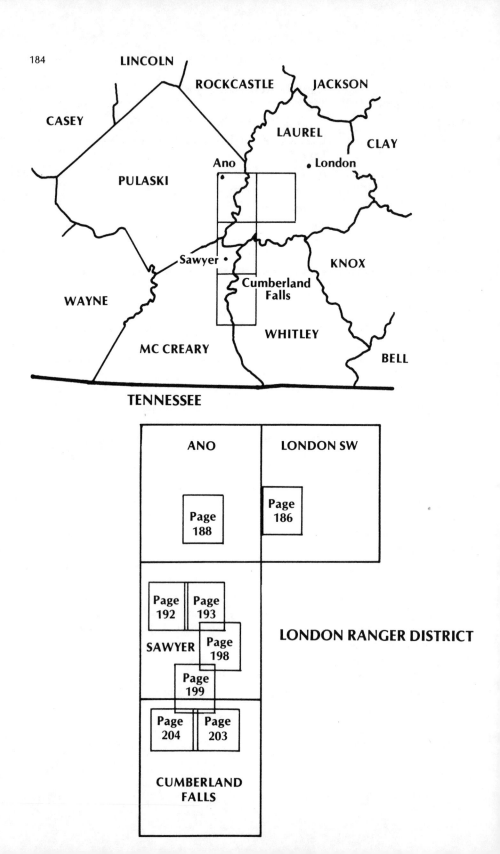

184

LINCOLN

ROCKCASTLE JACKSON

CASEY

LAUREL

CLAY

Ano

London

PULASKI

Sawyer

KNOX

Cumberland
Falls

WAYNE

WHITLEY

MC CREARY

BELL

TENNESSEE

ANO	LONDON SW

Page
188

Page
186

Page
192

Page
193

Page
198

SAWYER

Page
199

LONDON RANGER DISTRICT

Page
204

Page
203

CUMBERLAND
FALLS

LONDON RANGER DISTRICT

The London Ranger District encompasses 88,694 acres of federally owned lands in Laurel, Rockcastle, and Whitley counties. The twelve trails in the district (a total of 39.6 miles) are concentrated in three areas—the east bank of the Narrows of the Rockcastle River, Rockcastle Recreation Area, and Cumberland River–Lake Cumberland between Cumberland Falls and the Laurel Recreation Area.

The trail system in the London Ranger District includes three Adirondack-type shelters, two of which are on the Moonbow Trail and the other is at the mouth of Twin Branch Creek.

London Ranger District, Daniel Boone National Forest, Box G, London, Kentucky 40741. (606) 864-4163.

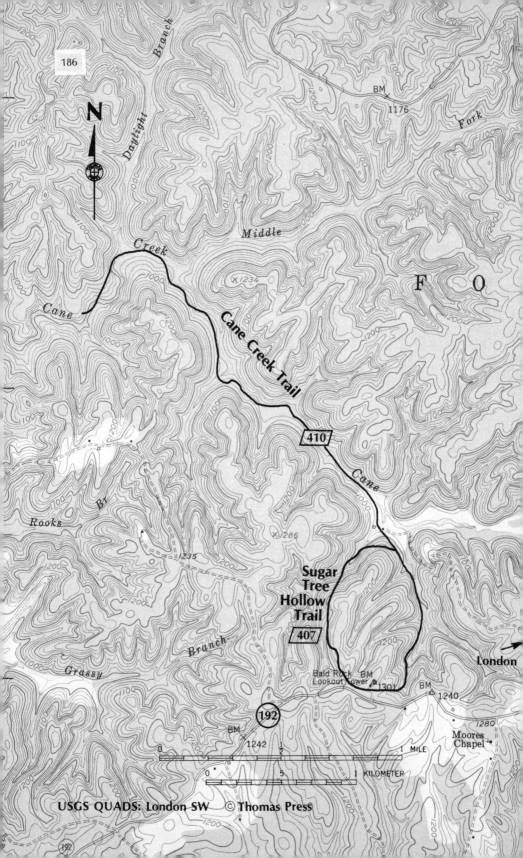

186

N

USGS QUADS: London SW © Thomas Press

NAME OF TRAIL:	Sugar Tree Hollow Trail (FS #407)
MAP ON PAGE:	186
START:	Bald Rock Picnic Area, approximately 10 miles southwest of London on KY 192
END:	Bald Rock Picnic Area
TRAIL CONNECTIONS:	Cane Creek Trail (FS #410)
USGS QUADS:	London SW
COUNTIES:	Laurel
RATING:	Easy; 1.7 mi.; footpath; +200 ft.

The Sugar Tree Hollow Trail is a 1.7-mile loop trail that ascends 200 feet from the Cane Creek bottoms to the former site of the Bald Rock Lookout Tower. The trail passes through stands of hardwoods with scattered pines. Water is seasonally available from Cane Creek; the trail was cleared in summer of 1978 under the Older Americans program.

NAME OF TRAIL:	Cane Creek Trail (FS #410)
MAP ON PAGE:	186
START:	Cane Creek bottoms at intersection of Sugar Tree Hollow Trail (FS #407)
END:	Deadends on Cane Creek
TRAIL CONNECTIONS:	Sugar Tree Hollow Trail (FS #407)
USGS QUADS:	London SW, Ano
COUNTIES:	Laurel
RATING:	Easy; 2.0 mi.; footpath; −100 ft.

The Cane Creek Trail is a 2-mile trail that goes from the Bald Rock Picnic Area (via 0.8 miles of the Sugar Tree Hollow Trail) down Cane Creek to the east. To reach the trailhead, hikers must first hike half of the Sugar Tree Hollow loop trail that encircles the woodlands southwest of the Bald Rock Picnic Area.

The Cane Creek Trail descends along Cane Creek approximately 100 feet. The gently rolling trail passes through a moist creek bottom rich in ground vegetation—rhododendron, mosses, ferns, and wildflowers. Water is available year-round, and there are some impressive stands of timber in the side hollows. Camping space is limited.

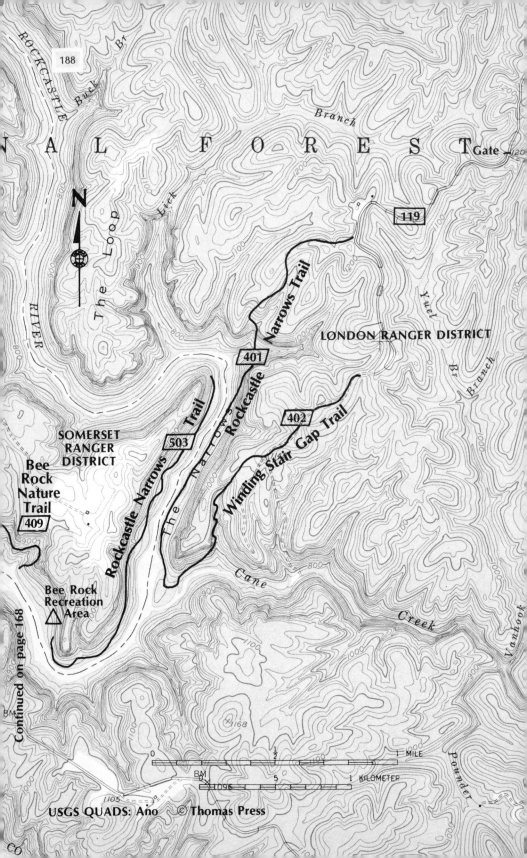

188

NATIONAL FOREST

Gate

119

N

The Loop

Buck Br

ROCKCASTLE

RIVER

Lick

Branch

Narrows Trail

401

LONDON RANGER DISTRICT

Yuel Br Branch

SOMERSET RANGER DISTRICT

Rockcastle Narrows Trail

503

The Narrows

Rockcastle

402

Winding Stair Gap Trail

Bee Rock Nature Trail

409

Bee Rock Recreation Area

Cane

Creek

Vanhook

Continued on page 168

BM

1168

BM

1105

1095

0   ½   1 MILE

0   5   1 KILOMETER

USGS QUADS: Ano   © Thomas Press

CO

NAME OF TRAIL:	Rockcastle Narrows Trail (FS #401)
MAP ON PAGE:	188
START:	FS Road 119, entrance to Cane Creek Wildlife Management Area
END:	Lower narrows of the Rockcastle River at the junction with Winding Stair Gap Trail (FS #402)
TRAIL CONNECTIONS:	Winding Stair Gap Trail (FS #402)
USGS QUADS:	Ano
COUNTIES:	Laurel
RATING:	Moderate; 2.4 mi.; footpath and logging road; −500 ft.

Rockcastle Narrows Trail parallels the east bank of the Rockcastle River across the lower narrows from the other Rockcastle Narrows Trail (FS #503). Hikers must walk about 1.5 miles on the gravel road (FS Road 119) before actually reaching the trailhead. This is because of the designation of 6,700 acres as the Cane Creek Wildlife Management Area. A locked gate keeps hikers from driving to the end of the road. In the spring of 1978 twenty whitetail deer were stocked in the area in hopes of establishing a resident population. Biologists have determined that the area has adequate habitat to support a small herd.

Walking down the gravel road, hikers should keep a sharp lookout for the trailhead on the right side of the road at a pull-off. There's a trail sign at the edge of the woods. The Rockcastle Narrows Trail is 2.4 miles long and begins as a logging road atop the ridge. The entire length of the trail was cleared in the summer of 1978 under the Older Americans program. A footpath finally branches off the logging road amid open forest of mixed hardwoods and pine. Continuing to descend for a total of 500 feet, the trail passes a side branch where water is available seasonally. Then it parallels the river through boulder fields and rhododendron thickets along rock ledges out of sight of the river, just above the floodplain.

NAME OF TRAIL: Winding Stair Gap Trail (FS #402)
MAP ON PAGE: 188
START: End of FS Road 119
END: Intersection with Rockcastle Narrows Trail, (FS #401)
TRAIL CONNECTIONS: Rockcastle Narrows Trail (FS #401)
USGS QUADS: Ano
COUNTIES: Laurel
RATING: Easy; 1.7 mi.; logging road; −300 ft.

Winding Stair Gap Trail is 1.7 miles long and descends 300 feet from the ridgetops to the Rockcastle River. Hikers can't actually drive to the trailhead because of a locked control gate on FS Road 119. It's about a 2-mile walk on the gravel road to the trailhead in the woods at the end of the road. The Winding Stair Gap Trail was cleared in the summer of 1978 under the Older Americans program, so hikers shouldn't have any trouble locating the trail, which descends through deciduous woods and parallels an abandoned logging road. Impressive patches of pink lady's slipper and several species of edible mushrooms are found along the trail in the spring. The trail is steep as it descends through the cliffline and there's a brief period where hikers must scramble around huge boulders littering the trail. There are numerous switchbacks. Good rockhouses along the trail are suitable for "holing up" in case of sudden thunderstorms. There are impressive cliffs to the right of the trail near its intersection with Cane Creek.

Daniel Boone National Forest. Photograph courtesy of the Commonwealth of Kentucky, Department of Public Information.

192

N

Gulf

ole

Tweed

Branch

Ridge

Bridge

1136

BM 1077

Peter

Branch

122A

1146

Branch

Lakeside North Trail

ROCKCASTLE

411

Ned Branch Trail

405

Parking

Peter Branch Trail

BM 1002

501

Rockcastle Recreation Area

Dutt

Scuttle Hole Trail

404

PULASKI CO

LAUREL CO

C

Continued on page 193

ERLAND

MC CREARY CO

Ridge

953

BM 734

1072

BM 1128

BM 1125

1193

Goodin Br

1000

Ike Branch

412

1125

1125

Campbell Br

0   ½   1 MILE

0   ½   1 KILOMETER

BM 5
1125

Lakeside South Trail

RIVER

Campbell Bottom

875

519

USGS QUADS: Sawyer

© Thomas Press

1029

BM

LAKE   CUMBERLAND

NORMAL POOL ELEV 723
Continued on page 174 1609

Sawyer Recreation Area

NAME OF TRAIL: Lakeside North Trail (FS #411)
MAP ON PAGE: 192
START: Intersection with Ned Branch Trail (FS #405)
END: Rockcastle River
TRAIL CONNECTIONS: Ned Branch Trail (FS #405)
USGS QUADS: Sawyer
COUNTIES: Laurel
RATING: Easy; 2.9 mi.; footpath; −100 ft.

The 2.9-mile Lakeside North Trail is below the cliffline for its entire length. It parallels the east bank of the Rockcastle River and eventually peters out. Off to the right of the Ned Branch Trail you'll find the trailhead deep in the woods. If you don't mind fighting the rhododendron, this trail is a good start for a cross-country jaunt to KY 192 at Bee Rock Recreation Area. Tweed Branch, 2 miles up the Rockcastle River, is an isolated creek with impressive cascading falls.

NAME OF TRAIL: Scuttle Hole Trail (FS #404)
MAP ON PAGE: 192
START: KY 1193, 1 mile east of Rockcastle Recreation
                      Area
END: Rockcastle Recreation Area
TRAIL CONNECTIONS: None
USGS QUADS: Sawyer
COUNTIES: Laurel
RATING: Easy; 1.1 mi.; footpath; −300 ft.

The 1.1-mile Scuttle Hole Trail begins on the ridgetop. It is a very scenic trail for those who like sweeping views of forestland. The trail actually splits into two footpaths. The northern, or upstream, section leads to an overlook that provides hikers a great view up Rockcastle River (to the right). The trail descends 300 feet through the headwaters of Dutch Branch and then climbs to the ridgetop overlooking the river. The lower section of the trail, which heads off to the left, crosses Dutch Branch through a maze of boulders. The trail actually is cut between two large rocks. Cliffs surround the valley, and hemlocks canopy the forest floor. The trail follows the creek to its mouth and coninues downstream to the Rockcastle Recreation Area.

NAME OF TRAIL: Lakeside South Trail (FS #412)
MAP ON PAGE: 192–193
START: Intersection of Twin Branch Trail (FS #406)
END: Rockcastle Recreation Area
TRAIL CONNECTIONS: Twin Branch Trail (FS #406)
USGS QUADS: Sawyer
COUNTIES: Laurel
RATING: Easy; 6.0 mi.; footpath; −100 ft.

The 6-mile long Lakeside South Trail parallels the northern bank of Lake Cumberland from the Twin Branch Shelter to the Rockcastle Recreation Area. The trail was brushed out in the summer of 1978 after years of neglect. It is not a popular trail and isn't that interesting as it's high above the lake in the woods. Campbell Bottom, a small resort community reached via FS Road 1125, is 2.5 miles downriver. At Ike Branch there's a footbridge over the creek. A practically level trail with no water available until Ike Branch, the Lakeside South Trail passes through mixed hardwoods and scattered stands of rhododendron. One interesting thing about the hike, though, is the large number of species of mushrooms encountered along the trail.

NAME OF TRAIL: Ned Branch Trail (FS #405)
MAP ON PAGE: 192–193
START: KY 1193 at former site of Pond School, approximately 2.5 miles east of Rockcastle Recreation Area
END: Intersection with Lakeside North Trail (FS #411)
TRAIL CONNECTIONS: Lakeside North Trail (FS #411)
USGS QUADS: Sawyer
COUNTIES: Laurel
RATING: Easy; 1.7 mi.; footpath; −300 ft.

The 1.7-mile Ned Branch Trail descends 300 feet to the Rockcastle River. It's not as attractive a trail as Bark Camp, Dog Slaughter, or Moonbow, by any means. But sometimes the trails in Daniel Boone National Forest seem to spoil you. The ever-present stands of towering hemlocks, rhododendron, and clean streams all begin to look alike after a while. There are many rockhouses along the Ned Branch Trail, one of which has a small branch flowing beneath it. It's a roller-coaster trail, descending and crossing the creek, then climbing slightly. The head of the trail is the most scenic. The small creek provides a year-round water source.

NAME OF TRAIL:	Twin Branch Trail (FS #406)
MAP ON PAGE:	193
START:	KY 1193, 2.5 miles east of the mouth of the Rockcastle River, near the site of Pond School
END:	Twin Branch Shelter
TRAIL CONNECTIONS:	Lakeside South Trail (FS #412)
USGS QUADS:	Sawyer
COUNTIES:	Laurel
RATING:	Easy; 1.1 mi.; footpath; −300 ft.

The 1.1-mile Twin Branch Trail descends 300 feet from KY 1193 in ridge-top woods to Lake Cumberland (at the junction of Upper and Lower Twin Branch Creeks). On the ridgetops, there are some impressive stands of pine and mixed hardwoods. One interesting feature of the trail is how it passes through two distinct forest types, which provide hikers with a practical lesson in forest ecology. The trail begins in a ridgetop zone with species of vegetation that can thrive in so-called dry sites. When the trail enters the creek bottoms, hikers walk through a zone called slope forest. The transition in vegetation types unfolds before the hiker's eyes.

The trail splits at the lake; the path to the right goes to Twin Branch Shelter, an Adirondack structure that sleeps six comfortably. There are a fire pit and picnic table beside the shelter, which is often used by fishers who boat in.

The trail winds through fields of boulders that are draped in vegetation. Towering hemlocks shade the sun. Rhododendron thickets line the trail. The impressive cliffs, which reach high above the valley, seem bolder than ever in the afternoon sun.

On the ridge between the two creeks there's an overlook with a grill and picnic table, which offers scenic views of the lake.

Continued on page 193

Cliffside Trail

519

198

896

Hamilton
Cem

△ Laurel
Recreation
Area

MC CREARY CO

WHITLEY CO

Fishing

Creek

1277

715

×1076

×1085

F O R E

×1133

Moonbow
Trail

CUMBERLAND RIVER

RIVER

Bark Camp Creek Trail

Camp

716

×1132

Bark

Bark Camp
Shelter

Creek

Jackie

eek

Continued on page 199

193

CURD

Devil

Grassy

| 0 | | ½ | | 1 MILE |

| 0 | 5 | 1 KILOMETER |

USGS QUADS: Sawyer   © Thomas Press

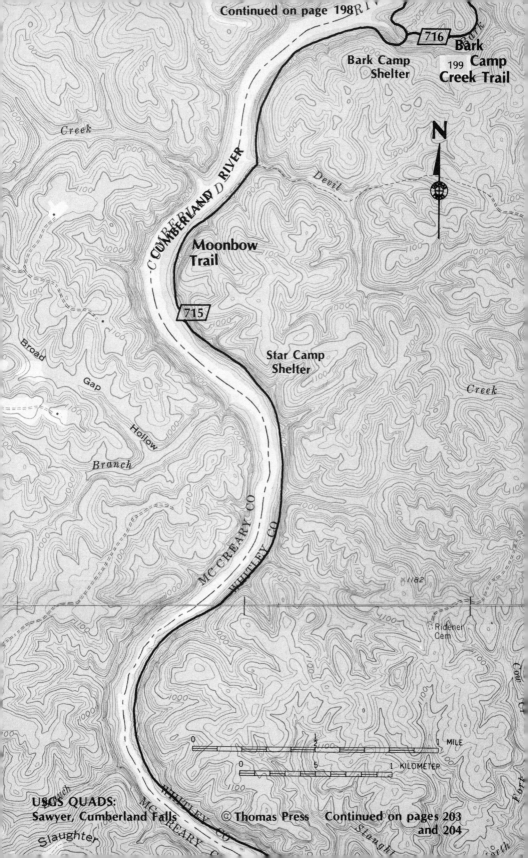

Continued on page 198

Bark Camp
Shelter

716 Bark
199 Camp
Creek Trail

N

Creek

CUMBERLAND RIVER

Devil

Moonbow
Trail

715

Star Camp
Shelter

Creek

Broad

Gap

Hollow

Branch

MC CREARY CO
WHITLEY CO

x 1182

Ridener
Cem

| 0 | | | | 1 | MILE |
| 0 | | 5 | | 1 | KILOMETER |

WHITLEY CO
MC CREARY CO

Slaughter

USGS QUADS:
Sawyer, Cumberland Falls   © Thomas Press

Continued on pages 203
and 204

NAME OF TRAIL:	Moonbow Trail (FS #715)
MAP ON PAGE:	198, 199, 203, 204
START:	Cumberland Falls
END:	KY 1277 at the mouth of the Laurel River (Laurel Recreation Area)
TRAIL CONNECTIONS:	Dog Slaughter Trail (FS #714) and Bark Camp Creek (FS #716)
USGS QUADS:	Cumberland Falls, Sawyer
COUNTIES:	Whitley
RATING:	Strenuous; 12.0 mi.; footpath and logging road; −200 ft.

The 12-mile Moonbow Trail begins at the downstream end of the concrete walkway that leads to the base of Cumberland Falls. The Moonbow Trail actually begins as Trail 2, a Cumberland Falls State Resort Park day-hiking trail. Trail 2 parallels the river past the old beach. There are huge piles of driftwood along the trail. A maze of boulders litters the channel of the river.

The trail stays below the cliffline and is intersected twice by day-hiking Trail 7, which ends on KY 90. Below Cumberland Falls is one of the most scenic and awesome stretches of white water in Kentucky, a Class-III and Class-IV river when the water flow is above 300 cubic feet per second. About 2.7 miles below the falls, the trail leaves the park boundary and enters the federally owned lands of Daniel Boone National Forest. Just beyond the boundary of the state resort park is the mouth of Catfish Creek. If you hike up the creek, you'll come to a delightful waterfall.

At this point, the trail is very close to the river, so close that during high water stretches of it may be inundated. The boulder-strewn, white water river and the high bluffs to the right that shelter pockets of towering timber give the hike a true wilderness quality. About 3.3 miles from Cumberland Falls, Moonbow Trail intersects with the Dog Slaughter Trail.

Dog Slaughter Falls, which plummets 25 feet off a rock lip, is just a short hike up the creek. It's nestled in a narrow gorge and is well worth the detour off Moonbow Trail. Below the mouth of Dog Slaughter Creek there are numerous rockhouses along the cliffline. Some are used as permanent summer homes by local fishers. The trail passes under Wedge Rock, a boulder suspended over the trail, before reaching Star Camp.

At 5.4 miles into the trail is Star Camp, the first of two Adirondack shelters between Cumberland Falls and the Laurel Recreation Area. There's a concrete grill (just below the shelter in a rockhouse) and a pit toilet. Since the shelter is a convenient halfway point on the trail, it is often full during the spring and fall. Fishers also use the shelter quite a bit, especially during the March and April white bass run. The availability of drinking water from springs is seasonal; the side branches often dry up in the summer. Water taken from the river must be boiled or chemically treated.

Just past the Star Camp Shelter there's a 70-foot-high waterfall. This section of the trail passes through canebrakes and stands of beech and sycamore. In springtime the drumming of ruffed grouse is often heard along this stretch of the trail. At mile 7.2, the footpath intersects a logging road. To continue on the Moonbow Trail, follow the footpath that branches to the left. The logging road heads up Devils Creek to the right.

At mile 8.5 (the mouth of Bark Camp Creek) is another Adirondack shelter that sleeps six to eight people. The Bark Camp Shelter has a picnic table, pit toilet, and fire pit. About 100 yards north of the shelter are the remains of an old homeplace. The chimney makes an excellent fireplace. A picnic table and fire pit were added to the "campsite."

Where the Moonbow Trail crosses Bark Camp Creek is one of the most beautiful spots on the trail. Bark Camp Creek Falls, which cascades over four ledges, can be seen from the mouth of the creek. From Bark Camp Creek to the Laurel Recreation Area is 3.5 miles. In this section the trail rises and falls along small hills below the cliffline and provides hikers with numerous view of the headwaters of Lake Cumberland as the river begins to pool. The trail sign at the Laurel Recreation Area has been vandalized so it's difficult to find it along KY 1277. If you follow the bank paths made by fishers, you'll eventually end up at the boat dock at the mouth of the Laurel River.

NAME OF TRAIL: Bark Camp Creek Trail (FS #716)
MAP ON PAGE: 198
START: FS Road 193, west of Corbin; reached via
                        U.S. 25W, KY 1277, then 1 mile south on FS
                        Road 193
END: Intersection with Moonbow Trail (FS #715)
TRAIL CONNECTIONS: Moonbow Trail (FS #715)
USGS QUADS: Sawyer
COUNTIES: Whitley
RATING: Moderate; 3.0 mi.; footpath; −200 ft.

Bark Camp Creek is a 3-mile long footpath that descends 200 feet through an absolutely beautiful gorge. Stocked with rainbow trout May through June, the creek offers some excellent fishing. Dense stands of rhododendron, towering hemlocks, and tulip poplars shade the cool, crystal-clear waters. But, for the most part, the trail is above the creek and only occasionally drops to the water's edge. The sprawling sand- and pebble-bottomed pools in the stream are simply beautiful and inviting during the hot summer months. Near the mouth there's a big rockhouse, a favorite camping spot for fishers. The trail ends with a cascading, stairstep waterfall. A wooden bridge was constructed to help hikers make it across the mouth of the creek (on the Moonbow Trail).

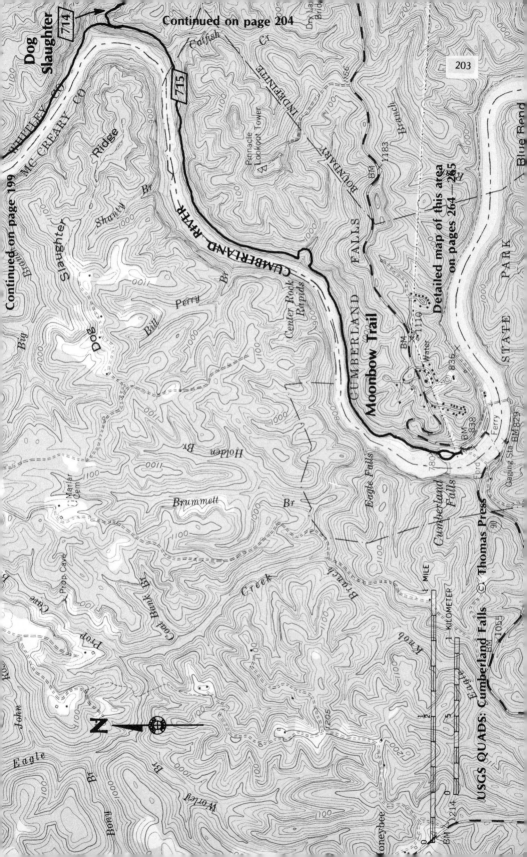

Continued on page 204

Continued on page 199

WHITLEY CO

MC CREARY CO

Dog
Slaughter

714

715

Catfish Cr

Dry Lau
Bridg

1200

INDEPENDENCE

Pinnacle
Lookout Tower

BOUNDARY

Branch

BM 1183

BM

Blue Bend

STATE PARK

Slaughter Ridge

Br

Shanty

1000

900

CUMBERLAND RIVER

CUMBERLAND FALLS

Detailed map of this area
on pages 264 – 265

Dog

Big Branch

Br

Perry

Bill

Dog

Center Rock
Rapids

Moonbow Trail

BM

Water

1110

× 836

BM 838

Ferry

BM 829

Holden Br

Marlar
Cem

1100

Brummett

Br

Eagle Falls

780

836

Gaging Sta

Cumberland Falls

© Thomas Press

90

Prop Cave

Cave Row

Coal Bank Br

Creek

Branch

1100

Knob

MILE

KILOMETER

1055

BM

John

Prop

1205

1200

N

1100

Eagle Br

Worley Br

Boxy Br

1214

BM

USGS QUADS: Cumberland Falls

oneybee

1100

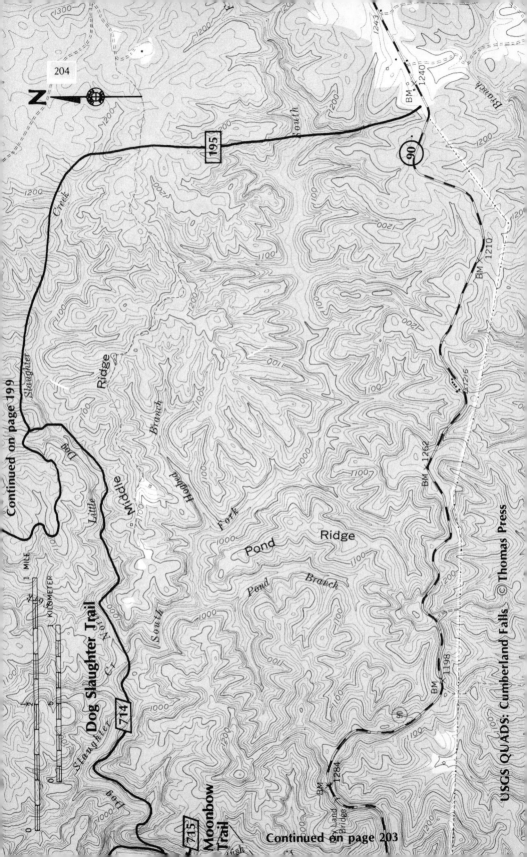

204

N

Continued on page 199

195

South

90

BM 1240

Branch

1210 BM X

1216

BM X 1262

Creek

Slaughter

Ridge

Dog

Little

Middle

Branch

Holyford

Fork

Pond

Ridge

Pond Branch

Pond

South

Cr.

1 MILE

KILOMETER

Dog Slaughter Trail

714

Slaughter

Creek

Fish

715

Moonbow
Trail

BM 1198

90

BM X 1284

Dry Land
Bridge

Continued on page 203

USGS QUADS: Cumberland Falls ©Thomas Press

NAME OF TRAIL: Dog Slaughter Trail (FS #714)
MAP ON PAGE: 203, 204
START: FS Road 195 over Dog Slaughter Creek
END: Intersection with Moonbow Trail (FS #715)
TRAIL CONNECTIONS: Moonbow Trail (FS #715)
USGS QUADS: Cumberland Falls
COUNTIES: Whitley
RATING: Moderate; 4.0 mi.; footpath; −500 ft.

The 4-mile long Dog Slaughter Trail parallels the southern bank of the creek through a rocky gorge and has a 25-foot-high falls near its mouth. The trailhead is approximately 1.5 miles west of the junction of KY 90 on FS Road 195, although, 2 miles farther down FS Road 195, there's another access point at a footbridge off to the left.

From the road to the trail's intersection with the Cumberland River, Dog Slaughter Trail descends approsimately 500 feet. The creek bottoms are lined with massive boulders. Water is available year-round. Like Bark Camp Creek, Dog Slaughter Creek has some excellent rainbow trout fishing. The U.S. Fish and Wildlife Service stocks the stream in March, April, and May. Impressive stands of tulip poplars and hemlock line the trail as it winds through thickets of rhododendron.

STEARNS RANGER DISTRICT

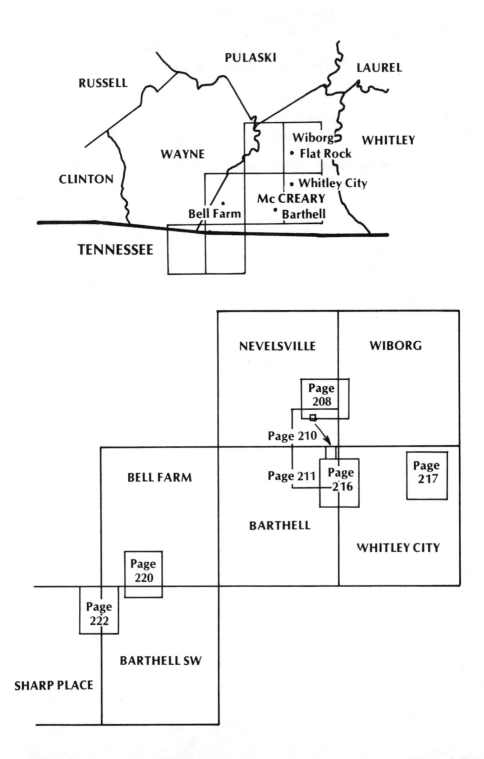

STEARNS RANGER DISTRICT

The Stearns Ranger District is 130,000 acres of land under public owner-ship in Whitley, Wayne, and McCreary counties. The southernmost of Daniel Boone National Forest's seven ranger districts, the Stearns unit has some of Kentucky's most remote woodlands and several fine fishing and canoeing streams.

There are eleven hiking trails in the Stearns Ranger District. The Yahoo Falls Scenic Area is a popular spot for day-hiking that has four trails that total 1.8 miles. For those interested in long, multi-day backpacking trips four trails in the district are often hiked consecutively (Yahoo Falls Trail, Lakeside Trail, Yamacraw Trail, and Lick Creek Trail) for a distance of 20.1 miles. The trek begins at Flat Rock, on U.S. 27 and ends at Whitley City after passing through Yahoo Falls Scenic Area, paralleling the Cumber-land River, and climbing to the headwaters of Lick Creek.

There are 29.4 miles of trail in the Stearns Ranger District. Two of the trails, Mark Branch and the Parker Mountain Trail, are in the vicinity of Rock Creek, which flows northeastward from Pickett State Park in Tennes-see and empties into the Big South Fork of the Cumberland River near Stearns. Rock Creek, a designated Kentucky Wild River, is an excellent trout fishing stream stocked with rainbow trout from March through Oc-tober. If you're interested in a combination hiking and fishing trip to the area, perhaps the best bet would be to camp at the Great Meadow Camp-ground on FS Road 139, which is reached via KY 1363 and FS Road 566 from Yamacraw (five miles west of Whitley City on KY 92). Open year-round, the campground has eight campsites, pit toilets, drinking water, picnic tables, and grills. There's a 22-foot maximum limit for recreational vehicles at the campground.

For those interested in cross-country "bushwack" hiking, the triangle of land between the Big South Fork and Little South Fork of the Cumber-land River, known as the Yellow Cliffs area, is probably your best bet. The area is north of KY 92. There are numerous logging roads through the woods.

Stearns Ranger District, Daniel Boone National Forest, P. O. Box 459, Whitley City, Kentucky 42653. (606) 376-5323.

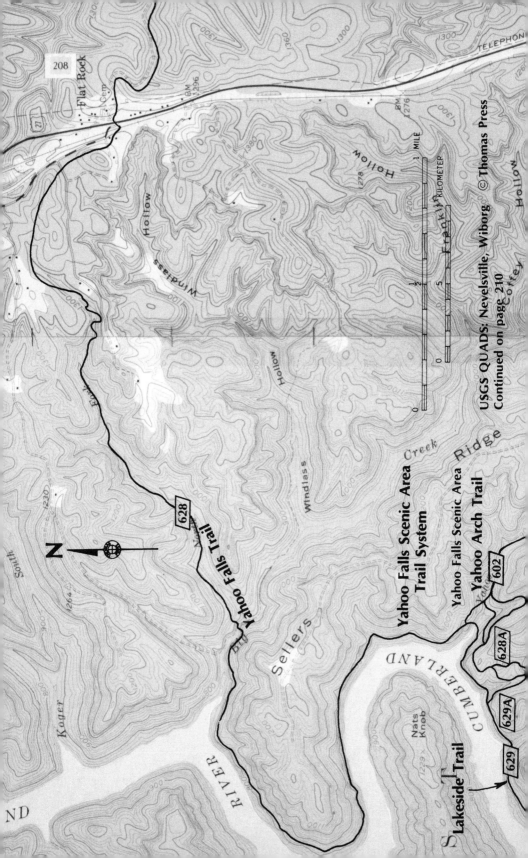

208

Flat Rock

Cem

BM 1296

TELEPHONE

BM 1276

Windless Hollow

Hollow

Hollow

Hollow

Windless

Creek

Ridge

Yahoo Falls Scenic Area
Trail System

Yahoo Falls Scenic Area

Yahoo Arch Trail

Koger

South

N

628

Yahoo Falls Trail

Sellers

Nats Knob

CUMBERLAND

602

628A

629A

629

RIVER

ND

Lakeside Trail

S

1 MILE

KILOMETER

Franklin

Coffey Hollow

1/2

5

0

0

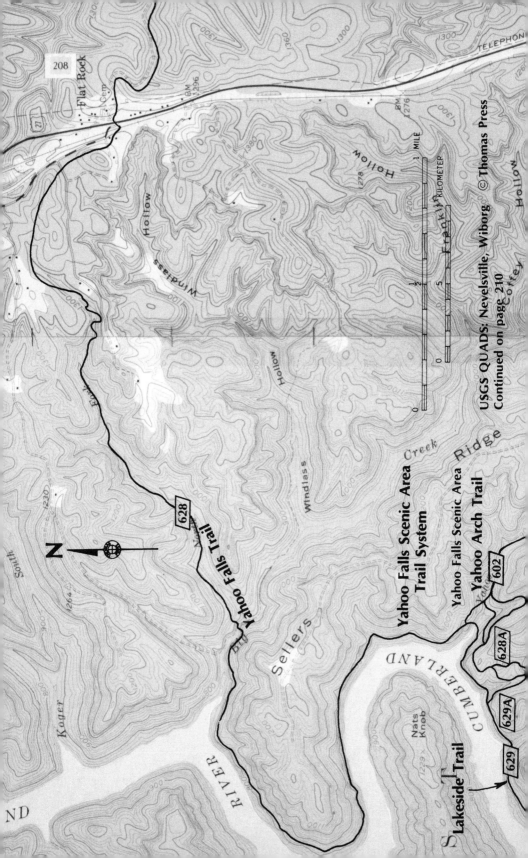

USGS QUADS: Nevelsville, Wiborg, ©Thomas Press
Continued on page 210

NAME OF TRAIL:	Yahoo Falls Trail (FS #628)
MAP ON PAGE:	208
START:	Northern bank of Yahoo Creek at its mouth
END:	U.S. 27 at Flat Rock
TRAIL CONNECTIONS:	Lakeside Trail (FS #629) and Yahoo Falls Scenic Area Trail System
USGS QUADS:	Nevelsville, Wiborg
COUNTIES:	McCreary
RATING:	Strenuous; 10 mi.; footpath and logging road; +600 ft.

This 10-mile trail parallels the Cumberland River below the cliffline until it reaches Big Creek where it climbs high above the water, and passes through hemlocks, rhododendron, and mixed hardwoods over very steep terrain. The trail then crosses Big Creek and parallels its North Fork. It's uphill most of the way to U.S. 27 with the trail snaking through creek bottoms; then it's elevated above a gorge. A spectacular hemlock grove can be seen below. There is a steep climb when the trail leaves the creek, and there are numerous switchbacks as the trail climbs 600 feet.

The section of the trail from the mouth of Big Creek to U.S. 27 at Flat Rock was completed in the summer of 1978. YACC trail crews cut about 3 miles of new trail (an important link in Sheltowee Trace) and maintained the entire right-of-way. Sections of old logging roads were used. Water availability is good year-round below the cliffline.

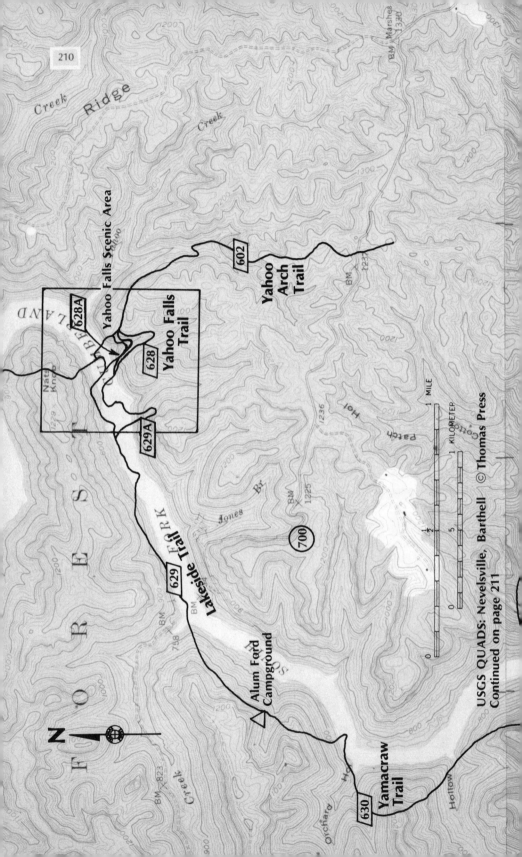

210

Creek Ridge

Creek

Yahoo Falls Scenic Area

602

Yahoo Arch Trail

BM

628A

Yahoo Falls Trail

628

Yahoo Falls Trail

629A

Nat Knob

F O R E S T

Jones Br

629

Lakeside Trail

BM 758

BM

Patch Hol

1236

BM 1225

700

MILE

KILOMETER

© Thomas Press

Alum Ford Campground

N

BM 823

Creek

Yamacraw Trail

630

USGS QUADS: Nevelsville, Barthell

Continued on page 211

Continued on page 210

Continued on page 216

Roaring
Rocks
Trail

Cliffside
Trail

Skyline
Trail

(Enlarged)

211

Hickman Falls

N

631

Lick Creek Trail

Lick Creek

630

Yamacraw Trail

CUMBERLAND

Negro

Hill Top

BM
1253

Chitwood

Koger
Spring

BM
793

92

RIVER

Yamacraw
Yamacraw

1 MILE

1 KILOMETER

5

Hollow

Ridge

SOUTH

BM

Wolf Creek
Sch

Creek

Ten

River

BM
775

Fishtrap

Wolf

USGS QUADS: Barthell
© Thomas Press

NAME OF TRAIL: Lakeside Trail (FS #629)
MAP ON PAGE: 210
START: Alum Ford Campground on Lake Cumber-
                      land at western end of KY 700
END: Yahoo Falls Scenic Area
TRAIL CONNECTIONS: Yahoo Falls Scenic Area Trail System and
                      Yamacraw Trail (FS #630)
USGS QUADS: Nevelsville
COUNTIES: McCreary
RATING: Easy; 2.0 mi.; footpath; +200 ft.

The 2-mile Lakeside Trail is an excellent trail along the eastern bank of the Cumberland River (headwaters of Lake Cumberland). Between Alum Ford and Yahoo Creek the trail hugs precipitous sandstone cliffs with many views of the river. There are lush stands of rhododendron, rockhouses, and pockets of towering hemlocks and tulip poplars in the side hollows, many of which have cool springs at their headwaters. It is an easy, practically level, but very scenic hike.

NAME OF TRAIL: Yahoo Arch Trail (FS #602)
MAP ON PAGE: 210
START: KY 700, approximately 1.5 miles east of Alum
                      Ford Campground
END: Intersection of Skyline and Cliffside trails
TRAIL CONNECTIONS: Skyline and Cliffside trails
USGS QUADS: Nevelsville
COUNTIES: McCreary
RATING: Easy; 1.8 mi.; footpath; −400 ft.

The Yahoo Arch Trail is eight-tenths of a mile long. Yahoo Arch, a 10-foot-high, 25-foot-wide bare span, is the major attraction of the trail. Beginning on a ridgetop (1300 feet above sea level) of mixed hardwoods and pine, the trail descends about 400 feet to a junction of color-coded day-hiking trails (Skyline is white, the Cliffside is blue) in the Yahoo Falls Scenic Area. The trail is easy; there is no water on the ridgetop.

NAME OF TRAIL: Yahoo Falls Scenic Area Trail System
MAP ON PAGE: 210–211
START: Parking area off KY 700, one-half mile east of
                      Alum Ford Campground
END: Parking area
TRAIL CONNECTIONS: Lakeside Trail (FS #629), Yahoo Falls Trail (FS
                      #628), and Yahoo Arch Trail (FS #602)
USGS QUADS: Nevelsville
COUNTIES: McCreary
RATING: Easy; 1.0 mi.; footpath; −200 ft.

The Yahoo Creek drainage has been set aside by the U.S. Forest Service as a protected scenic area because of its outstanding beauty. It provides a marvelous combination of high cliffs, a towering 113-foot waterfall, crystal-clear streams, and impressive stands of timber.

Pronounced "Yae-hoe" by many local residents, the cathedral-like hollow has a system of three loop trails. The trails cover about 1 mile of footpath and criss-cross the ridges, boulder fields below the cliffline, and creek bottoms clothed in dense stands of rhododendron. A system of twenty consecutively numbered signs help hikers locate their position in the maze of footpaths.

The **Skyline Trail,** coded in a white blaze, begins at its junction with the Yahoo Arch Trail above the falls. The Skyline Trail is four-tenths of a mile long and ends (two-tenths of a mile west of its junction with the Cliffside Trail) at the parking lot and picnic grounds at the main entrance off KY 700, which is a half mile east of the Alum Ford Campground.

The **Cliffside Trail,** blazed in blue, begins at its junction with the Skyline and Yahoo Arch trails (trail sign #11). It passes through stands of mature hemlock, tulip poplar, basswood, magnolia, buckeye, and oaks to the base of Yahoo Falls, a ribbonlike waterfall set deep in a cavernous hollow. There's a rockhouse the size of a football field behind the 113-foot-high falls that defies belief. Cliffside Trail ends at trail sign #6 at its intersection with the Skyline Trail.

The two-tenths-mile long **Roaring Rocks Trail** is perhaps the most unusual in the system. Hikers must literally get down on their hands and knees to negotiate the trail, which parallels a cascading stream twisting through a field of house-sized boulders that have fallen down into the valley from the ridgetops. The Roaring Rocks Trail begins at trail sign #12 on the Cliffside Trail and ends at trail sign #15 on the Cliffside Trail.

There's about two-tenths of a mile of connector trail. One section is a short link between trail sign #13 on the Cliffside Trail and trail sign #16 at the beginning of the Yahoo Falls Trail. The other connector is between trail sign #17 on the Cliffside Trail and the end of Lakeside Trail.

NAME OF TRAIL:	Yamacraw Trail (FS #630)
MAP ON PAGE:	210–211
START:	Yamacraw at the KY 92 bridge over the South Fork of Cumberland River
END:	Alum Ford Campground
TRAIL CONNECTIONS:	Lakeside Trail (FS #629) and Lick Creek Trail (FS #631)
USGS QUADS:	Nevelsville, Barthell
COUNTIES:	McCreary
RATING:	Moderate; 6.0 mi.; footpath and logging road; +100 ft.

The 6-mile Yamacraw Trail parallels the east bank of the South Fork of the Cumberland River from the Yamacraw bridge to Alum Ford Campground at the backwater of Lake Cumberland. YACC crews cleared the entire length of the footpath during the summer of 1978 as high water in the past few years practically destroyed the trail by causing deadfalls and washouts.

The section of the trail from the Yamacraw bridge to the mouth of Lick Creek is an old logging road. The section after the footbridge is a narrow trail. There are many crossings of small streams. Some of the side hollows through which the trail passes are quite lovely with mature timber, boulders matted with ferns and lush stands of rhododendron. A footbridge was recently constructed over Negro Branch where hikers formerly had to climb across a rock at the head of a gorge, exposing themselves to a potentially dangerous situation—a fall to the creek below. The tape-blazed trail at the footbridge leads to a waterfall up the creek.

There's an Adirondack shelter at Cottonpatch Ridge that is open to hikers on a first come, first served basis. Just beyond the shelter, though, there is an old homeplace with the chimney still intact that is an excellent place to tent camp. There are many places along the trail where hikers can lunch amid the huge rocks that line the river. The trail is easy; there are a few climbs in side hollows. Water is available year-round. It is good trail to hike in the spring during the white bass run when the fishing is excellent.

NAME OF TRAIL: Lick Creek Trail (FS #631)
MAP ON PAGE: 211, 216
START: Lick Creek Road off U.S. 27, one-half mile
                        south of downtown Whitley City
END: Intersection with Yamacraw Trail (FS #630)
TRAIL CONNECTIONS: Yamacraw Trail (FS #630)
USGS QUADS: Whitley City, Barthell
COUNTIES: McCreary
RATING: Easy; 3.2 mi.; footpath and logging road;
                        −500 ft.

Lick Creek Trail, a 3.2-mile trace, begins on a ridgetop west of Whitley City and descends 500 feet along Lick Creek to the river bottoms of the South Fork of the Cumberland River. The trailhead is on Lick Creek Road, off U.S. 27 within the city limits of Whitley City (trail sign on right side of road heading south). There's a concrete parking area and a gate at the entrance to a logging road, which is the first mile of the trail. The ridgetop woods were logged in the early 1970s and are now grown up in bushes and small trees. A trail sign at a fork of the logging road is the beginning of the section of narrow footpath.

The trail descends through a steep cliff by metal stairs and then follows the cliffline. Towering hemlocks and lush stands of rhododendron flank the trail. At one time, rainbow trout were stocked in Lick Creek, which is a clear, free-flowing stream with numerous ledges, riffles, and gravel pools. An excellent source of water, there are numerous cool springs flowing into the creek. About halfway to the river, on a side trail to the left, is Hickman Falls, a stunning 50-foot-high waterfall that spills over a rock lip and rains down on boulders below. The waterfall is tucked away in a steep-walled side hollow with a loose sand and gravel floor. Lush mosses, lichens, and ferns give the spot a special beauty. Below Hickman Falls the trail skirts the creek; at times it is high above the water, and then it threads through rocks at streamside. The next attraction along the trail is Princess Falls, a series of ledges over which the creek cascades in stair-step fashion. Near the mouth of Lick Creek the trail crosses a footbridge. Campsites are plentiful at the trail's junction with Yamacraw Trail.

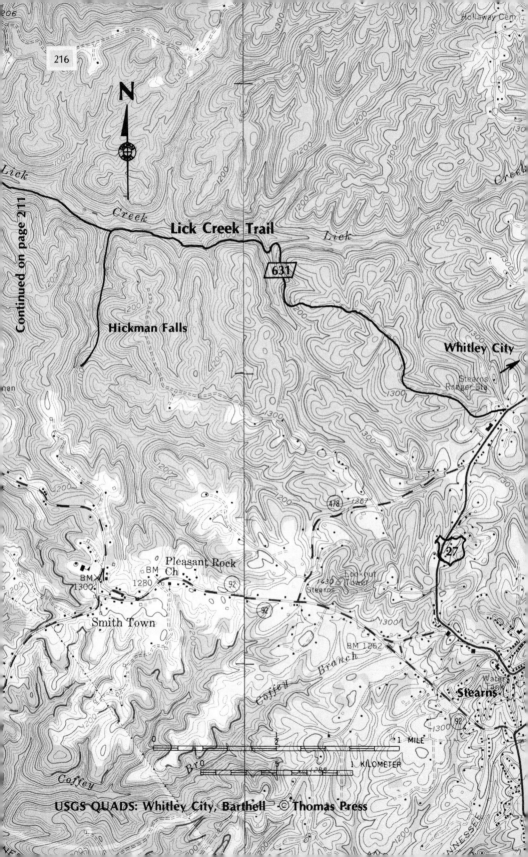

N

Continued on page 211

Lick

Creek

Lick Creek Trail

Lick

631

Hickman Falls

Lick

Creek

Whitley City

Stearns
Ranger Sta

1300

478   1367

1300

27

Pleasant Rock
BM   Ch
1280
BM
1300

92

Smith Town

Lookout
Tower
1630
Stearns

1300

BM 1262

Coffey   Branch

Water
Tank

Stearns

1300   92

Bro

Coffey

1   MILE

1   KILOMETER

USGS QUADS: Whitley City, Barthell   © Thomas Press

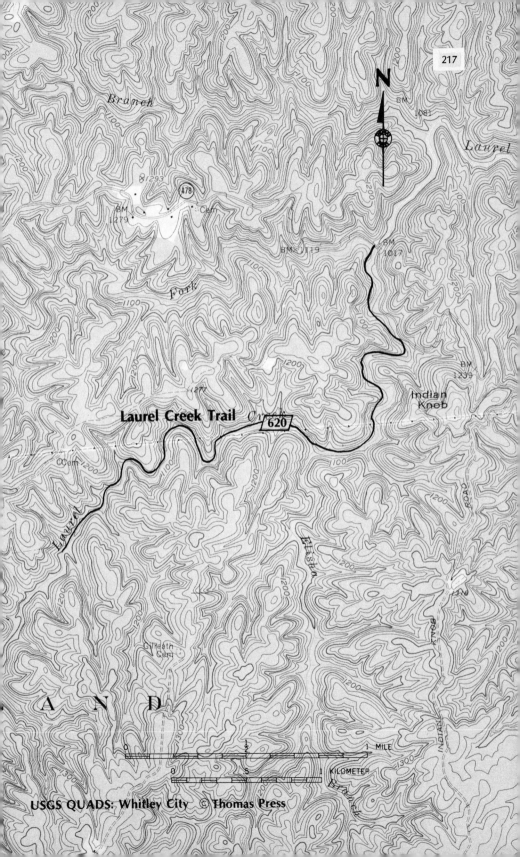

Branch

Laurel

N

BM
1081

BM
1017

8 1293

A78

Cem

BM
1279

BM 1119

BM
1239

Fork

Indian
Knob

1277

1200

Laurel Creek Trail
Creek
620

Cem

1100

Laurel

Elisha

ROAD

Gilreath
Cem

A N D

0   1/2   1 MILE

0   .5   1 KILOMETER

ROAD

INDIAN

Branch

USGS QUADS: Whitley City   © Thomas Press

NAME OF TRAIL: Laurel Creek Trail (FS #620)
MAP ON PAGE: 217
START: Bridge over KY 478, 1.5 miles east of Whitley
                        City
END: Laurel Creek
TRAIL CONNECTIONS: None
USGS QUADS: Whitley City
COUNTIES: McCreary
RATING: Easy; 2.5 mi.; footpath; −100 ft.

The Laurel Creek Trail is a practically level creek bottom trace popular with both hikers and horseback riders. It is approximately 2.5 miles long, and begins at the metal highway bridge on KY 478 and deadends along Laurel Creek. There's a wooden bridge at the approach to the trail. Water is available year-round; the trail passes through mixed hardwoods and rhododendron. It is an easy trail with spacious creek bottoms for camping.

Breaks Interstate Park. Photograph courtesy of the Commonwealth of Kentucky, Department of Public Information.

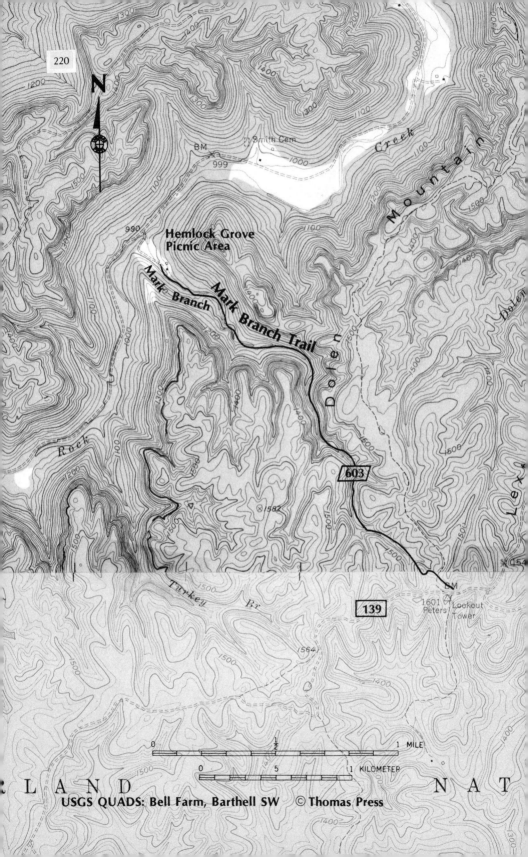

220

N

Creek

Mountain

Smith Cem

BM
999

1000

990

**Hemlock Grove
Picnic Area**

Mark Branch

Mark Branch Trail

Dolen

Rock

603

⊗ 1582

Lex

Turkey   Br

139

BM
1601
Peters Lookout
Tower

1564

0   ½   1 MILE

0   5   1 KILOMETER

L A N D   N A T

USGS QUADS: Bell Farm, Barthell SW   © Thomas Press

NAME OF TRAIL: Mark Branch Trail (FS #603)
MAP ON PAGE: 220
START: Former site of Peter Mountain lookout tower
                      on FS Road 139
END: Clearing across Rock Creek from Hemlock
                      Grove Picnic Area
TRAIL CONNECTIONS: None
USGS QUADS: Bell Farm, Barthell SW
COUNTIES: McCreary
RATING: Easy; 2.4 mi.; footpath; −500 ft.

Mark Branch Trail is a 2.4-mile footpath that descends almost 500 feet from Laurel Ridge to Rock Creek (southwest of Dolen Mountain). The exceptionally beautiful trail is above the cliffline for the first quarter mile or so, but soon hikers find themselves on the edge of a gorge with the valley floor a vast garden of rhododendron. Towering hemlocks and tulip poplars reach skyward; the crowns of the majestic trees viewed from above seem like an ocean of leaves between rock shorelines. There are numerous clear views of the cliffs across the gorge on the descent to the valley floor. About a mile from the trailhead there's a 50-foot waterfall off to the right in a side hollow. The trail actually passes beneath the falls, although hikers are protected from getting drenched by a rockhouse. The mist from the falls nurtures lush gardens of ferns and mosses. Once in the valley floor, the trail crosses the creek several times. Mark Branch Trail ends in a clearing east of (across from) Rock Creek, and hikers must hop the rocks to get to Hemlock Grove Picnic Area. Water availability below the cliffline is good year-round. The trail is frequented by horseback riders.

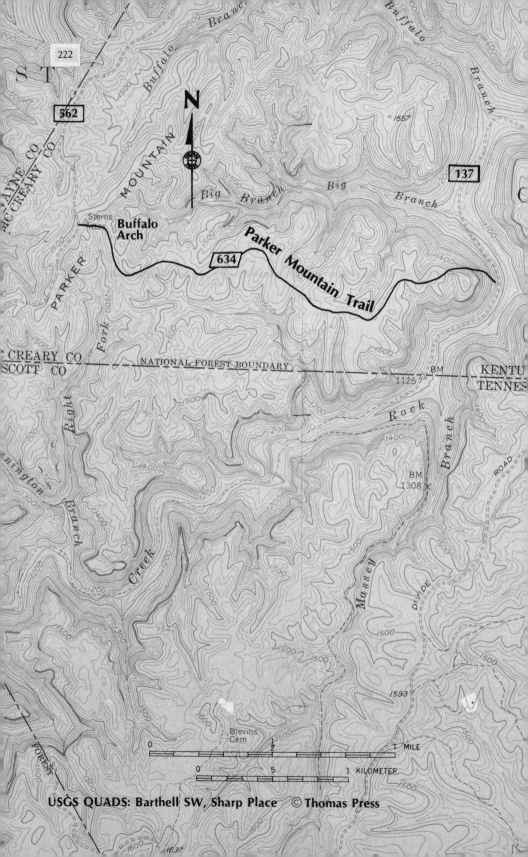

USGS QUADS: Barthell SW, Sharp Place   © Thomas Press

NAME OF TRAIL: Parker Mountain Trail (FS #634)
MAP ON PAGE: 222
START: FS Road 562, approximately 7 miles south of
                        intersection with FS Road 137
END: FS Road 137
TRAIL CONNECTIONS: None
USGS QUADS: Barthell SW and Sharp Place (TN)
COUNTIES: McCreary
RATING: Easy; 4.0 mi.; footpath and logging road;
                        −400 ft.

The Parker Mountain Trail is a 4-mile trail on which the main point of interest is Buffalo Arch. The trailhead is difficult to find as there is no sign along FS Road 562; there is just a logging road going off to the left (at a clearing approximately 7 miles south of junction of FS roads 137 and 562). Continue to the right on this logging road until you come to a trail blaze on the left. This is where the trail actually begins.

It really is a confusing situation because there's also a blaze to the right, and a trail sign. This sign and marking are not for the main trail but for a quarter-mile spur that leads to Buffalo Arch. There's a small footpath off the logging road that leads to the arch, one of the largest in McCreary County. Evergreens and rhododendron are in abundance.

The Parker Mountain Trail is a ridgetop trail, so water isn't available. The average elevation of the trail is 1300 feet, which makes the walk one of the highest in the Daniel Boone National Forest.

The trail is relatively flat and has some sections of old roadbed. Blackberries and blueberries are abundant. The trail has a few deadfalls across it. Woods, clearings, and reverting fields are passed while hiking the Parker Mountain Trail. The last half-mile of the trail is a 400-foot descent into Rock Creek through boulder fields, past rockhouses and stands of impressive timber. The trail intersects FS Road 137, 3.5 miles south of the Great Meadow Campground. There's a trail sign at its junction.

To reach the trail's end on FS Road 137 requires a 3.5-mile ride over a road passable only for four-wheel-drive vehicles. vehicles. (It might be a good idea to leave one car at the trail's end and another at the Great Meadows Campground, which is six miles north of the marked trailhead. The area around the trailhead is not well patrolled and vandalism is sometimes a problem.)

Fall foliage, Pine Mountain State Resort Park. Photograph courtesy of the Commonwealth of Kentucky, Department of Public Information.

REDBIRD RANGER DISTRICT

The Redbird Ranger District is 140,000 acres of federally owned lands in Clay, Knox, Perry, Bell, Owsley, Harlan, and Leslie counties. The compartments of land were purchased in 1964, seventeen years after the U.S. Forest Service made its initial acquisitions in 1937 for what was then called Cumberland National Forest.

A major trail is being developed in the Redbird Ranger District, but there are no other trails in the district at this time. The Redbird Crest Trail will be approximately 60 miles long when completed.

Redbird Purchase Ranger District, P. O. Box 1, Big Creek, Kentucky 40914. (606) 598-2192.

226

N

Redbird Crest Trail

Temporary route

Proposed route

US Forest Service map
Redbird Ranger District
© Thomas Press

0   ½   1 MILE

0   5   1 KILOMETER

NAME OF TRAIL: Redbird Crest Trail
MAP ON PAGE: 226
START: KY 66, two miles south of Daniel Boone Park-
                       way
END: KY 66 at Peabody
TRAIL CONNECTIONS: None
USGS QUADS: Big Creek, Hyden W, Hoskinston, Beverly,
                       Helton, and Creekville
COUNTIES: Clay, Leslie, and Bell
RATING: Strenuous; 60.0 mi.; footpath and logging
                       road; +800 ft.

The Redbird Crest Trail, under construction at this writing, is an approximately 60-mile loop footpath that begins and ends at the Redbird Ranger
District Headquarters on KY 66 at Peabody. Construction began in the
summer of 1977. Both Youth Conservation Corps (YCC) and Young Adults
Conservation Corps (YACC) crews helped build the 13.23 miles already
completed. Much of the trail is still on the drawing board; only 1.51 miles
(other than that section completed) have been flagged.
     The Redbird Crest Trail follows the watershed divide of the Red Bird
River, a tributary to the South Fork of the Kentucky River. Since the trail is
predominantly on the ridgetop, water availability is seasonal at best. The
proposed corridor is all on federally owned lands. The following is a
quadrangle by quadrangle breakdown of the status of the trail:
          BIG CREEK: 8.51 miles completed.
          HYDEN W: 1.51 miles completed.
          HOSKINSTON: 1.51 miles flagged; 11.17 miles proposed; and
                      1.13 miles completed.
          HELTON: 8.90 miles proposed.
          BEVERLY: 14.96 miles proposed.
          CREEKVILLE: 10.03 miles proposed; and 2.08 miles com-
                      pleted.

228

1 STRICKLETT
2 CRANSTON
3 FARMERS
4 MOREHEAD
5 SALT LICK
6 BANGOR
7 SCRANTON
8 SLADE
9 POMEROYTON
10 COBHILL
11 ZACHARIAH
12 LEIGHTON
13 HEIDELBERG
14 SAND GAP
15 MC KEE
16 LIVINGSTON
17 PARROT
18 BILLOWS
19 BERNSTADT
20 ANO
21 LONDON SW
22 HAIL

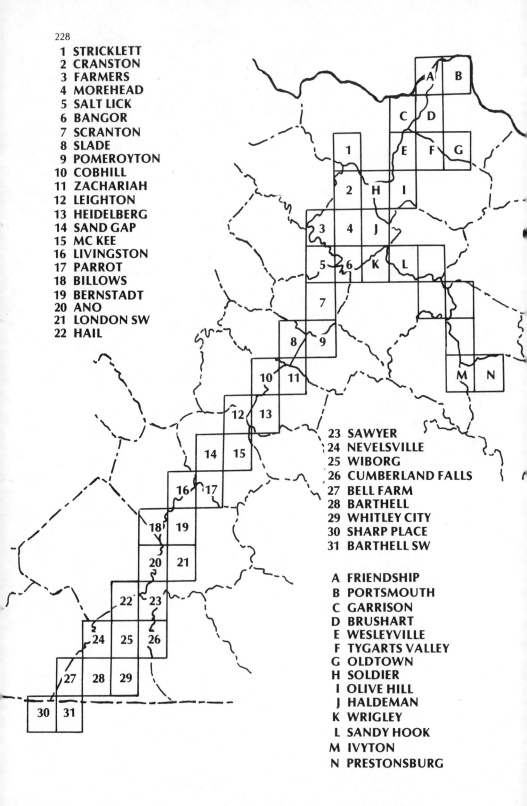

23 SAWYER
24 NEVELSVILLE
25 WIBORG
26 CUMBERLAND FALLS
27 BELL FARM
28 BARTHELL
29 WHITLEY CITY
30 SHARP PLACE
31 BARTHELL SW

A FRIENDSHIP
B PORTSMOUTH
C GARRISON
D BRUSHART
E WESLEYVILLE
F TYGARTS VALLEY
G OLDTOWN
H SOLDIER
I OLIVE HILL
J HALDEMAN
K WRIGLEY
L SANDY HOOK
M IVYTON
N PRESTONSBURG

6
Trails of Special Mention

The miles of trail open to hikers in Kentucky have dramatically increased since 1976. In that year, the planning, funding, and actual construction began on what will prove to be the two most important long-distance hiking trail systems the Commonwealth has ever known. Although both the Jenny Wiley Trail System and the Sheltowee Trace have not been completed (at this writing), more than 250 miles of trail have been cut. When finished, the two systems combined will be more than 500 miles long (including the combined 33 miles of the Simon Kenton and Michael Tygart Trails, both completed spurs off the Jenny Wiley Trail).

The Sheltowee Trace, nominated for National Trails status, is being planned and built by the U.S. Forest Service with the help of private individuals and state and private organizations. At this writing, approximately 178.65 miles have been completed. The Sheltowee Trace will pass through some of the most spectacular and remote lands in Kentucky and will provide an important link in the national trails system. When completed, it will no doubt be the most popular and most heavily used footpath. Its length and difficulty will make it tremendously popular with the growing numbers of hikers from Kentucky and the Midwest.

Another trail included in this chapter about footpaths of special mention is the Jenny Wiley Trail. It is indeed the most fascinating story in trail development. Built and managed by the Jenny Wiley Trail Conference and the Fivco Area Development District (a state agency), the trail became a reality by hard lobbying (for funding), meticulous planning, and innovative construction. It is a first in Kentucky trails as it passes through privately owned lands for more than ninety percent of its right-of-way. The hard work of a few dedicated individuals and the cooperation of landowners have made for a trail that combines glimpses into mountain heritage, a truly demanding walk, and innovative facilities (Adirondack shelters and cleverly devised cisterns). It is a hiking experience not to be missed by the serious trail traveler.

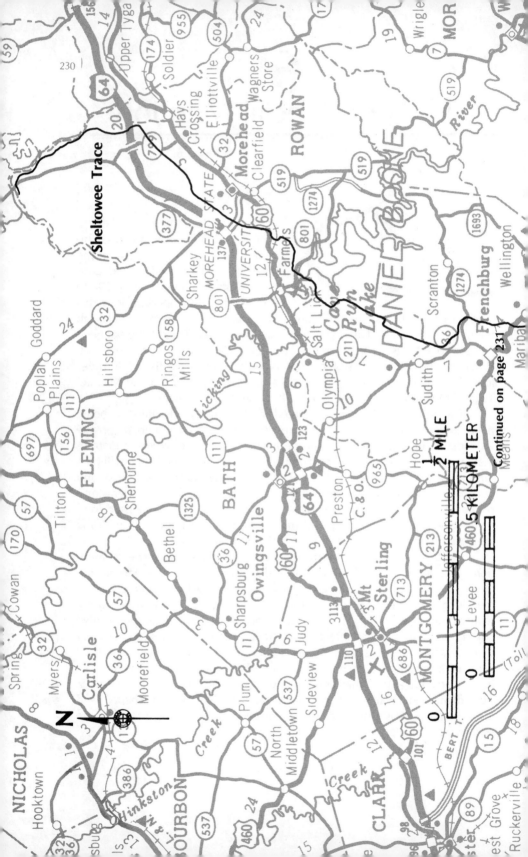

Sheltowee Trace

Continued on page 231

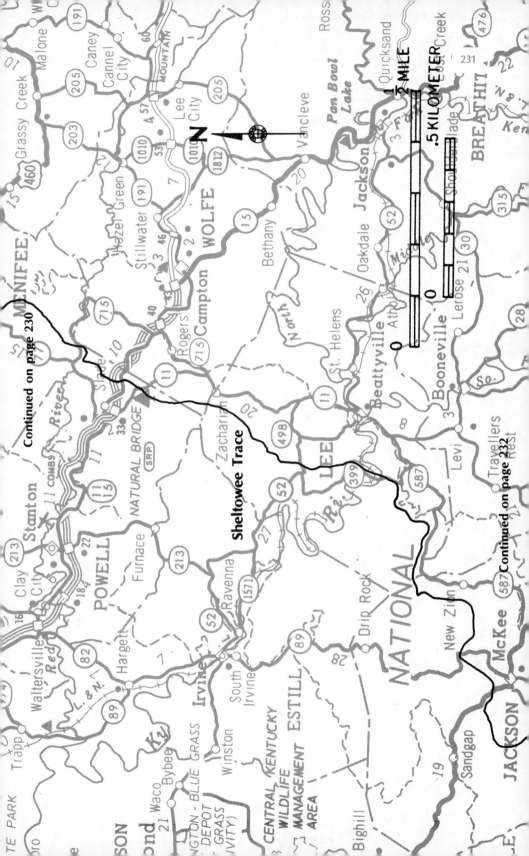

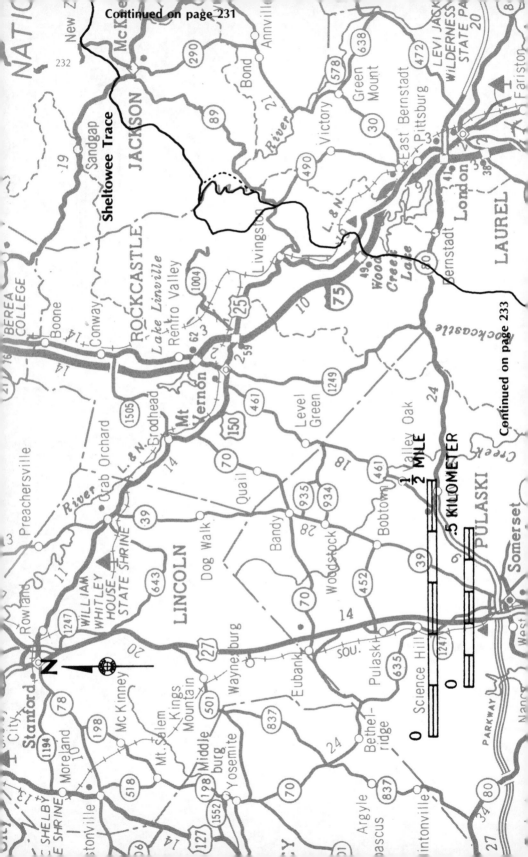

Continued on page 231

Continued on page 233

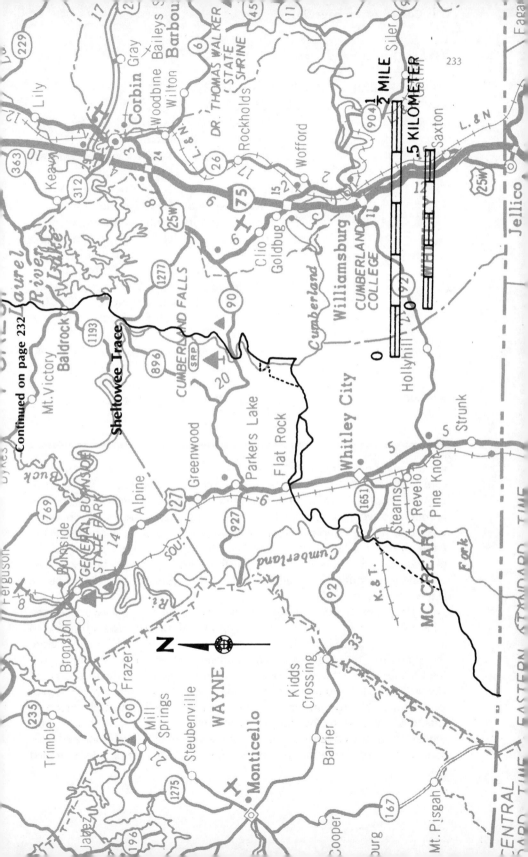

NAME OF TRAIL: Sheltowee Trace
MAP ON PAGE: 230–231, 232–233
START: KY 377 north of Morehead Pickett State Park, west of Oneida, Tennessee
END: Pickett State Park, west of Oneida, Tennessee
TRAIL CONNECTIONS: North Country Trail (Ohio), Jenny Wiley Trail, and John Muir Trail (Tennessee)
USGS QUADS: Stricklett, Cranston, Soldier, Morehead, Bangor, Farmers, Salt Lick, Scranton, Pomeroyton, Slade, Zachariah, Cobhill, Heidelberg, Leighton, McKee, Sandgap, Parrot, Livingston, Bernstadt, London SW, Ano, Sawyer, Cumberland Falls, Wiborg, Nevelsville, Barthell, Bell Farm, Barthell SW, and Sharp Place (TN)
COUNTIES: Rowan, Bath, Menifee, Powell, Wolfe, Estill, Jackson, Rockcastle, Laurel, Pulaski, McCreary, Whitley, and Scott (TN)
RATING: Strenuous; 300 mi.; footpath and logging road; +1000 ft.

On the night of February 8, 1778, during a snowstorm, Daniel Boone was surprised and pulled off his horse. He was returning laden with buffalo meat for the thirty men he led to Blue Lick Springs from Fort Boonesborough to secure a supply of salt, an all-important substance for preserving meat. Boone's capture by Indians was not unusual (it happened many times during his life), but it turned out that this capture was one of the more important events in the western theater of the Revolutionary War. It ultimately prevented an attack on Fort Boonesborough at a time when it surely would have fallen.

The night of Boone's capture, he was taken to a backwoods camp where white renegades, British officers, and Shawnees were all gathered around a blazing log fire. Restrained as a prisoner, he was brought before the Shawnee Chief Blackfish. What transpired is one of the most fascinating chapters in Kentucky history. In a masterpiece of backwoods oratory, Boone talked the Indians out of attacking Fort Boonesborough (thus preventing a massacre), surrendered his men at Blue Licks, and agreed to submit to questioning by the British in Detroit. (Unfortunately, this "surrender" was not understood by all. Some settlers accused Boone of treason.) While appeasing the Indians and British, who triumphantly marched their captives northward, Boone gained valuable time for the men and women on the Kentucky frontier. In the next three months, Boone eventually was adopted as a son of Chief Blackfish, and lived the life of a Shawnee Indian encamped at the winter quarters of the tribe near Little Chillicothe, Ohio. A proficient hunter and proven warrior; Boone gained the respect of the Indians because of his marksmanship and his skill as a gunsmith. The Indian name given to Boone was *Sheltowee* (Big Turtle).

Boone's escape in the spring was just in time to warn Fort Boonesborough of an impending attack. Boone ran away from the Indians while on a hunting trip. He rode a stolen horse into the ground, swam the Ohio River, and ran the rest of the way to the frontier outpost. It was one of the most exciting adventures in Boone's life, which was one escapade after another anyhow.

It is fitting that the north–south hiking trail through Daniel Boone National Forest should be named for the adopted son of a great Shawnee chief, a white man who opened Kentucky (America's fifteenth state) to settlement.

The Sheltowee Trace is a backpacking trail that will traverse the entire length of Daniel Boone National Forest. When completed (the target date is 1979), the trail will be approximately three hundred miles long and will cross some nine eastern Kentucky counties southward from its beginning near Morehead. Nominated to the National Trails System, the Sheltowee Trace will end at Pickett State Park in Tennessee where it will intersect the John Muir Trail (which connects with the Appalachian Trail). The idea for the trail was first proposed twenty years ago, but it wasn't until 1976 that the actual planning began.

The Sheltowee Trace is marked with a five-inch, white diamond blaze (standard U.S. Forest Service blaze) or the turtle-shaped blaze (from Daniel Boone's Indian name).

At this writing, approximately 178.65 miles of the trail is completed. Since public ownership encompasses only thirty percent of the lands within the forest's demarcation boundary, it's unavoidable that the Sheltowee Trace must cross some private lands. Gaining the right-of-ways (ROWs) isn't always easy, and without the help of private agencies, the Forest Service's job would be all but impossible.

When completed, the Sheltowee Trace will be Kentucky's longest continuous footpath and will pass through the Pioneer Weapons Hunting Area, the Red River Gorge Geological Area, the Turkey Foot Recreation Area, the S Tree Recreation Area, Yahoo Falls Scenic Area, and the proposed Big South Fork National Recreation Area. The trail will also cross the Cave Run Dam and the Laurel River Dam and pass through Natural Bridge and Cumberland Falls State Resort Parks. Other points of interest include four Kentucky Wild Rivers—the Red, Rockcastle, Upper Cumberland, and

Big South Fork of the Cumberland—and historic areas such as portions of the original Wilderness Road (Boone's Trace), iron furnaces, caves (Wind and Big Salt Peter), and the Wildcat Mountain Battlefield, the site of a Civil War skirmish.

Verne Orndorff, landscape architect for the U.S. Forest Service in Winchester, has worked hard on laying out the Sheltowee Trace, sixty miles of which will use existing trails. He personally inspects the work being done on the trail in the field periodically.

In the summer of 1976, a corridor for the trail was approved by the forest supervisor and district rangers. Construction of the trail (and flagging) is being done by joint efforts of the U.S. Forest Service, Sierra Club, Boy Scouts, Older Americans, Youth Conservation Corps (YCC), and the Young Adults Conservation Corps (YACC). Trailhead parking lots and bridges are major construction projects related to the actual cutting of the footpath.

The following is a quad-by-quad breakdown of the status of the trail at this writing.

STRICKLETT:	1.89 miles completed; 0.94 miles of right-of-way (ROW) sought by Fivco Area Development District.
CRANSTON:	2.65 miles flagged (ROW over existing private roadway sought by Fivco Area Development District); 2.46 miles completed.
SOLDIER:	4.15 miles are flagged; 0.57 miles of ROW needed; and 1.70 miles are completed. Jenny Wiley Trail intersects with the Sheltowee Trace on this quadrangle.
MOREHEAD:	2.26 miles of ROW is needed; 1.13 miles are under construction; and 10.21 miles are completed. Students at Morehead State University built sections of the trail on this quadrangle. ROW is being acquired by Fivco Area Development District. U.S. Forest Service Trail #109 (FS #109), Big Limestone Trail, intersects Sheltowee Trace on this quad.
BANGOR:	0.56 miles completed
FARMERS:	0.56 miles completed
SALT LICK:	5.19 miles flagged; 0.75 miles of ROW needed; and 10.96 miles completed. The trail passes through Pioneer Weapons Area after crossing Cave Run Dam.

Bridges are needed over Caney and Clear creeks.

SCRANTON: 2.65 miles flagged; 4.35 miles of ROW needed; and 4.35 miles completed. Part of the complete section parallels KY 1274. All ROWs are being negotiated by the Fivco Area Development District.

POMEROYTON: 2.46 miles flagged (Laurel Branch, Aladic Creek); and 4.35 miles completed in Red River Gorge Geological Area.

SLADE: 0.75 miles ROW is being secured by Kentucky Trails Association; and 9.46 miles completed. Sheltowee Trace mileage on this quad is all in Red River Gorge Geological Area; there are connections with FS trails #223, 205, 217, and day-hiking trails in Natural Bridge State Resort Park.

ZACHARIAH: 3.02 miles of ROW being sought by Lee County Board of Education; and 6.80 miles completed. Bridges are needed at Hawk Branch and Big Sinking Creek.

COBHILL: 1.69 miles of ROW needed; and 0.56 miles completed.

HEIDELBERG: 1.13 miles flagged; 7.57 miles ROW needed; and 6.43 miles completed. The completed section is a dirt road along Sturgeon Creek.

LEIGHTON: 5.30 miles completed.

Mc KEE: 9.84 miles completed. A bridge is needed over Big Buck Lick; the trail here passes Turkey Foot Recreation Area.

SANDGAP: 11.17 miles completed.

PARROT: 2.27 miles completed; two alternate routes proposed off KY 89.

LIVINGSTON: 2.65 miles flagged; 6.43 miles of ROW needed (Tri-County Development District); and 13.82 miles completed, including 4.54 miles of old Daniel Boone Trace. A bridge is needed over Horse Lick Creek. Three alternate routes have been suggested, variously flagged, and

	completed (old logging roads, passable by four-wheel-drive vehicles).
BERNSTADT:	11.75 miles completed.
LONDON SW:	0.75 miles flagged; and 1.70 miles ROW needed (Tri-County Development District). A bridge is needed over Big Sinking Creek.
ANO:	0.37 miles ROW needed; and 7.57 miles completed. Bridges are needed over Cane and Pounder creeks.
SAWYER:	11.75 miles completed; trail crosses Laurel River Dam and uses FS (trail) #715. The bridge is completed at Bark Camp Creek. There are Adirondack shelters at Bark Camp and Star Camp.
CUMBERLAND FALLS:	1.51 miles ROW needed; and 11.36 miles completed (of which 3.03 miles are a completed alternate). 8.33 miles is FS (trail) #715. ROW is being acquired by the McCreary County Hiking Club.
WIBORG:	4.73 miles flagged; and 7.0 miles completed (3.03 miles of which are an alternate route). Four bridges are needed over Railroad Branch and Barren Creek.
NEVELSVILLE:	6.81 miles completed using FS (trails) #628, 629, and 630 passing through Yahoo Falls Scenic Area and Alum Ford Campground.
BARTHELL:	2.46 miles flagged; 0.37 miles ROW needed (McCreary County Hiking Club); and 10.02 miles completed.
BELL FARM:	2.84 miles completed.
BARTHELL SW:	2.65 miles completed to Kentucky–Tennessee line; and 2.27 miles of unimproved road in Tennessee.
SHARP PLACE (TN):	3.21 miles completed.

The author at Breaks Interstate Park. Photograph by Marty Colburn.

Portsmouth

125

240

Rome
(Stout P. O.)

Friendship

South Portsmouth

South Shore

Wheeler:

C. & O.

784

Firebrick

GREENUP

Buena Vista

52

10

23

784

Letitia

Grays
Branch

7

52

8

Quincy

Garrison

Lynn

827

23

Haverhi

Vanceburg

N

1306

Greenup

1

Rad
Flatwoo

59

Jenny Wiley Trail

784

Warnock

Argillite

207

Kinniconick

Michael Tygart Trail

Kehoe

GREENBO LAKE

SRP

2

Camp Dix

474

Carter

2
7

GREENUP

A

56

MEAD
FOREST

21

2

784

Hopewell

207

Wesleyville

Simon Kenton Trail

7

1

10

59

CARTER
CAVES

Tygarts

River

18

SRP

16

172

14

Rush

5

60

11

85

156

2

11

Grayson

C. & O.

64

14

182

CARTER

Hitchins

Denton

20

Upper Tygart

Olive Hill

Leon

773

Shelltowee Trace

174

Grahn

GRAYSON LAKE
STATE PARK

1

1496

Soldier

955

Gimlet

Grayson
Lake

Willard

Continued on page 230

504

504

Bruin

Webbville

35

re ad
arfield

649

7

ROWAN

Wagners
Store

24

Ordinary

416

0

2 MILE

Newfoundland

409

0

5 KILOMETER

201

173

Sandy
Hook

ELLIOTT

32

486

Cherokee

Blaine

19

Continued on page 241

Little Sandy

Isonville

16

Blaine

32

Mazie

NAME OF TRAIL: Jenny Wiley Trail
MAP ON PAGE: 240, 241
START: Trailhead park, South Portsmouth, Kentucky,
                        on the Ohio River at U.S. 23 (U.S. Grant
                        Bridge)
END: Jenny Wiley State Resort Park
TRAIL CONNECTIONS: Michael Tygart Trail and Simon Kenton Trail
USGS QUADS: Portsmouth, Friendship, Brushart, Garrison,
                        Wesleyville, Olive Hill, Soldier, Haldeman,
                        Wrigley, Sandy Hook, Ivyton, and Prestons-
                        burg
COUNTIES: Greenup, Lewis, Carter, Elliott, Rowan, Mor-
                        gan, Floyd, Magoffin, and Johnson
RATING: Strenuous; 123.75 mi.; footpath, gravel road,
                        and logging road; +700 ft.

When completed, the Jenny Wiley Trail will pass through nine northeastern Kentucky counties. At this writing, 123.75 miles of the trail have been
completed. The 97.75-mile "north" section between South Portsmouth,
Kentucky and the Morgan–Elliott county line, was completed in 1977. A
23-mile "south" section, beginning on KY 114 in Magoffin County at the C
& O Railroad Bridge and ending at the Goble Creek Campground in Jenny
Wiley State Resort Park, is also finished and open to the public. Approximately fifty miles of trail that would link these two systems is now under
construction.

    The Jenny Wiley Trail is a joint effort of the Jenny Wiley Trail Confer-
ence and Fivco Area Development District. Funding started in November
of 1975 when the Fivco Area Development District received a grant of
$150,000 from the Appalachian Regional Commission (funding through
May of 1977). Construction of the trail began in January 1976 about the
time the Jenny Wiley Trail Conference was formed.

    In October of 1976, additional funding ($92,000 for one year's op-
eration), was received from the Kentucky Department for Human Resources (CETA financed).

    Additional funds for the construction of shelters, footbridges, trail
upgrading, and maintenance were received in January, 1978 when the
Kentucky state legislature awarded the development district $200,000 for
two years' work and made it guardian of the "Eastern Kentucky Trail
System"—twenty miles of the Sheltowee Trace that crosses privately
owned lands, the Jenny Wiley Trail, and two spur trails that connect to
state resort parks, the Michael Tygart and Simon Kenton Trails.

The Jenny Wiley Trail is a first in Kentucky since seventy-five percent of the trail crosses privately owned lands (over two hundred landowners), necessitating massive easement lease agreements for the six-foot right-of-ways. The trail uses woodland footpaths (2" x 12" blue rectangular blaze), dirt logging and agricultural roads, pipeline right-of-ways, gravel roads, and in some cases, paved highways when right-of-way across privately owned lands cannot be secured. Trail re-routing in the future will eliminate many of these sections of the trail. The trail passes through rural farmlands, pine and cedar thickets, stands of mixed hardwoods, abandoned mines, and small communities. Water from surface sources (ponds and streams) as well as tapped springs and cisterns (located at many of the trail shelters) is considered unfit for human consumption without boiling or chemical treatment. Natural water sources are scarce because much of the trail is on ridgetops along county boundaries.

At the present time, twelve trail shelters have been constructed along the two sections of the Jenny Wiley Trail open to hikers. The wood frame, Adirondack-type shelters sleep six to eight persons. Frost-free spigots have been installed at all water sources located at the shelters. The shelters were named, in most cases, after the landowner on whose land they are located. Stiles were built to keep hikers from breaking down fences, and to eliminate the need for opening and closing gates (and also to prevent the possibility of livestock escaping).

All the cisterns installed along the trail operate by gravity flow and use rainwater off the shelter roof. The water is stored in buried 500-gallon tanks.

From the trailhead to the Scaff Shelter, the Jenny Wiley Trail ascends Springville Hill with numerous switchbacks and goes past a radio tower with an excellent view of Portsmouth, Ohio across the river. The trail continues along the ridgetop until it reaches Scaff Shelter, 6.6 miles south of the trailhead. Cistern water is available.

Intermittent views of the Ohio River continue until the trail drops off ridgetop. To the right is the junction with the Lozier Trail, a 1½-mile, privately owned footpath that begins at Kellen Hollow Road, off KY 10.

Before reaching Scaff Shelter, the trail passes some clay pits and one old stripmine. The woodland trace has numerous fence crossovers beyond Scaff Shelter. It's 10 miles to Briery Shelter, the second of the ten on the 97.75-mile "north" section. Cistern water is available at Briery Shelter. There is a gigantic dump on the county line where Dry Fork Road crosses the trail. Some stretches of gravel roads, old farm roads, and apple orchard with pond are noted along the trail.

From the Briery Shelter it's 8.2 miles to the Buzzard Roost Shelter. The trail cuts through the woods until it reaches Schultz Creek Ridge Road where it is on and off the pavement for about 4 miles since the right-of-way for the trail could only be secured atop the ridge where the road is located. The Buzzard Roost Shelter is just off KY 784 (Schultz Creek Ridge Road); cistern water is available. Michael Tygart Trail intersects at shelter #3.

It's 10.9 miles from the Buzzard Roost to William's Shelter. The trail follows gravel road for 3 miles, beginning one mile south of the Buzzard Roost Shelter. Then the trail goes into the woods to William's Shelter, passing through stands of mixed hardwoods, agricultural lands, and reverting fields (cedar thickets). A cistern is located at William's Shelter.

The trail is 9.75 miles long between William's and Danner shelters. It crosses KY 474, following it in some sections, and intermittently uses farm access roads. The trail passes through the front yard of Virgie and Labe Auxier. Before reaching the Danner Shelter, the trail passes some clay pits.

The Danner Shelter is located on an old county road that is no longer in use by vehicles. Cistern water is available.

It's 10 miles from the Danner Shelter to the Henderson Shelter. About 3 miles south of the Danner Shelter, the Simon Kenton Trail intersects the Jenny Wiley. The trail crosses KY 59 at Rose Hill and again it follows the pavement intermittently through the woods and over a gravel road (Walnut Hill Road). There's a cistern at the Henderson Shelter.

It's 11 miles to Easterling Shelter from Henderson Shelter. On this stretch of trail, Interstate 64 is crossed. The trail passes under the elevated roadway at Fleming Fork Creek. Then the trail ascends to the ridgetop again and goes through stands of hardwoods and past old farm buildings on the edges of fields. Spring water is available at the Easterling Shelter.

The 8.4-mile section from Easterling to Thomas Shelter passes near Hays Crossing and Globe. From Soldier, off KY 174 in Carter County, the trail ascends the ridge and again drops into the valley at Haldeman. Cistern water is available at the Thomas Shelter.

The 9.2-mile section of the trail between the Thomas and Royce shelters is mostly on the ridgetops and uses old logging roads. About 6 miles south of Thomas Shelter, the trail crosses KY 32 at Elliottville.

The 10-mile section from the Royce to the Howard Shelter includes a 5-mile stretch along KY 173 that eventually will be relocated through the Minor Shop Hollow. The last 3.7 miles of the north section of the trail passes through stands of mixed hardwoods such as tulip poplars and hemlock, with some stretches through rhododendron thickets at the bases of clifflines. There are a few waterfalls in the area.

The 23-mile south section of the trail has a lot of up-and-down stretches and is considered only for experienced hikers in excellent shape.

Stretches of the trail need improvements. It is a rocky, strenuous trail. Beginning west of trail shelter #18, the Francis Shelter (cistern water available), the trail is on the C & D Railroad Bridge, then it follows the tracks for about 3.2 miles, crossing KY 114, and ascends the steep ridge to Francis

Shelter. The 12-mile stretch of trail from Francis Shelter to Arms Shelter is the most difficult of the entire Jenny Wiley system. Eventually a primitive campsite will be established between the two shelters because it's a strenuous 12 miles and not everyone will want to tackle it in one day. Cistern water is also available at the Arms Shelter.

The last 7.8 miles of the trail crosses dense mountainous woodlands with some stretches along clifflines and valleys of thick stands of hardwoods, and some beautiful mountain woodlands, especially after entering the state resort park boundary. The trail ends at the Goble Creek Campground.

Jenny Wiley Trail, c/o Brian Mattingly, Trail Director, P. O. Box 636, Catlettsburg, Kentucky 41129. (606) 739-5191.

NAME OF TRAIL: Michael Tygart Trail
MAP ON PAGE: 240
START: Jesse Stuart Lodge, Greenbo Lake State Re-
                        sort Park
END: Intersection with the Jenny Wiley Trail at trail
                        shelter #3, the Buzzard Roost Shelter, off KY
                        784
TRAIL CONNECTIONS: Jenny Wiley Trail
USGS QUADS: Brushart, Tygarts Valley, and Oldtown
COUNTIES: Greenup
RATING: Strenuous; 24.0 mi.; footpath, logging road,
                        and gravel road; +450 ft.

The Michael Tygart Trail is a 24-mile trail that runs from east to west across Greenup County. Named for the eighteenth century explorer and scout profiled in the book, *The Frontiersmen,* by Allan Eckert, the Michael Tygart Trail was completed on August 12, 1978. There are three shelters on the trail. The Blackberry Shelter (no water available) is 3.3 miles west of Greenbo Lake State Resort Park. The first 8.4 miles of trail is through ridgetop hardwoods and pine thickets and uses gravel roads, dirt footpaths, and logging roads.

From Hall's Shelter, the trail passes along the paved Tygarts Road (the trail is in the process of being re-routed at this writing) and plunges into the creek bottoms at Johnson's swimming hole, a good place to relax and cool off in warm weather. Tygarts Creek is a year-round water source; chemical treatment or boiling of all drinking water is advised.

Then the trail ascends and descends rapidly from ridge to creek bottom along a woodland trace and farm access road. After crossing the creek by swinging bridge, the trail parallels KY 2 and KY 7 at Kehoe, then ascends Tick Ridge on woodland trace and farm roads, and crosses two pipeline right-of-ways.

Greene's Shelter is 18.6 miles west of trailhead. Cistern water is available at this point. From Greene's Shelter it's 5.4 miles to the junction with Jenny Wiley Trail. Ridgetop logging roads are used on this last section of the trail. There are numerous wet-weather side drainages. The trail ascends approximately 450 feet from Tygarts Creek to its junction with Jenny Wiley Trail.

NAME OF TRAIL:	Simon Kenton Trail
MAP ON PAGE:	240
START:	Parking area of beach, Carter Caves State Resort Park
END:	Intersection with Jenny Wiley Trail, 2.7 miles west of Bethel Church off KY 2
TRAIL CONNECTIONS:	Jenny Wiley Trail
USGS QUADS:	Olive Hill, Wesleyville
COUNTIES:	Carter
RATING:	Moderate; 9.0 mi.; footpath and logging road; +300 ft.

The 9-mile Simon Kenton Trail is named in honor of the frontier scout who saved Daniel Boone's life during the siege of Fort Boonesborough in the year of the "Bloody Three Sevens," 1777. The Simon Kenton Trail passes through a natural arch within the boundary of Carter Caves State Resort Park amid rocky clifflines and stands of towering hemlocks, tulip poplars, and dense "fields" of rhododendron.

The James Shelter is 3.1 miles west of the trailhead, just outside the boundary of Tygarts State Forest. There's a spring at the shelter; two tributaries of Buffalo Creek are crossed along the trail, which follows ridgetops and then skirts along pasture after leaving the state-owned lands. A short section of the trail, 0.2 miles, is along KY 2. The trail ascends approximately 300 feet from the creek bottoms to the ridgetops at the junction of the Jenny Wiley Trail (5.9 miles west of James Shelter).

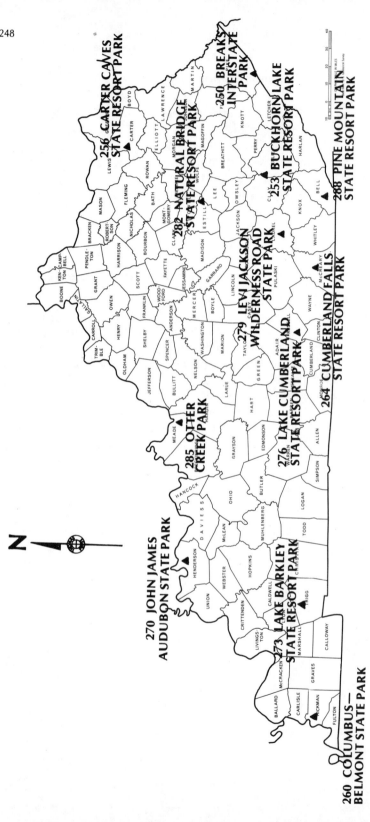

256 CARTER CAVES STATE RESORT PARK

250 BREAKS INTERSTATE PARK

282 NATURAL BRIDGE STATE RESORT PARK

253 BUCKHORN LAKE STATE RESORT PARK

288 PINE MOUNTAIN STATE RESORT PARK

279 LEVI JACKSON WILDERNESS ROAD STATE PARK

264 CUMBERLAND FALLS STATE RESORT PARK

276 LAKE CUMBERLAND STATE RESORT PARK

285 OTTER CREEK PARK

270 JOHN JAMES AUDUBON STATE PARK

273 LAKE BARKLEY STATE RESORT PARK

260 COLUMBUS— BELMONT STATE PARK

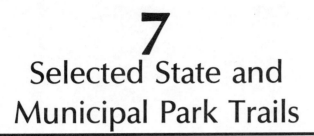

7
Selected State and
Municipal Park Trails

In this chapter, the day-hiking trails in ten selected state parks, one interstate park, and one City of Louisville–owned park will be described. The ten state parks selected are known for their emphasis on day-hiking and nature study. Many of the other state parks in the system not listed in this chapter are water-oriented and have only casual footpaths for stretching your legs after dinner. There is a total of 95.80 miles of trail in the ten state parks. John James Audubon State Park has the most miles of day-hiking trails, 15.75; followed by Cumberland Falls State Resort Park, 14.25; Columbus–Belmont Battlefield State Park, 11.5; Natural Bridge State Resort Park, 9.75; Wilderness Road State Park, 9.0; Carter Caves State Resort Park, 7.75; Pine Mountain State Resort Park, 6.8; Lake Barkley State Resort Park, 6.0; Lake Cumberland State Resort Park, 4.0; and Buckhorn Lake State Resort Park, 2.0.

Otter Creek Park, owned by the City of Louisville, was included in this unit because of its popularity with picnickers and casual hikers from the Louisville area. Otter Creek is a favorite with those hikers who prefer to pack a lunch in a rucksack and spend the day exploring the wooded knobs and river-bottom forest along the Ohio. There are 9.7 miles of trail in the park.

Breaks Interstate Park is unique in that it was developed jointly and is run by a cooperative agreement between the commonwealths of Kentucky and Virginia. The scenery in the park is nothing short of spectacular, and the rental cottages are private and rustic. The park is a perfect get-away spot with plenty of interesting trails to explore. There are approximately 10 miles of trail in Breaks Interstate Park.

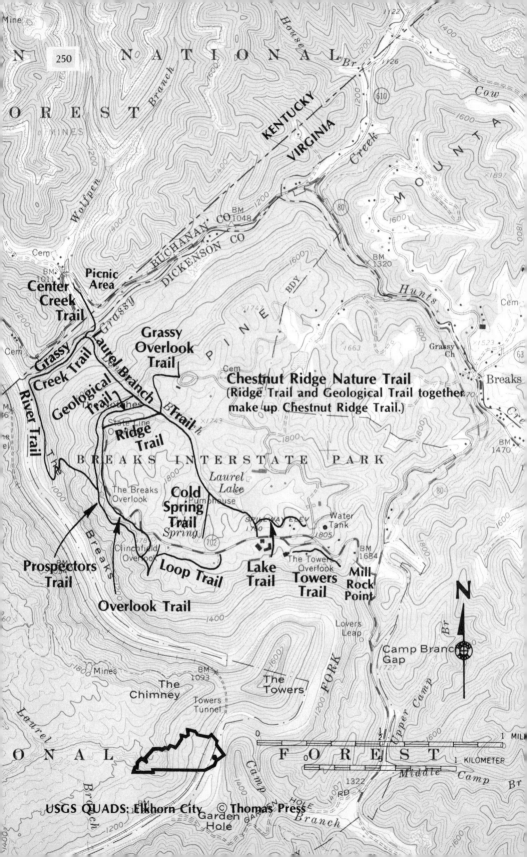

250

N A T I O N A L

F O R E S T

Mine

Houser Br.

KENTUCKY

VIRGINIA

Cow

MOUNTA

Cem

Picnic Area

BM 1048

BUCHANAN CO.

DICKENSON CO.

BM 1320

Hunts

Center Creek Trail

PINE

Grassy Overlook Trail

Cem

Chestnut Ridge Nature Trail
(Ridge Trail and Geological Trail together make up Chestnut Ridge Trail.)

Breaks

Grassy Ch.

Grassy Creek Trail

Laurel Branch

Trail

Geological Trail

Ridge Trail

River Trail

BM 1470

B R E A K S   I N T E R S T A T E   P A R K

Laurel Lake

The Breaks Overlook

Cold Spring Trail

Pumphouse

Water Tank

SPILLWAY ELEV 1760

Spring

BM 1684

Clinchfield Overlook

Prospectors Trail

Loop Trail

Lake Trail

The Towers Overlook

Towers Trail

Mill Rock Point

Overlook Trail

Lovers Leap

N

Camp Branch Gap

Mines

BM 1093

The Chimney

The Towers

Laurel

Towers Tunnel

0   ½   1 MILE

N A L   F O R E S T

1 KILOMETER

Camp

Middle Camp Br.

USGS QUADS: Elkhorn City   © Thomas Press

Garden Hole

NAME OF TRAIL: Breaks Interstate Park Trail System
MAP ON PAGE: 250
START: (See map)
END: (See map)
TRAIL CONNECTIONS: None
USGS QUADS: Elkhorn City
COUNTIES: Pike (KY) and Dickenson (VA)
RATING: Easy; 10 mi.; footpath; +300 ft.

Breaks Interstate Park, straddling the Kentucky–Virginia border, has some of the most awesome and impressive scenery in the Cumberlands. Just over 170 miles southwest of Lexington via the Mountain Parkway to Prestonsburg, then via KY 80 to Elkhorn City, the park encompasses 2,860 acres of woodlands, rock cliffs, and skyscraping mountain scenery. Nestled in the hills of eastern Kentucky's Pike County and Virginia's Dickenson County in the Jefferson National Forest, the park's past is woven with legends about vast fortunes in silver hidden by Englishman, John Swift, the Hatfield–McCoy feud, sacred Indian grounds, and explorer and settler, Daniel Boone.

Breaks Interstate Park was created by joint action of the Kentucky and Virginia legislatures in 1951. Development of the facilities began in 1958. The central attraction at the park is Breaks Canyon, a five-mile-long, 1,600-foot-deep horseshoe-shaped chasm. Russell Fork of the Big Sandy River, a raging white-water river, cuts through the narrow gorge; forest lands and an imposing rock knob called the Towers overlook the river's twisting path. Geologists believe that the rock formations are of the Pennsylvanian, late Palezoic era.

Breaks Interstate Park is open year-round, but its lodge and restaurant are only open from April 1 to October 31. There are thirty units in the motor lodge that rent for $16 single occupancy, $19 double. All rooms have two double beds and one bedroom. There are four two-bedroom housekeeping cottages (open year-round) that may be rented on a weekly basis for $25 a night. The Rhododendron Lodge houses the gift shop and restaurant.

The park's campground, also open seasonally, has 44 recreational vehicle sites with water, electric, and sewer hookups; 20 sites for tents only; and 85 sites with water hookups only. Flush toilets, showers, and drinking water are available at the campground's bathhouse. Picnic tables and grills are at each campsite. There are five picnic shelters on the grounds. During the summer, outdoor dramas and special programs such as nature slide shows are held in the park's amphitheater.

There are approximately 10 miles of day-hiking trails in the park. The **Prospectors Trail** leads from the Russell Fork overlook on VA 647 to its intersection with the **River Trail,** which descends with numerous switchbacks to the bank of the Russell Fork. The **Laurel Branch Trail** also intersects the Prospectors Trail near the state line overlook. The **Ridge Trail** and **Geological Trail** intersect the Laurel Branch Trail at the Notches, a rock formation. The **Center Creek Trail** and **Grassy Creek Trail** intersect KY 80 at the Kentucky–Virginia line at the north end of the park. There are no established day-hiking trails in the vicinity of the Lover's Leap, Mill Rock Point, or the Towers overlook, but there are footpaths along the canyon rim. The **Chestnut Ridge Nature Trail** incorporates sections of the Ridge Geological, and Laurel Branch trails. It is a self-guided nature and geological interpretive trail with 27 numbered stops. A booklet available at the Visitors' Center and Nature Museum explains the forest types, the predominant species of shrubs and wildflowers, and the origins of rock formations in the park. Exhibits of area history (antiques, moonshine stills, farm implements), plant and animal communities, an audio-visual birdsong display, and a park facilities map are located in the visitors' center. The recreational facilities also include an Olympic-size swimming pool (open Memorial Day to Labor Day), 12-acre Laurel Lake (paddle boat rentals available), horseback riding, nature interpretive programs, and nature walks.

Breaks Interstate Park, Breaks, Virginia 24607. (703) 865-4413.

USGS QUADS: Buckhorn

© Thomas Press

Leatherwood Trail

Moonshiners Hollow Trail

Lodge

BUCKHORN LAKE STATE RESORT PARK

NAME OF TRAIL: Buckhorn Lake State Resort Park Trail System
MAP ON PAGE: 253
START: North side of the entrance road, east of the lodge
END: North side of the entrance road, east of the lodge
TRAIL CONNECTIONS: None
USGS QUADS: Buckhorn
COUNTIES: Perry
RATING: Easy; 2.0 mi.; footpath and logging road; +100 ft.

Construction on Buckhorn Lake began in 1956, and the project was completed four years later. The 1,200-acre, 21-mile-long reservoir, built by the U. S. Army Corps of Engineers, Louisville District, lies in Leslie and Perry counties of eastern Kentucky, west of Hazard. The Buckhorn Dam is located on the middle fork on the Kentucky River, 43 miles upstream from Beattyville where the three forks of the Kentucky River converge.

The lake's primary recreational development is Buckhorn Lake State Resort Park, 15 miles west of Hazard off KY 28 on KY 1833. The 856-acre park is open from May 1 to October 31. Construction of the lodge, campgrounds, and recreational facilities was completed in 1962. All of the 36 lodge rooms are equipped with 2 double beds, a ceramic tile bath with tub and shower, color TV, telephone, air conditioning, and private patio or balcony with lake view. The 200-seat dining room in the lodge is open for breakfast from 7:00 to 10:30 A.M., for lunch from 11:30 A.M. to 2:30 P.M., and for dinner from 5:30 to 9:00 P.M. A gift shop, with a large assortment of Kentucky-made dolls, and a recreation room with air hockey, foosball, table tennis, and video games are also located in the lodge. Naturalist-led programs, bicycle rentals, miniature golf, two tennis courts and swimming pool (open from Memorial Day to Labor Day; for lodge guests only), and seasonal beach and bathhouse complex are available.

There are two day-hiking trails in the park, the Leatherwood and Moonshiners Hollow trails. The system has a total of two miles of footpath and logging road. An interpretive booklet with illustrations is available for the **Moonshiners Hollow Trail.** The loop trail for the most part follows an old logging road through this mixed hardwood forest. The forest, bedrock, soil, the contours of the land, and evidences of disturbance by man are discussed at eighteen interpretive stations.

The **Leatherwood Trail** is a quarter-mile trail that ascends to an overlook at the lakeshore. Like the Moonshiners Hollow Trail, the Leatherwood

Trail begins 200 yards northeast of the lodge. Both trails are marked by signs. Picnic tables, shelter, and stands of pines and hardwoods are found along the trail.

The park's campground, located at the Gays Creek site three miles west of the lodge, is open May 1 to Labor Day, and has 112 sites—72 with electrical hookups and 40 primitive. Flush toilets, showers, drinking water, a dumping station, ice, picnic tables, and grills are available. The Buckhorn Lake State Resort Park Marina, adjacent to the lodge, is open May 1 to October 31 and has 100 open slips. A restaurant at the marina is open from May to Labor Day. Rental fishing boats, live bait (minnows, crickets, and worms), tackle, a fish cleaning station, freezer space, and a boat launching ramp are available. Buckhorn Lake State Resort Park, Buckhorn, Kentucky 41721. (606) 398-7510, marina extension 120.

NAME OF TRAIL: Carter Caves State Resort Park Trail System
MAP ON PAGE: 256
START: (See map)
END: (See map)
TRAIL CONNECTIONS: Simon Kenton Trail
USGS QUADS: Wesleyville, Tygarts Valley, and Grahn
COUNTIES: Carter
RATING: Easy; 7.75 mi.; footpath, and logging road;
                        +300 ft.

This northeastern Kentucky park in Carter County can be reached by driving five miles east on U.S. 60 from Olive Hill, then three miles north on KY 182. It is noted for the cave system that honeycombs the hills in the thousand-acre, state-owned park, its splendid woodlands, and nearby Tygarts Creek, a fine canoeing and fishing stream. Opened in the 1940s, Carter Caves State Resort Park has a full selection of recreational pastimes.

There are five color-coded day-hiking trails in the park; they total 7.75 miles. The **Red Trail,** the longest, is 5 miles long and climbs 200 feet. The trail passes through deciduous forest with lots of rhododendron and tall hemlock trees. Hiked counterclockwise from the lodge, the trail first passes Smokey Bridge, the first of three natural rock arches on the trail. Smokey Bridge is the largest natural arch in Kentucky. It is more than 70 feet high and 40 feet wide. It's a tunnel-like rock span, 220 feet through a narrow ridge. Steps lead to the base of the arch. The next arch to be encountered on the Red Trail is the Raven Bridge, which can be reached by a spur trail. Raven Bridge is 40 feet wide and 15 feet high.

Draped in ferns and set amid a jumble of boulders, the Fern Bridge is a 90-foot-high, 100-foot-wide natural arch. Just past Fern Bridge, the Red Trail passes the cottages, trading post and miniature golf course.

The **Blue Trail** is an easy, three-quarter-mile ridgetop trail that begins at the lodge and ends at Raven Bridge. The **Yellow Trail** is a half-mile loop at the base of a cliff that connects the Blue and Red trails. The **Green Trail** is a 1-mile trail that begins near the auxiliary parking lot of the trading post. It ends in Horn Hollow east of Laurel Cave. By permission from the park naturalist, hikers may enter the short cave that exits through a cliffline into a forest of hemlocks, rhododendron, and tall stands of deciduous trees. The **Natural Bridge Trail** is a half-mile trail that begins at the trading post and descends past the picnic grounds to a huge natural arch. The trail can be hiked as a loop by using the main entrance road to the park on the return hike. This road actually is on top of Natural Arch, a 45-foot-high, 40-foot-wide span. The trail passes through mixed stands of hardwoods and crosses on stream on a footbridge. The massive horseshoe-shaped arch has a stream flowing under it.

The trail system at Carter Caves State Resort Park is more than twenty years old. Aside from the five natural arches—the largest number in any state park in Kentucky—Carter Caves State Resort Park is known for its underground wonders.

There are four cave tours. Tickets for the X Cave and Saltpetre Cave tours can be purchased at the park's trading post, open 9:00 A.M. to 7:00 P.M. daily. Prices range from 35¢ to $1.00. Group rates are available. The Cascade Visitors' Center, open from 9:00 A.M. to 5:00 P.M. daily, sells tickets for the Cascade Cavern Tour. The tour costs less than a dollar for adults and children.

There are seven Cascade Cavern Tours daily. The hour-long leisurely walk features the Counterfeiters Room, "Hanging Gardens of Solomon," and numerous formations typical of limestone caves. The Saltpetre Cave Tour, held only on weekends, is a 45-minute tour about one mile long. Naturalists talk on the War of 1812 saltpeter mining operations, Indian Princess Grave, inscriptions, part of the Legend of the Lost Miner, and "Devil's Dome," a highlight of the tour.

The X Cave Tour gets its name from an unusual formation X-shaped of stalactites, stalagmites, and flowstone curtains. The easy tour only lasts 40 minutes and is about a quarter of a mile long.

The two strenuous tours offered at Carter Caves State Resort Park are the Bat Cave Tour and the Laurel Cave–Horn Hollow Cave Tour. The Bat Cave Tour is by reservation only and is offered on Tuesdays, Wednesdays, Saturdays, and Sundays. The two-hour tour covers about two miles, with extended stooping and squatting required. During the tour, participants must wade in water; flashlights, old clothes, sturdy shoes, and jackets are advised. Children under 16 must be accompanied by adults. The highlight of the tour is a discussion and observation of a colony of rare bats in Kentucky. The Laurel Cave–Horn Hollow Cave Tour departs from the Trading Post at 2 P.M., and is offered only on Thursdays. It includes 1½ miles overland hiking and a half mile of walking in caves. It is a strenuous hike that lasts about two hours and is the only tour at Carter Caves State Resort Park that is free of charge. Preschool children are not permitted because of the wading in deep water and the exhausting stooping and crawling. Sturdy shoes, a flashlight, and warm clothes are advised.

In season, park naturalists conduct canoeing trips on Tygarts Creek, a smooth water, Class-I stream bordered by dense woodlands and farmlands. It's known for good fishing for muskellunge, smallmouth bass, and panfish. The canoe trips are free and reservations are required. The informal, un-scheduled trips are limited to persons 14 years old and older, those under 16 years of age must be accompanied by an adult. Canoe trips are limited to ten persons. There's a good chance of sighting wildlife—kingfishers, turtles, wood ducks, and maybe even a deer during the canoe outings.

The lodge, swimming pool for guests only, 45-acre lake and beach house, nature center (with interpretive exhibits on geology, plants, and animals), and cave tours are open from April 1 to October 31; the house-keeping cottages and campground are open year-round.

The campground's services and facilities include showers, flush toilets, dump stations, ice, a playground for youngsters, picnic and shelter houses. Firewood is available. Carter Caves Resort Park, Olive Hill, Kentucky 41164. (606) 286-4411.

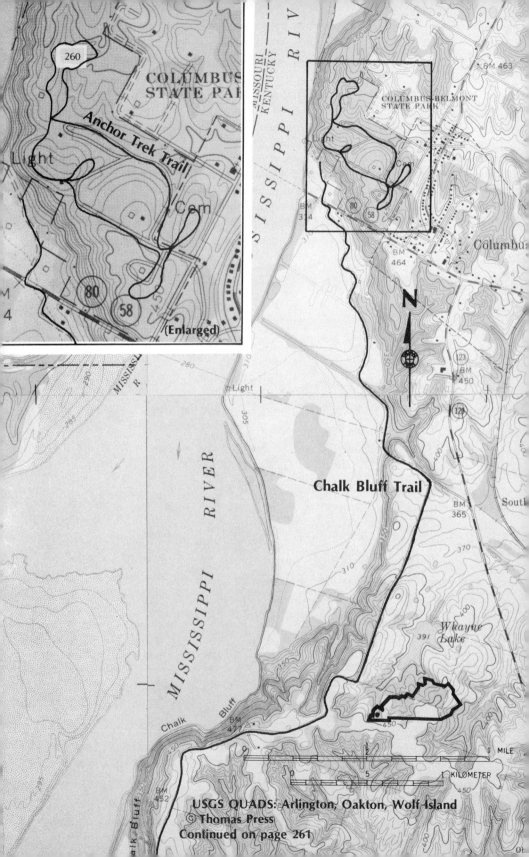

COLUMBUS
STATE PARK

260

Anchor Trek Trail

Light

Cem

80

58

(Enlarged)

MISSOURI
KENTUCKY

MISSISSIPPI RIVER

COLUMBUS-BELMONT
STATE PARK

BM 463

Light

Cem

80

58

BM
314

BM
464

Columbus

N

123
BM
450

South

128

Chalk Bluff Trail

BM
365

370

400

Whayne
Lake

391

MISSISSIPPI RIVER

310

305

290

280

285

295

310

350

350

330

310

400

450

450

450

450

400

450

Chalk   Bluff

BM
427

BM
452

1 MILE

1/2

0

5

KILOMETER

USGS QUADS: Arlington, Oakton, Wolf Island
© Thomas Press
Continued on page 261

Continued on page 260

BM 429

1 MILE

0   5   1 KILOMETER

339

Hollingswor

360

350

Chalk Bluff Trail

380

350

BM 382

380

350

320

380

N

123

350

Hailwell

312

BM 367

400

Three Ponds Blu

USGS QUADS: Oakton, Wolf Island
© Thomas Press

BM 363

Three

NAME OF TRAIL:	Columbus–Belmont State Park Trail System
MAP ON PAGE:	260, 261
START:	Columbus, on KY 80 at state park museum
END:	(See map)
TRAIL CONNECTIONS:	Chalk Bluff Trail
USGS QUADS:	Arlington, Wolf Island, and Oakton
COUNTIES:	Hickman
RATING:	Easy; 11.5 mi.; footpath and logging road; +300 ft.

In September of 1861 a garrison of more than nineteen thousand Confederate troops fortified the bluffs overlooking the Mississippi River at Columbus. An extensive network of trenches and breastworks was built, and 140 heavy guns, mostly 32- and 64-pounders, were positioned to guard against attack on both the river and inland fronts. Further fortified by floating batteries and a huge, mile-long chain stretched across the Mississippi to prevent Union gunboats from penetrating this all-important route to the heart of the South, the outpost became known as the "Gibraltar of the West."

Successfully defended in the Battle of Belmont of November 7, 1861, and during flanking skirmishes on the Kentucky side of the river, the position finally had to be abandoned the next spring when the Confederates were flanked by Grant's troops. The Union army moved into Tennessee with the capture of Fort Donelson and Fort Henry on the Tennessee and Cumberland rivers. Columbus was then occupied by Union forces who held it for the remainder of the Civil War.

Today, the battleground is a Kentucky State Park. Civil War cannon and a wrought-iron fence surrounding an old cemetery where many of the battle's dead are buried are the first things visitors see when they arrive at 156-acre Columbus–Belmont State Park.

There are approximately 11.5 miles of trail in the park. The **Anchor Trek Trail** is entirely within the park. It is 3.5 miles long and begins at the museum. It passes the most interesting attraction to history buffs the park has to offer—an actual section of the chain that Confederate forces stretched across the Mississippi and the giant anchor used to secure it to the bluffs on the Kentucky side. Each link in the chain is said to weigh fifteen pounds and is more than a foot long. That would make the entire weight of the chain in excess of 39 tons. Anchor Trek Trail winds through the Confederate trenches to Arrowhead Point, an observation post. After going through the cemetery, the trail takes hikers to more cannon trenches and skirts the campground. The dirt and pavement trail is nearly level; soft drinks and water are available at the concession area.

Between the campground and the museum the Anchor Trek Trail intersects the **Chalk Bluff Trail,** an 8-mile trail that descends the bluff (crossing KY 58) overlooking the Mississippi River, leaves the park and follows two dirt and gravel roads southward. The first road is Battery Road. There's an overlook on the bluff of a huge sandbar in the river. Just before reaching South Columbus and KY 123, the trail crosses the Chalk Bluff Road. The trail ascends 300 feet; water is available at Columbus–Belmont State Park. The trail was laid out by local Girl Scouts.

The story of Columbus–Belmont's fortification and the battle in 1861 are told by numerous historical markers on the grounds and a diorama in the park's museum. Displays of Indian relics—birdstones, skinstones, arrow points, and other artifacts recovered from Indian campsites unearthed locally are featured in the three-room museum, which is housed in a crica 1852 home where the mayor of Columbus once lived. Personal correspondence between a Union officer and his commander and sketches of the fortifications published in *Harper's Weekly* during the Confederate occupation are displayed beside powder flasks, cannonballs, canister shot, and glass-enclosed cases filled with flintlock and percussion cap rifles and shotguns.

Minie balls, bullet molds, and an interesting collection of ordnance found in 1916 by Alfred A. Scott, are on exhibit as are a Union officer's dress uniform, a medical kit, and a hospital scene. Admission to the museum is 50¢ for adults and 25¢ for children.

Picnickers will find tables and grills around the park and three shelter houses for eating outside during inclement weather. There are swings, monkey bars, and sand pits for the children, and a railing around the steep bluff from which barges may be seen negotiating the bend at Wolfe Island, downstream from the Columbus ferry that shuttles the historic Mississippi.

Open from April 1 to October 31, Columbus–Belmont Battlefield State Park is in Hickman County at Columbus, on KY 80. The campground, adjacent to the cemetery where those who lost their lives in the Battle of Columbus–Belmont were laid to rest, has 24 sites equipped with electrical hookups for either tents or recreational vehicles. The campground's services and facilities include drinking water, showers, flush toilets, picnic tables, and a shelter. Columbus–Belmont Battlefield State Park, Columbus, Kentucky 42032. (502) 677-2327.

0   ½   1 MILE

0   .5   1 KILOMETER

264

N

Brummett Br

Holden Br

Bill Perry

Continued on page 265

Center Rock Rapids

CUMBERLAND

Eagle Falls

9

10

12

90

BM

Cabin Group

1110

780

Water

4

5

Cumberland Falls

6

6

6

835

2

Motor Lodge

BM 838

Dupont Lodge

2

Ford

Ferry

Gaging Sta

BM 829

STATE

Continued on page 203

Moonbow Trail

715

N

Pinnacle
Lookout Tower

INDEFINITE

Catfish

Cr

2

Dry Land
Bridge

BOUNDARY

11

1156

90

LLS

BM

1183

Branch

2

2

Ryan

2

GS QUADS: Cumberland Falls   © Thomas Press

Blue Bend

NAME OF TRAIL: Cumberland Falls State Resort Park Trail Sys-
                        tem
MAP ON PAGE: 264–265
START: DuPont Lodge
END: DuPont Lodge
TRAIL CONNECTIONS: Moonbow Trail (FS #715)
USGS QUADS: Cumberland Falls
COUNTIES: Whitley
RATING: Easy; 14.25 mi.; footpath and logging road;
                        +500 ft.

In January 1931, a $400,000 bequest in the will of former Kentuckian, Senator T. Coleman DuPont, of Delaware, made possible the purchase of 500 acres adjacent to Cumberland Falls and the establishment of one of Kentucky's foremost state parks.

Today, Cumberland Falls State Resort Park is a showplace in the system. Plummeting 67 feet into a rocky gorge, Cumberland Falls, nicknamed "Niagara of the South," because it is the highest falls in the eastern United States south of Niagara, presents a rare phenomenon: a moonbow, which appears in the mist of the thundering waterfall when the moon is full. Unique to the western world, the only other such moonbow occurs at Victoria Falls in Africa.

The 1,794-acre park, open all year, is in southeastern Kentucky's Whitley County in Daniel Boone National Forest off Interstate 75 (from the Corbin and Williamsburg interchange), eight miles south on U.S. 25W, then seven or eight miles west on KY 90. The lodge, woodland suites, and cottages have both heat and air conditioning for year-round comfort.

At this writing, there are eight day-hiking trails open to visitors in Cumberland Falls State Resort Park, a total of 14.25 miles of dirt footpath. All trails are marked by signs; some have square blazes of yellow numbers in a red background.

The longest day-hiking trail in the park is **Trail 2.** It begins at the picnic grounds behind DuPont Lodge on the banks of the Cumberland River. Trail 2 is a 7-mile loop that basically parallels the river through mixed hardwoods and pine and stands of hemlocks and rhododendron, and it ascends 500 feet to Pinnacle Knob Lookout Tower, which is open and affords those who climb to the top a breathtaking view of the surrounding forest. Sections of Trail 2 use an old logging road and the trail crosses KY 90. Trail 2 intersects trails 5, 7, and 11.

Trail 4 is a 1-mile, self-guided nature trail that begins at the east side of DuPont Lodge. Booklets describing the natural features of the walk are available at the trailhead display case and at the lodge. There are approximately eighty steps on the trail; one spur leads to the picnic grounds, the other to trail 5 at cabin group 2.

Trail 5 is a short, quarter-mile trail that connects cabin group 2 with trails 3 and 2. At the intersection with Trail 2, there's a set of wooden stairs.

Trail 6 is a half-mile (one-way) trail that begins in front of DuPont Lodge (at the picture display). The trail is above the cliffline most of the way and offers hikers an excellent view of the river and Gatliff Bridge (the concrete bridge on KY 90 over the Cumberland River). A side trail leads to Cumberland Falls. Trail 6 is one of the most popular hikes in the park.

Trail 7 is a short (quarter- to three-quarter-mile) trail that begins a quarter mile east of DuPont Lodge on KY 90 (left side of the road). It is a maze of loops with spurs that connect with trail 2 and 11.

Trail 9 is temporarily closed for the safety of visitors. The trail overlooks Cumberland Falls and is the most scenic hike in the park. Steps and railings are needed as it is a precipitous climb above a rocky gorge; Eagle Falls is the highlight of the walk.

Trail 10 is a 2-mile loop that connects with Trail 9. It can be reached by hiking from the Holiday Motor Lodge west of the park on KY 90. There's a lookout shelter on the trail. Trees have been cut away so that the river can be seen.

Trail 11 is a 2-mile trail that begins a half mile east of the park entrance on KY 90. The highlight of the walk is a huge rhododendron grove and some sizeable stands of impressive beech trees. There's also a small picnic shelter that was built by the CCC (Civilian Conservation Corps) in the 1930s. Benches and a fireplace are at the shelter. Trail 11 crosses the bridle path and intersects Trail 2 near the Pinnacle Knob Lookout Tower.

Trail 12 is a 1.25-mile trail that begins at camping area 1. A big grove of hemlocks is an attraction. Most of the walking is above the cliffline; a spur trail leads to Cumberland Falls.

During the summer, naturalist-led hikes are conducted each morning and evening. During the off-season, the hikes are by appointment only (groups preferred). All hikes originate from DuPont Lodge. With the completion of the park's nature museum in the fall of 1979, all guided hikes will begin at the new facility.

Cumberland Falls State Resort Park is one of the few parks with planned recreational programs even in the winter. Seasonal programs highlight the park's natural history. There are occasionally seminars on nature photography, special horseback rides, demonstrations of mountain crafts, and square-dancing at an outdoor pavilion.

The Cumberland River flows through the wooded plateau land and is a white-water river, one of Kentucky's Wild Rivers, protected from development by law. Downstream from Cumberland Falls, the river is con-stricted into narrow chutes and flows rapidly over rock shoals. It's con-sidered to be one of the most difficult canoeing runs in the state.

There are two campgrounds with a total of 73 sites with electrical hookups for either tents or recreational vehicles (RVs). Dump stations are at both areas; water is unavailable in the winter. The grocery and laundry facilities are open from April 1 to October 31.

The following are rules of the park that day-hikers are asked to ob-serve.

1. Do not hike alone. In the event of an accident, someone must be able to summon aid.
2. Always let someone know of your hiking plans.
3. Do not hike at night, many park trails are bordered by cliffs that are not visible at night.
4. It is advisable to carry a supply of drinking water and snack items on the longer trails, according to your individual needs.
5. Wear comfortable, well-broken-in footgear. Care should be taken to protect the ankles from strain, particularly on the "difficult" trails.
6. Overnight camping on state park property is permitted only in designated areas.
7. No fires are permitted along these trails.
8. Help maintain trails as you hike them by removing rocks, fallen trees, and branches on the trail.
9. Do not smoke while hiking a trail. It's a rule in many forests, and a good habit in all of them. Forests destroyed by wildfires take many years to restore.
10. When hiking up or down steep terrain, stick to the trail. Never take a shortcut through a series of switchbacks; you'll start erosion and ruin the trail system.
11. Help us keep your state parks clean by bringing everything back that you take on a trail. Thanks for not being a litterbug!
12. Report hazards such as washed-out trail sections, fallen trees, and other problem areas to park personnel.
13. Insect repellent may be advisable at certain times of the year.
14. Concerning wildflowers . . . observe them, enjoy them, photograph them, but leave them for the next party to see.
15. Do not disturb wasp, hornet, yellow jacket, and bumblebee nests. These are useful creatures . . . also, they have their own way of getting even with molesters!!!
16. Cumberland Falls State Resort Park has two types of poison-

ous snakes: The copperhead and the timber rattlesnake. Neither snake is aggressive, but both protect themselves when danger is sensed. Leave all snakes alone. They are protected by law. Poking and molesting will only aggravate them and increase your chances of being bitten. Poisonous snakes are rarely seen in the park.

Cumberland Falls State Resort Park, Corbin, Kentucky 40701. (606) 528-4121.

270

BM ×381

1
641

414

BM ×376

N

389

400

390

450

Wilderness
Lake
Trail

500

AUDUBON

Museum
Trail

MEMORIAL STATE PARK

450

Museum

King Benson
Trail

567 ⊗

Park
Office

450

500

450

25

0   ½ MILE

0   .5 KILOMETER

USGS QUADS: Evansville South   © Thomas Press

AUDUBON

NAME OF TRAIL: John James Audubon State Park Trail System
MAP ON PAGE: 270
START: Museum
END: Museum
TRAIL CONNECTIONS: None
USGS QUADS: Evansville South, Henderson
COUNTIES: Henderson
RATING: Easy; 15.75 mi.; footpath and logging road; −200 ft.

John James Audubon State Park in western Kentucky memorializes the nineteenth-century naturalist who roamed the backwoods of the American frontier and became one of the great animal and birdlife artists. During his lifetime (1785–1851), Audubon spent a total of 14 years in Kentucky. He lived in Louisville and in Red Banks (later named Henderson), where he was partner in a store and grist mill. A woodsman, hunter, and naturalist first, Audubon took little interest in business affairs and spent much time afield. His knowledge of the techniques of art was acquired through experimentation, with only limited instruction.

The print collection of the John James Audubon Memorial Museum includes 126 of the originals from *The Birds of America,* his best-known work. The folio edition was published in England from 1827 to 1838. Its aquatint engravings were made from copper plates on sheets 39½'' x 26½''. The impressions were then water-colored by hand. The four-volume set sold for $1,000 and fewer than 200 complete sets were made up.

The exhibits in the castlelike museum are based largely on three of Audubon's published works: *The Birds of America, The Ornithological Biography,* and *The Quadrupeds of North America.* In addition to prints and oil paintings of birds and animals, exhibits include family mementos such as watches, antique jewelry, silver spoons, forks, and candleholders; an oil portrait of Audubon by Nicola Marchall; pewter teapots and plates; a riverboat "captain's chair"; a beaded deerskin shirt believed to have been worn by Audubon during his Missouri expedition in 1843; manuscripts and journals; and a portrait of Daniel Boone by Audubon.

John James Audubon State Park is in Henderson on U.S. 41. Added to the Kentucky State Park System in 1934, the park was originally located on 275 acres of land purchased by the community as a memorial to the wildlife artist whose works have never been equaled. Today the park consists of 692 acres of heavily forested, hilly woods with two small lakes of 28 and 12 acres. The park is a nature lover's paradise as there are extensive stands of beech, hickory, and oak trees, and scattered wetlands. Bird-life, small mammals, and a few deer inhabit the park.

There are three day-hiking trails in the park. The multi-use **Museum Trail** is a 1200-foot paved loop beginning and ending at the museum and gardens, east of the main entrance. The level trail passes through deciduous forest. There are many wildflowers. There is a possibility in the future that interpretive signs in Braille could be placed along the trail, which was built especially for the handicapped and blind.

The **King Benson** interpretive trail is approximately 2,000 feet long. It was named for the naturalist at the park who recently retired after nineteen years of service. It is a woodchip and paved loop trail that begins and ends at the east end of the parking lot. At the trailhead there are a sign and several steps. The terrain is hilly though the trail descends only slightly. There are 14 self-guided interpretive signs describing mammals, plantlife, and other natural subjects. The trail passes through deciduous forest of maples, tulip poplars, walnut, paw paw, and oak–hickory associations.

The **Wilderness Lake Trail** is a 1.75-mile loop trail that begins and ends at the parking lot of the park office. The first three-quarters of a mile of the trail is paved road (to interior of wildlife area), then the trail (alternately rock and dirt) turns north to the 8-acre Wilderness Lake, which was built by CCC workers in the 1930s. After encircling the lake, the trail takes hikers in the southwest direction back to the museum and gardens. The hilly trail passes through mixed deciduous forest with some impressive stands of beech trees. There is a sign at the trailhead. (There are two Boy Scout trails in the park, but they are not well maintained and not generally available to the public.)

In addition to the three day-hiking trails, there is approximately 1 mile of connector trails so that hikers can shorten or lengthen their walks easily. All the hiking trails are open year-round.

The rental cottages and museums are open daily from May 1 to October 31 and on Saturdays and Sundays from November 1 to April 30. The swimming lake, snack bar, and golf course are open from May 1 to October 31. The campground is open all year and has 58 sites (with electrical hookups). Drinking water, showers, flush toilets, a picnic ground and shelter, ice, and a dumping station are nearby. John James Audubon State Park, Henderson, Kentucky 42420. (502) 826-2247.

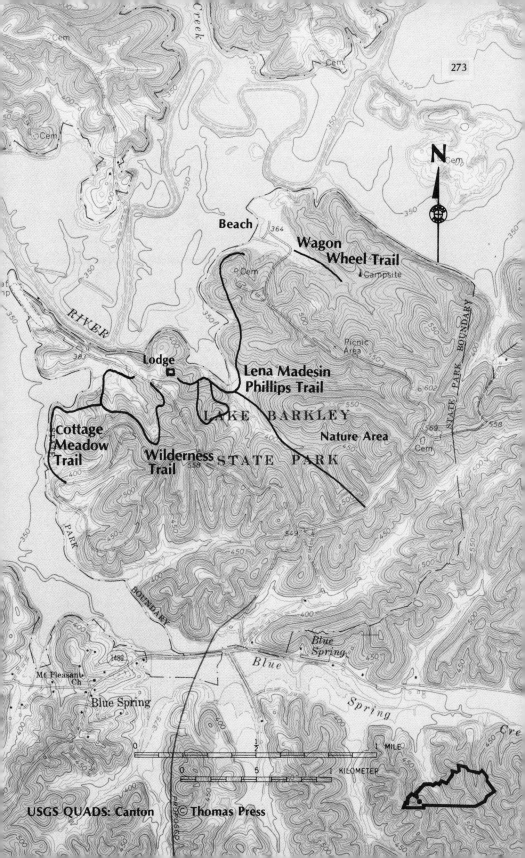

Beach

Wagon Wheel Trail

Campsite

RIVER

Lodge

Lena Madesin Phillips Trail

Cottage Meadow Trail

Wilderness Trail

LAKE BARKLEY

Nature Area

STATE PARK

PARK BOUNDARY

Blue Spring

Blue Spring

Mt Pleasant Ch

Blue Spring

273

N

0   ½   1 MILE

0   5   1 KILOMETER

USGS QUADS: Canton   © Thomas Press

NAME OF TRAIL: Lake Barkley State Resort Park Trail System
MAP ON PAGE: 273
START: Barkley Lodge
END: (See map)
TRAIL CONNECTIONS: None
USGS QUADS: Canton
COUNTIES: Trigg
RATING: Easy; 6.0 mi.; footpath and logging road; +200 ft.

Named in honor of the late Senator and Vice-President from Kentucky, Alben Barkley, Lake Barkley is a 118-mile-long impoundment of the Cumberland River that stretches from Dickson County, Tennessee, to Grand Rivers, Kentucky, in Lyon County. Barkley Dam is at mile 30.6 of the lower Cumberland River. Completed in 1966, the 7,985-foot-long dam, designed by the Nashville District, U.S. Army Corps of Engineers, and constructed under their supervision, is an earth and concrete structure with navigation locks, a canal, and a hydropower generating plant. The 115-foot-high dam, built at a cost of $145,000,000, forms a shallow, winding 57,920-acre lake (42,020 acres in Kentucky), whose main body is in Livingston, Lyon, Caldwell, and Trigg counties, Kentucky.

Kentucky's grandest vacation resort, Lake Barkley State Resort Park, is located on the Little River embayment seven miles west of Cadiz, off U.S. 68. The park entrance road winds through wooded hills, and at night the approach is lit with rows of lights that encircle the sprawling redwood lodge that overlooks the lake. Open year-round, the 3,600-acre park (the largest in the Kentucky state park system), and lodge offer some of the finest accommodations and recreational opportunities in the mid-South. Nationally acclaimed in travel magazines, Lake Barkley State Resort Park has an 80-site campground, 200-seat dining room, coffee shop (open from 7:00 A.M., Memorial Day to Labor Day), an indoor recreation room (billiards, table tennis, card tables, and video games) in the lodge, an eighteen-hole golf course, horseback riding stables (open seasonally), marina, heated swimming pool and sand beach with bathhouse (open seasonally), lighted tennis courts, and basketball courts. There are 120 lodge rooms and four lodge suites. The rooms are well appointed with tasteful furnishings, wall-to-wall carpeting, indirect lighting, individually controlled air conditioning, a split-area dressing room–bath with shower, and a private balcony. The lodge suites are equipped with kitchenettes. The nine executive cottages have custom kitchens, two studio couches that convert to double beds, two bedrooms with two double beds in each, a bath, air conditioning, and electric heat. Tableware, cooking utensils, and linens are furnished. Off-season rates are available for all accommodations. Specially equipped rooms for the handicapped are available. During the season, entertainment and planned recreation programs are held daily.

There are four day-hiking trails in the park, which cover approximately 6 miles. The **Wagon Wheel Trail** is two-tenths of a mile long and connects the camping area with the beach and bathhouse. The half-mile-long **Cottage Meadow Trail** parallels the shoreline of Lake Barkley from the cottage area to its intersection with the Wilderness Trail. There are numerous lake views from the Cottage Meadow Trail. The **Wilderness Trail** is a 2-mile loop that begins at the dormitories for the seasonal help and ends at the tennis courts. There are several natural history displays and two rest stops along the trail. Walks guided by the park's naturalist are often held on the Wilderness Trail. Future plans call for the construction of a wildlife observation station along the trail. Wildlife management practices such as food plots and the creation of woods openings are being implemented.

The **Lena Madesin Phillips Trail** is a three-quarter-mile loop along the lake that begins at the southeast edge of the parking lot at Barkley Lodge. A booklet describing the 18 interpretive stops on the trail is available at the trailhead. The trail honors the first woman to graduate from the University of Kentucky Law School, Lena Madesin Phillips, 1881–1955. Ms. Phillips was a pioneer in the Women's Movement in Kentucky. Funds for construction of the trail were donated by the Cadiz Chapter of the Business and Professional Women's Club. There are two spur trails off the Lena Madesin Phillips loop. One leads to the beach and bathhouse (1.75 miles), the other to the horseback riding stables (1.25 miles). The spur trail that leads to the beach and bathhouse complex passes through a field, a cedar thicket, a picnic shelter, and an oak–hickory forest along the lake.

The park's campground, also open year-round, has 80 campsites, all with water and electrical hookups. The campground's services and facilities include central service buildings with showers, flush toilets, and drinking water, ice, a launching ramp, picnic tables, grills, shelters, and a playground.

Fuel, grocery staples, fishing equipment and live bait (minnows, red worms, and night crawlers), and limited freezer space for cleaned fish are available. A boat launching ramp is nearby. Lake Barkley State Resort Park, Route #2, Cadiz, Kentucky 42211. Marina (502) 924-9954, lodge telephone (502) 924-1171.

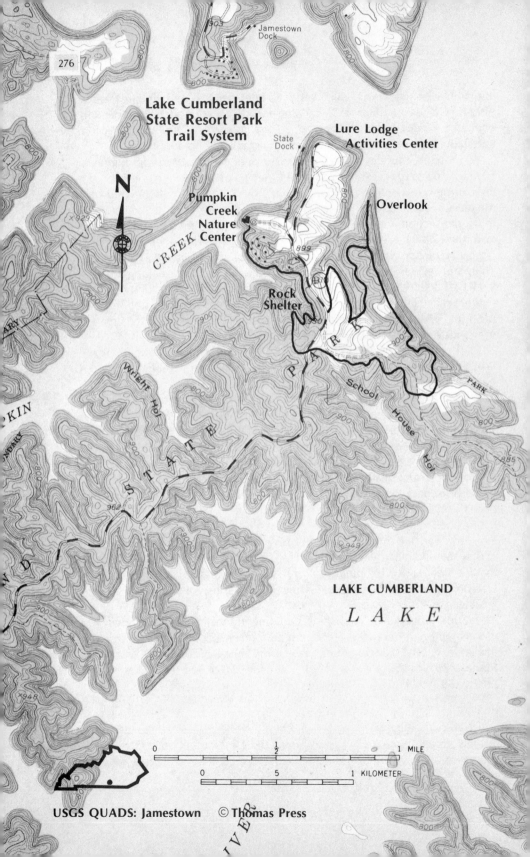

276

Lake Cumberland State Resort Park Trail System

Jamestown Dock

Lure Lodge Activities Center

State Dock

N

Pumpkin Creek Nature Center

Overlook

CREEK

899

Rock Shelter

STATE PARK

Wright Hol

School House Hol

PARK

885

PUMPKIN

BOUNDARY

962

949

LAND

1948

LAKE CUMBERLAND

L A K E

| 0 | | ½ | | 1 MILE |
| 0 | 5 | | 1 KILOMETER |

USGS QUADS: Jamestown   © Thomas Press

NAME OF TRAIL:	Lake Cumberland State Resort Park Trail System
MAP ON PAGE:	276
START:	Activities Center at Lure Lodge
END:	Nature Center at Pumpkin Creek Lodge
TRAIL CONNECTIONS:	None
USGS QUADS:	Jamestown
COUNTIES:	Russell
RATING:	Easy; 4.0 mi.; footpath; +100 ft.

Lake Cumberland (impounded in 1952) extends westward from Daniel Boone National Forest across Whitley, Laurel, Pulaski, Wayne, Russell, and Clinton counties of south central Kentucky. Steep rock cliffs border the headwaters in fjordlike grandeur. West of Mill Springs the lake widens; its serpentine path contours the forested hills of the Cumberland Plateau. At sunset, the azure waters glisten, highlighting rocky islands (once mountaintops) that jut from the cool depths.

Lake Cumberland, the largest of Kentucky's ten major impoundments (50,250 acres), is fed by mountain rivers and creeks and hundreds of springs that help keep the lake cool and clear. Dense woodlands are the backdrop for the 1,255 miles of rocky shoreline.

Lake Cumberland is accessible from the north by the Cumberland Parkway via a number of two-lane roads, mainly KY 92, U.S. 127, KY 196, KY 76, KY 761, KY 80, and U.S. 27. The southern shore of the lake is best reached via KY 90 from Burnside, near the headwaters, and Monticello on KY 1275, KY 789, KY 9, KY 1546, and KY 734. Lake Cumberland was built by the Nashville District, U.S. Army Corps of Engineers. The address of the lake's management office is: Route 8, Box 173 T, Somerset, Kentucky 42501, (606) 679-6337.

Lake Cumberland State Resort Park is a 3,000-acre peninsular park overlooking Pumpkin Creek and the main lake approximately 14 miles southwest of Jamestown, off U.S. 127 on KY 1370. Open all year, the full-facilities park has two lodges—Lure Lodge with 48 rooms, each with two double beds; and Pumpkin Creek Lodge, 15 rooms, each with one double bed. All rooms have telephone, television, climate control, and tile bath with tub and shower. Both one-bedroom and two-bedroom rental housekeeping cottages are available. Ten of the larger ones are special "wildwood cottages" with living–dining room, kitchen, bath, fireplace, porch deck, telephone, color television, electric heat, and air conditioning. Tableware, cooking utensils, and linens are furnished in all cottages. The dining room for the restaurant in Lure Lodge seats 160 and is open for breakfast, 7:00 to 10:30 A.M., lunch, 11:30 A.M. to 2:30 P.M., and dinner, 5:30 to 9:00 P.M.

There is one 4-mile day-hiking trail in the park. It begins at the activities center at Lure Lodge and ends at the Nature Center at Pumpkin Creek. There are numerous side trails and crossovers. A self-interpretive trail, there are nineteen metal plaques with information on flora, fauna, and wildlife on the trail. The improved dirt trail has ten wooden bridges, and erosion control devices. The trail passes through mixed hardwoods. There are two lake views along the trail and one rockhouse, reached via a side trail. The trail is open to day-hiking only.

Although there is only one trail in the park now, plans are being completed for a 20-mile trail on U.S. Army Corps of Engineers and state-owned lands that would connect Kendall Recreation Area at Wolf Creek Dam to Lake Cumberland State Resort Park. No date for completion has been set at this writing.

A gift shop, meeting room, hospitality hall (for groups up to 500 persons), recreation room (with billiards, cards, checkers, chess, table tennis, and foosball), and special accommodations for handicapped persons are included in the park's services and facilities. The Nature Center is complete with interpretive displays on area history and wildlife. Whitetail deer, raccoons, and foxes are often seen on the grounds. Naturalist programs are part of the planned recreation programs. The par-3, nine-hole golf course, Olympic-size swimming pool, tennis courts, horseback riding stables, and shuffleboard are open Memorial Day to Labor Day; the campgrounds, April 1 to October 31. There are 150 paved sites with electrical hookups. Drinking water, showers, flush toilets, a dumping station, picnic tables and shelters, grills, and firewood are available. Lake Cumberland State Resort Park, Jamestown, Kentucky 42629. (502) 343-3111.

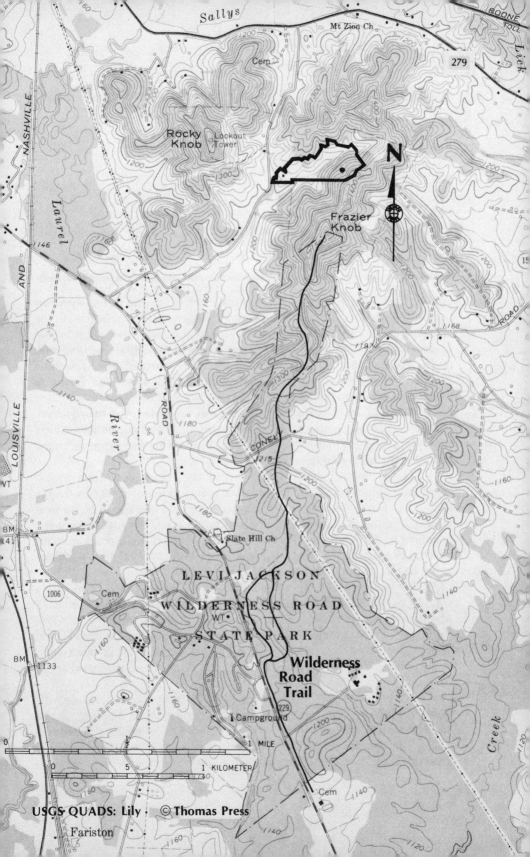

Sallys

BOONE TOLL

Mt Zion Ch

279

Lick

Rocky Knob

Lookout Tower

NASHVILLE

Laurel

Frazier Knob

N

River

AND

ROAD

CONELY

ROAD

LOUISVILLE

BM 141

Slate Hill Ch
Cem

LEVI JACKSON

1006

Cem

WILDERNESS ROAD

WT

STATE PARK

BM 1133

**Wilderness
Road
Trail**

229

Campground

1 MILE

1 KILOMETER

Creek

USGS QUADS: Lily · **©Thomas Press**

Fariston

NAME OF TRAIL:	Levi Jackson Wilderness Road State Park Trail System
MAP ON PAGE:	279
START:	Campground Control Building
END:	Fraziers Knob
TRAIL CONNECTIONS:	None
USGS QUADS:	Lily
COUNTIES:	Laurel
RATING:	Easy; 9.0 mi.; footpath and logging road; +500 ft.

Levi Jackson Wilderness Road State Park, named for one of the early settlers in this area, is part of the legend and history of Daniel Boone. In the late eighteenth century, a buckskin-clad frontiersman emerged from the wilderness to direct the white man's settlement of Kentucky. The land west of the Appalachians, deeded from the Cherokee Indians, was to become America's fifteenth state, and Daniel Boone's name was destined to be ineradicably linked with Kentucky's.

A trapper, market hunter, farmer, and land surveyor by vocation, Daniel Boone was perhaps the most important leader of pioneer settlers who journeyed from the Carolinas and Virginia to the game-rich land beyond the Cumberlands.

Colonel Boone, as he was called in later years, became a legend along the Kentucky frontier. A party of axemen under his direction cut the Wilderness Road, the first trans-Appalachian route. He was one of the most respected of the militia-elite, and he was the image of the rugged frontiersman fighting for land. His very name, and the legends that sprang from his adventures took root in Kentucky, where they grew into indelible additions to the history of the Commonwealth.

Levi Jackson Wilderness Road State Park, 2 miles south of London on U.S. 25, is located on a section of the path followed by Boone in 1775 when he led a party from Cumberland Gap to the confluence of Otter Creek and the Kentucky River, where a wooden stockade named Fort Boonesborough was built in his honor. The 815-acre park, open year-round is approximately 54 miles south of Fort Boonesborough State Park as the crow flies.

There are 9 miles of day-hiking trails in the park. The 3-mile long **Wilderness Road Trail** starts at the campground control building, circles the 3-acre lake, and passes part of the old trace Daniel Boone and his men cut. A 4-H camp, split-rail fences, historical markers, and the Wilderness Road Museum are highlights. Drinking water (from water fountains) is available at the beginning of the hike, which climbs 100 feet along its course. A trail brochure is provided on request.

The second trail in this park is a 6-mile spur off the Wilderness Road Trail that climbs to Fraziers Knob, the highest point in the park. No water is available on it; the trail is marked with sign. Deciduous forest and stands of pine are found along the trail, which climbs 500 feet. The trail ends in a clearing.

Open from 9:00 A.M. to 5:00 P.M., May 1 to November 30, the Mountain Life Museum is one of the main attractions at the park. The museum is a group of handhewn cabins furnished with authentic antiques. A two-room cabin once used as a schoolhouse now is filled with Indian artifacts and pioneer era guns. The household furnishings of an early settler and namesake of the park, Levi Johnson, are displayed in another cabin. Other interesting features are the Bald Rock Chapel, complete with collection plate, original pulpit, and 200-year-old rosewood piano and the blacksmith's cabin where his tools, anvil, and bellows are on display. Admission is less than $1 for both adults and children.

The recreational facilities at the park include a field archery range, a horseback riding stable, swimming pool (open Memorial Day to Labor Day), bathhouse, and snack bar.

From May through November a gift shop and grocery, at the entrance to the campground, are open. The campground at Levi Jackson Wilderness Road State Park is one of the finest in the system, with 200 paved sites, 125 which are equipped for recreational vehicles. All sites have electrical outlets and water hookups. Three central service buildings with flush toilets, showers, laundry facilities, and a TV room, serve the campers. Levi Jackson Wilderness Road State Park, London, Kentucky, 40741. (606) 864-5108.

282

BM 732

Granny Towns

Trail 5

745

N

Owls Window

Trail 4

Lovers Leap

Battleship Rock

Trail 6

I D G E

S T A T E   P A

Trail 3

Natural Bridge

BM 772

Natural Bridge

Balanced Rock

Trail 1

11

Trail 2

NATURAL BRIDGE STATE PARK

0   ½ MILE

0   .5 KILOMETER

USGS QUADS: Slade   © Thomas Press

NAME OF TRAIL: Natural Bridge State Resort Park Trail System
MAP ON PAGE: 282
START: Hemlock Lodge
END: Natural Bridge
TRAIL CONNECTIONS: Whittleton Branch Trail (FS #216)
USGS QUADS: Slade
COUNTIES: Powell
RATING: Moderate; 9.75 mi.; footpath and logging
                        road; +400 ft.

In 1926, the L & N Railroad donated 137 acres to the Commonwealth of Kentucky for a state park at the site of Natural Bridge, an 80-foot-long and 65-foot-high natural rock arch on the middle fork of the Red River in Powell and Wolfe counties. The scenic area had been a whistlestop since the 1890s when the Kentucky Union Railroad Company first laid tracks into the mountains. Natural Bridge State Resort Park is south of the Mountain Parkway at the Slade exit on KY 11. Open year-round, the 1,899-acre park has full facilities—a central lodge, cottages, a dining room that seats 175, meeting rooms, a nature center, and a calendar of entertainment and recreation events. The 35-room Hemlock Lodge is equipped with air conditioning, wall-to-wall carpeting, telephones, color TVs, and private balconies. All rooms have either two double beds or a double bed and a studio couch. Daily maid service is available to lodge guests.

There are six efficiency cottages, all fully furnished with cooking utensils and linens, air conditioning, color TVs, telephones, and electric heat. These cottages all have a combination living room–bedroom, a kitchen, and a bath. The four one-bedroom cottages also have a kitchen, a living room, and a bath.

The lodge gift shop has the largest selection of American Indian turquoise jewelry in Kentucky's state park system. The lodge rooms overlook 54-acre Mill Creek Lake and Hoedown Island and are open from Memorial Day to Labor Day. Square-dancing is held nightly at the lodge. The park's activity center, open seasonally, houses the nature center. Interpretive guided tours of nearby Red River Gorge Geological Area are held during the summer. Other seasonal activities include horseback riding, a skylift, a community pool free to lodge and cottage guests, and planned recreation programs. A canoe and paddle boat rental service is available daily and on weekends in the spring and fall.

There are six day-hiking trails in the park that total 9.75 miles. All trails are marked with signs denoting the trail number and arrows indicating their direction. All trails are surfaced with dirt, gravel, or wood shavings.

Trail 1 is a half-mile trail that begins behind Hemlock Lodge and ascends 300 feet to Natural Bridge. It passes through a hollow clothed in mixed hardwoods and parallels a wet-weather stream. **Trail 2** also ascends to Natural Bridge although it is a great deal harder to climb than Trail 1. The three-quarter mile Trail 2 begins behind Hemlock Lodge. There are about 500 steps on the trail, which ascends approximately 400 feet. **Trail 3** is a nine-tenths-mile-long ridgetop trail that starts at Natural Bridge, takes hikers to Lookout Point, then descends approximately 100 feet to Devils Gulch, and intersects Trail 1 at a small arch. **Trail 4** is a 1.6-mile trail that ascends approximately 100 feet to Natural Arch from Hemlock Lodge (at the intersection of Trail 1). Wildflowers are abundant along this trail in the spring. **Trail 5** is the longest and most strenuous of the six day-hiking trails in the park. It takes practically all day to hike the 6 miles (at a leisurely pace). It begins at Natural Arch Bridge and descends 500 feet by way of Trail 2, passes the skylift area, and follows the paved road to Hemlock Lodge. There are numerous scenic overlooks on the ridgetop section of the trail. **Trail 6** is a quarter-mile footpath spur that takes hikers from Devils Gulch to Lovers Leap along a ridgetop of hardwoods and mixed pine.

During the off-season the nature center is open by appointment with the park naturalist. Informal walks and nature talks are often held. Plantlife includes hemlock, beech, tulip poplar, oaks, and pine trees, spring blooming rhododendron, mountain laurel, and magnolias. As many as seventy-five species of birdlife have been identified in the park in a single day. Wildflower buffs flock to the park in March, April, and May for the annual appearances of jack-in-the-pulpit, May apples, bloodroot, pink lady's slipper, and countless varieties of ferns. Occasionally fox, deer, raccoons, and other mammals are seen.

The geology of the park is similar to the entire Cumberland Plateau Region, with deep ravines, high-walled cliffs, and towering rock formations of conglomerate sandstone, claystone, and siltstone. A folding of the earth's crest raised many of these layers off the bottoms of inland seas, and erosion took place from rainfall and the freezing and thawing action of dramatic seasonal upheavals. The most interesting geologic formations of Natural Bridge State Resort Park are Pivot Rock, Balancing Rock, Battleship Rock, Profile Rock and Owls Window, Devils Gulch, Lookout Point, Lovers Leap, and the spectacular Natural Bridge.

The park's campground is open year-round and has 95 sites, all with water and electrical hookups, drinking water, flush toilets, showers, a dumping station, ice, a playground and picnic tables, are all available at the campground. Natural Bridge State Resort Park, Slade, Kentucky 40376. (606) 663-2214.

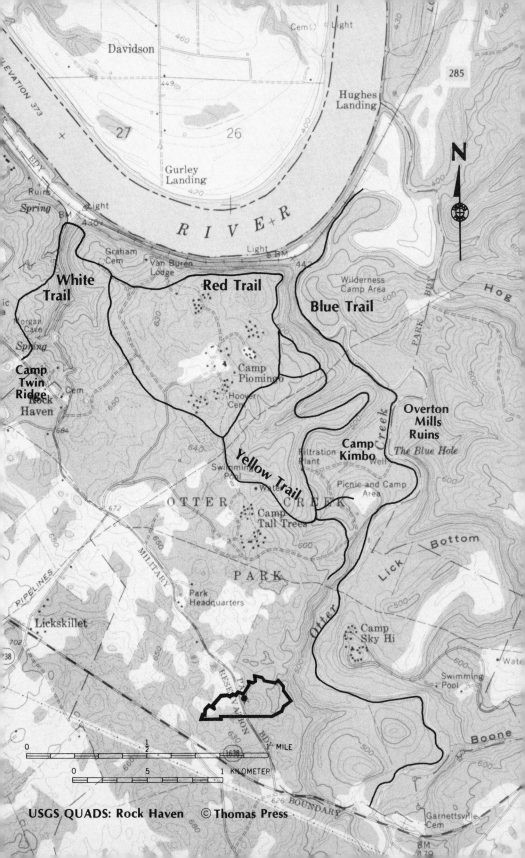

Davidson

Hughes
Landing

285

Gurley
Landing

N

RIVER

Ruins
Spring

Graham
Cem

Van Buren
Lodge

Light

Wilderness
Camp Area

**White
Trail**

Red Trail

Blue Trail

Morgan
Cave
Spring

Camp
Piominco

**Camp
Twin
Ridge**

Cem

Hoover
Cem

**Overton
Mills
Ruins**

Rock
Haven

The Blue Hole

684

Filtration
Plant

**Camp
Kimbo**

Creek

Yellow Trail

Swimming
Pool

Water

Well

Picnic and Camp
Area

OTTER

CREEK

672

Camp
Tall Trees

PARK

Lick

Bottom

MILITARY

Park
Headquarters

Otter

RIPELINES

Lickskillet

38

702

Camp
Sky Hi

Swimming
Pool

Water

Boone

RESERVATION BDY

0   ½   1 MILE

0   5   1 KILOMETER

Garnettsville
Cem

BOUNDARY

BM

USGS QUADS: Rock Haven   © Thomas Press

NAME OF TRAIL: Otter Creek Park Trail System
MAP ON PAGE: 285
START: Rock Haven Picnic Area or Garnettsville Pic-
                      nic Area
END: Ohio River
TRAIL CONNECTIONS: None
USGS QUADS: Rock Haven
COUNTIES: Meade
RATING: Easy; 9.7 mi.; footpath and logging road;
                      +250 ft.

Otter Creek Park is owned by the City of Louisville although it is 25 miles southwest of the heart of town on KY 1638 off U.S. 31W (Dixie Highway) west of Muldraugh. Open from March 15 to December 31, the 2,000-acre park lies along the Ohio River.

There are four day-hiking trails in the park that total 9.75 miles. The **Red Trail** is a 2.5-mile loop beginning and ending at the Rock Haven Picnic Area. Trees along the footpath and logging-road sections of the trail are blazed in red, hence the name. The trail begins at a picnic shelter (grills and picnic tables but no drinking water available), passes through the Graham Cemetery (grown up in weeds), and rises 250 feet through rolling to hilly woods of oak, hickory, and maple to the North Point Lookout at the bluffs overlooking the Ohio River. The trail crosses several wet-weather streams on wood footbridges and ends at the Van Buren and Haven Hill Lodges, both of which sleep 30.

The **Yellow Trail** is a 2-mile footpath that passes through hilly woods of mixed deciduous trees and cedars. The trail begins a quarter of a mile southwest of Otter Creek at its intersection with the Red Trail, and it ends 100 yards south of Camp Piomingo on the Red Trail. The trail passes the filtration plant at Camp Kimbo (which has cabins with bunks to sleep 40) and crosses several wet-weather streams on footbridges. The trail is marked with a yellow blaze and ascends 250 feet.

The longest of the four day-hiking trails in the park is the **Blue Trail.** It begins at the Garnettsville Picnic Area on KY 1638, and ends at the Ohio River. The trail, blazed in blue, follows the west bank of Otter Creek. It is 4.5 miles long and is both footpath and overgrown logging road. Hikers on this trail cross several wet-weather streams, pass the ruins of Overton Mill canal, and pass beside the park's 200-acre wilderness camp area, which is grown up in cottonwoods, ash, sycamore, and willows. The trail is a favorite with fishers who either walk the banks or boat in during the spring to fish for sauger (early March) or jig for largemouth bass in April. The **White**

Trail is simply a three-quarter-mile spur connecting Camp Twin Ridge (a Girl Scout camp) with the Rock Haven Picnic Area and boat ramp.

There are four campgrounds (all open April 1 to November 1) at Otter Creek Park. The largest campground has 150 campsites, all with water and electrical hookups (16 also have sewer hookups). Flush toilets, showers, drinking water, a grocery, ice, picnic tables, grills, boat launching ramp on river, four swimming pools (open Memorial Day to Labor Day), a dumping station, a laundry, a visitor center with local flora, fauna, and geology exhibits (closed Mondays), and a playground with basketball, tennis courts, and a miniature golf course are available. There's one campground especially for tents; all sites are primitive. Two of the campgrounds are for groups larger than 50 persons on a weekly basis only; the fee is $12.50 a person per week.

Accommodations at the park include 12 lodges; six two-family lodges that sleep up to 12 each and rent for $32.50 a night Monday through Friday, $37.50 a night on weekends; four family-size lodges, $20 a night, Monday through Friday, $25.00 a night on weekends; and two large lodges for groups of up to 30, $4.00 a person on weekends, and $3.50 a night Monday through Friday.

There are three picnic areas, all with flush toilets, grills, tables, and shelters. Otter Creek Park, Route #1, Vine Grove, Kentucky 40175. (502) 583-3577.

NAME OF TRAIL: Pine Mountain State Resort Park Trail System
MAP ON PAGE: 288
START: (See map)
END: (See map)
TRAIL CONNECTIONS: None
USGS QUADS: Pineville, Middlesboro North
COUNTIES: Bell
RATING: Moderate; 6.8 mi.; footpath and logging road; +300 ft.

Pine Mountain State Resort Park, Kentucky's first state park, is sandwiched between Kentucky Ridge State Forest and the town of Pineville along the Cumberland River. In 1924, citizens of Pineville secured a 2,000-acre tract of mountainous woodlands and offered it to the state for a recreation and conservation area, which was known as Cumberland Park until 1938. There was little development of facilities at the park in the early years. In 1933, the first real improvements were initiated by the Emergency Conservation Work Program through the Civilian Conservation Corps (CCC). The CCC laborers built roads, trails, picnic tables, shelters, cabins, footbridges, and a road leading to the top of Pinnacle Point. They also built an amphitheater that was filled with 6,000 people for the inaugural Mountain Laurel Festival held on May 31, 1935.

The 2,500-acre mountain park is 36 miles southeast of Corbin (off Interstate 75), on U.S. 25E at Pineville in Bell County. Open year-round, Pine Mountain State Resort Park is a perennial favorite with nature lovers. The 30 lodge rooms (each with modern conveniences, two double beds, wall-to-wall carpeting, air conditioning, electric heat, full bath and shower, and private balcony), overlook some of the most magnificent scenery in the Cumberland Mountains. From April 1 to November 15, rental cottages are available, including seven rustic log cabins with a combination living room–bedroom, a kitchen, and a bath; three one-bedroom cottages with living room, kitchen, and bath; and ten two-bedroom cottages with living room, kitchen, and bath. All cottages have telephone, television, air conditioning and electric heat, tableware, cooking utensils, and linens. They range in price from $18 to $38 a night. The two-bedroom cottages are open year-round.

The park facilities include a dining room (which overlooks the mountains), open daily for breakfast from 7:00 to 10:30 A.M., for lunch from 11:30 A.M. to 2:30 P.M., and dinner from 5:30 to 9:00 P.M., a craft and gift shop, meeting room, lodge, swimming pool (for guests only), horseback riding stables (seasonal), indoor recreation room, playground, and day-hiking trails are also available.

In all, there are eight day-hiking trails that cover 6.8 miles. All the trails have a dirt tread and are marked by signs. A trail maintenance program and trails brochure are planned. Each year, during the last weekend in April, a wildflower weekend is held at the park that draws nature enthusiasts who walk the trail system in search of pink lady's slipper and other forest beauties. West of the park, off KY 382, there's a lookout tower that was once used by the Division of Forestry employees to keep watch over Kentucky Ridge State Forest, which borders the state park lands. It is no longer in use. It affords those who climb it a spectacular view of the Pine Mountain Range. But a word to the wise: The lookout tower isn't in good repair, and those who climb it do so at their own risk.

The **Living Stairway Trail** is a half-mile loop beginning and ending at the lodge. It is a nearly level trail that passes through mixed hardwoods and a ravine of rhododendron and hemlocks. The high point of the trail is the Living Stairway, a tulip poplar tree that leans across a rocky cliffline. In the 1930s CCC workers reinforced the tree with concrete, forming a series of steps up the rock outcropping. The tree still lives today, thus the name Living Stairway. The tree is not used to get up the cliff now since a series of metal stairs was installed.

The **Lost Trail** is a half-mile loop that begins and ends at the lodge. It intersects the Living Stairway Trail, descends to a hollow along a cliffline, crosses a creek (water is available year-round, but chemical treatment is advised), and ascends approximately 200 feet.

The longest trail in the park is the **Honeymoon Falls Trail,** 1.5 miles that begin at the lodge and end at the trail's intersection with the park's horseback riding trail. If you want to shorten the walk, pick up the trail on the paved park road east of the lodge. The highlight of the trail is 20-foot high Honeymoon Falls (a year-round water source). During wet weather there's another falls in the area on a side branch. The trail climbs approximately 100 feet.

The **Fern Garden Trail** is a 1-mile loop extension of the Living Stairway Trail. The trail, which passes through stands of rhododendron and hemlock–poplar forest, rises approximately 100 feet. The main attraction is a massive fern garden, which is marked with a sign.

The **Hemlock Garden Trail** is a three-quarter-mile loop that begins and ends at the lodge. The highlight of the trail is a massive grove of hemlocks, some of which are believed to be virgin. At Boulder Alley, a maze of house-sized rocks, there's a wooden shelter built in the 1930s by the CCC. A two-tenths-mile spur off the main loop leads to Inspiration Point, which overlooks a huge rhododendron thicket.

The **Rock Hotel Trail** is a 1-mile trail, including the quarter-mile spur off the main loop. Beginning at the park lot for Chained Rock and ending at KY 382, the ridgetop trail ascends 100 feet through pines and mixed hardwoods. The main attraction of the trail is Rock Hotel, a huge rockhouse.

The **Laurel Cove Trail** is a 1.3-mile footpath that begins off the Chained Rock Trail and ends at Laurel Cove Amphitheater, where the Mountain Laurel Festival beauty pageant is held. The trail descends 200 feet. The highlight of the trail is a small natural arch; the trail passes through pine and mixed cove hardwoods. A spur off the trail leads to the Laurel Cove Amphitheater parking lot. The **Chained Rock Trail** is nearby. It is said that the citizens of Pineville, in the valley below, were fearful that the giant boulder outcropping that looms over the city would fall. They were so sure that the rock would come tumbling down that they anchored it to the cliffs by a mighty chain; thus, the name Chained Rock.

The campground at Pine Mountain State Resort Park, open April 1 to October 31, has 36 sites, all with electricity. Drinking water, flush toilets, and showers are available at the central service building. In July and August, "The Book of Job," a religious choral drama is presented in the Laurel Cove Amphitheater (daily except Sundays). Entertainment includes singing groups, square-dancing, arts and crafts fairs, guided nature walks, and special interest programs (nature photography, floral arrangements, wildlife seminars). A 36-acre lake, nature museum, and wildflower garden are on the grounds. Pine Mountain State Resort Park, Pineville, Kentucky 40977. (606) 337-3066.

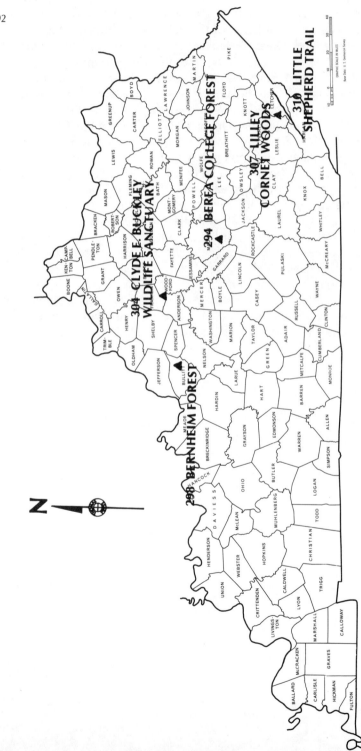

8
Nature and Scenic Areas

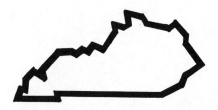

The five nature and scenic areas discussed in this chapter have trails that total 98.7 miles. They are areas set aside primarily for nature study, although hunting and primitive camping is allowed along the Little Shepherd Trail, which passes through Kentenia State Forest. Berea College Forest, Bernheim Forest, Clyde E. Buckley Wildlife Sanctuary, and Lilley Cornett Woods are strictly preserves for day-use only. Some of the finest day-hiking trails in Kentucky are in these areas.

Funding for these areas comes from private foundations, colleges, the Commonwealth of Kentucky, and nature conservacy groups. The Sierra Club and the National Audubon Society frequently conduct organized hikes and nature seminars in these areas. Persons interested in bird watching, plant and animal studies, wildlife management, and timber management should enjoy visiting these areas. They are alternatives for hiking in state and national parks, national forests, and TVA's Land Between the Lakes. Since they are not as popular with hikers as the well-known spots, the trails are less crowded and well worth the effort to explore. Kentucky's nature and scenic areas fill a need for the growing number of individuals who enjoy casual walking.

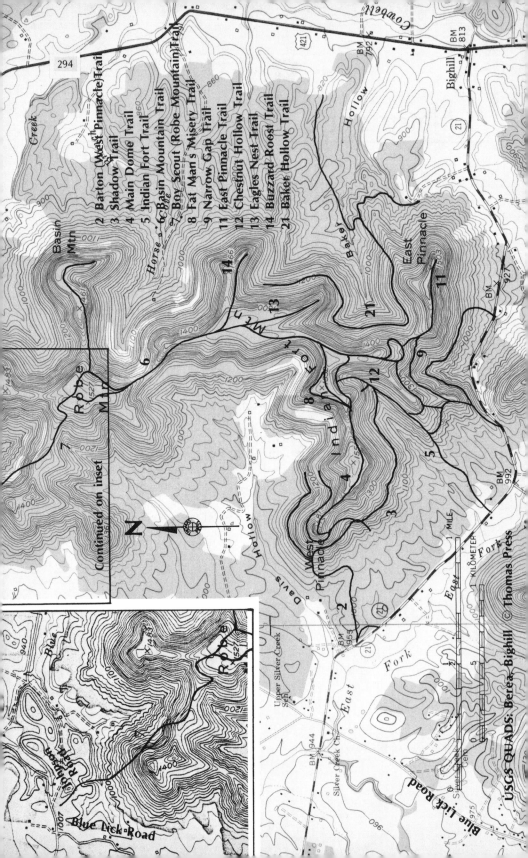

294

2 Barton (West Pinnacle) Trail
3 Shadow Trail
4 Main Dome Trail
5 Indian Fort Trail
6 Basin Mountain Trail
7 Boy Scout (Robe Mountain) Trail
8 Fat Man's Misery Trail
9 Narrow Gap Trail
11 East Pinnacle Trail
12 Chestnut Hollow Trail
13 Eagles Nest Trail
14 Buzzard Roost Trail
21 Baker Hollow Trail

Continued on inset

N

USGS QUADS: Berea, Bighill   ©Thomas Press

NAME OF TRAIL: Berea College Forest Trail System
MAP ON PAGE: 294
START: (See map)
END: (See map)
TRAIL CONNECTIONS: None
USGS QUADS: Berea, Bighill
COUNTIES: Madison, Rockcastle, and Jackson
RATING: Moderate; 19.2 mi.; footpath and logging
                       road; +500 ft.

Berea College Forest, 5,500 acres in Madison, Rockcastle, and Jackson counties of eastern Kentucky, is an outdoor laboratory for forestry students and an integral part in a demonstration project of water and timber management in the Appalachians. Berea College was a pioneer school of forestry education in America. The first general forestry course was offered by the college's agriculture department in 1898.

After the turn of the century, Berea College embarked on a land acquisition program. By 1910, sizeable tracts of valuable timber and year-round reliable water sources were purchased. The woodlands east of the city of Berea are today called Berea College Forest. They are bounded roughly by Blue Lick Creek on the north, U.S. 42 on the east, KY 21 on the south, and Davis Hollow on the west. In addition to providing land for recreational uses and forestry research, Berea College Forest protects the watershed from which the city of Berea gets its domestic and industrial water.

A liberal arts college, Berea College was founded in 1855 to provide educational opportunities to mountain youths with ability but limited economic resources. There is no tuition; every Berea College student must work to help meet the expense of bed and board. Since the school's founding, concern for the "dignity of labor and the preservation of Appalachian crafts" has led to the establishment of college-operated student industries offering more than sixty different kinds of jobs, many of which are in such Appalachian crafts as weaving, wood burning, antique furniture reproduction, broommaking, ceramics, baking, and cooking homestyle candies and jams. The nonsectarian, interracial college was founded to promote the ideal of Christian brotherhood. The college, with its attractive tree-lined campus in downtown Berea, is the cornerstone of the historic community, a model for all Appalachia. Berea is a center for the mountain arts. It has museums, galleries, and Boone Tavern, which offers fine accommodations and wholesome home-cooked regional foods.

There are thirteen day-hiking trails that total 19.2 miles. All the trails are numbered. The **Barton (West Pinnacle) Trail (2)** is 1 mile long. It begins on KY 21, a half mile southeast of Silver Creek Church and ends at the west pinnacle of Indian Fort Mountain after ascending 500 feet. No water is available. The 1.2-mile **Shadow Trail (3)** intersects Trail 2 and contours the west pinnacle. **Trail 4, the Main Dome Trail,** is 1.4 miles long and is a ridgetop trail on the west pinnacle. No water is available here either. **Trail 5** is the 2.2-mile **Indian Fort Trail,** which begins at the Indian Fort Theater and ascends 400 feet to Indian Fort Mountain; no water is available. The **Basin Mountain Trail (6)** is a 2.8-mile, ridgetop trail connecting Indian Fort Mountain to Basin Mountain. **Trail 7, the Boy Scout (Robe Mountain) Trail,** is 2.4 miles long and ascends 500 feet from Blue Lick Road to the top of Robe Mountain. **Trail 8, Fat Mans Misery,** is a seven-tenths-mile trail atop Indian Fort Mountain. It gets its name from the narrow-channel rock formation through which the trail winds. Trail 8 connects with trails 4 and 5. **Narrow Gap Trail (9)** is a 1.2-mile trail that begins on KY 21 one-half mile east of Indian Fort Theater. The loop trail has a spur off of it that ascends 300 feet up the east pinnacle of Indian Fort Mountain and intersects trails 5 and 11. **Trail 11** is the seven-tenths-mile **East Pinnacle Trail** that begins at the intersection of trails 5 and 9 and ascends 100 feet to the summit of east pinnacle of Indian Fort Mountain. **Chestnut Hollow Trail (12)** is a four-tenths-mile connector trail between trails 3 and 4; it ascends 200 feet. The **Eagles Nest Trail (13)** is a spur off Trail 5. It is practically level and is on the ridgetop; it has no water. The **Buzzard Roost Trail (14)** is a six-tenths-mile spur off Trail 6. The ridgetop trail is practically level.

The longest of the trails in the system is the 4.3-mile **Baker Hollow Trail (21)** that begins off KY 21 west of Bighill (at the base of east Pinnacle) on private property and contours Indian Fort Mountain. One spur of the trail heads due east. Water is available seasonally, but chemical treatment is advised.

The forest types are representative of those in the Cumberland Plateau. Virginia and short leaf pine, yellow poplar, hickory, and mixed oaks grow in drier sites atop ridges, with rich stands of yellow poplar in the moist cove sites at 1400 feet. At lower elevations in the creek valleys there's a multitude of herbaceous ground plants, mosses, ferns, and wildflowers. Basswood, walnut, ash, sugar maple, white oak, and hickory trees thrive under these conditions. Most of the timber in the area was cut in the 1880s but reforestation took place rapidly. Berea College Forest is now actively managed for timber through a cooperative program between the college and the U.S. Forest Service. Geologists estimate that the rock formations and soil types (heavy clay soils derived from carboniferous shales, gray-shale clay zone, and limestone soils) range from the Devonian to the Holocene Period. Geologic points of interest in Berea College Forest include Devils Slide, Devils Kitchen, and Fat Mans Misery.

The Pigg House, south of KY 21 near the Indian Fort Theater, can be reserved for Girl Scout, civic, religious, and nature study groups. The log home was donated to the college in the 1920s. Wooded hillsides surround Indian Fort Theater, the setting for the summertime outdoor drama "Wilderness Road," which is about mountain families caught in the turmoil of the Civil War. The drama, filled with dancing and singing, mountain music, colorful costumes, and thunderous battles, is a stirring testimony to the Civil War's tragic impact on the isolated and proud people of the Appalachians. Performances take place nightly except Sundays; curtain time is 8:30 P.M. The season runs from late June to Labor Day; admission prices (subject to change) range from $1.25 to $5.00.

Each spring and fall (May and October), the Kentucky Guild of Artists and Craftsmen holds its craft fairs in Berea's Indian Fort Theater and brings together as many as a hundred exhibitors displaying their Kentucky products, which include pottery, woven items, quilts, chairs, baskets, jewelry, paintings, prints, woodwork, sculpture, and candles. Daily craft demonstrations at the three-day fairs include the wheel-throwing of pottery, vegetable dyeing, silk screen painting, carving, and broommaking. Performances of Kentucky's music—ballads, bluegrass, folk, and country—are also given during these seasonal craft fairs, which are sponsored by the non-profit organization that is devoted to the preservation and development of Kentucky's arts and crafts.

Although primarily a day-use area, camping is allowed in the Berea College Forest by special permission. There's a state-maintained roadside picnic area on KY 21 near the Indian Fort Theater. Camping permission and reservations for accommodations in the Pigg House must be arranged through the Office of the Business Vice-President, College Post Office Box 3204, Berea College, Berea, Kentucky 40404, (606) 986-9341. For information concerning the trail system, telephone Mr. Jim King, Berea College Forester, (606) 986-4336.

Continued on page 299

Continued on page 298

299

Lotus

Spicewood
Flat

Double
Cabin
Hollow
Trail

Iron Ore Hill Trail

Pauls
Point
Loop

Ridgetop

Knob
Top
Trail

High
Point
Trail

Lookout
Tower

Tower
Loop

Overalls
Fork
Trail

Big Rock
Horse Trail

Fern Valley Trail

Shepler Hollow

Pond Ridge

West Fork

Middle Fork

East Fork

Rice Fork

Ashlock

Orchard

Overalls

Dunn Hollow

FOREST

USGS QUADS: Shepherdsville, Samuels   © Thomas Press

1 MILE

5   KILOMETER

NAME OF TRAIL: Bernheim Forest Trail System
MAP ON PAGE: 298–299
START: KY 245, one mile east of Interstate 65
END: (See map)
TRAIL CONNECTIONS: None
USGS QUADS: Samuels and Shepherdsville
COUNTIES: Nelson and Bullitt
RATING: Moderate; 23.5 mi.; footpath, logging road, and gravel road; +400 ft.

Bernheim Forest in Nelson and Bullitt counties is just a 45-minute drive south of Louisville. Opened to the public in 1950, the 10,000-acre area is managed by the Isaac W. Bernheim Foundation as a nature preserve and study area. Reached via U.S. 31E, U.S. 150, and KY 245, KY 61, and KY 245, or Interstate 65 and KY 245 (the Bernheim Forest ramp four miles south of the Shepherdsville Plaza), Bernheim Forest is open daily from 9:00 A.M. to sundown, March 15 to November 15.

Isaac W. Bernheim immigrated to the United States from Germany when he was 17 years old. When he reached New York he had less than four dollars in his pocket. He peddled hardware goods to colonies of German immigrants in Pennsylvania and eventually moved to Paducah, Kentucky, where he founded a wholesale whiskey business, which he operated in partnership with his brother. In 1872 Bernheim moved to Louisville and incorporated the Bernheim Distillers. Bernheim retired from business at the beginning of the Prohibition era and died in 1945 at the age of 96.

Bernheim purchased 13,000 acres of woodlands around 1928 and set up a foundation to protect and develop the acreage so that city dwellers could learn about nature. A trust fund provided money for maintenance and the construction of day-use facilities—arboretum center, picnic grounds, two small lakes, paved access roads, extensive gardens and an arboretum, nature trails, and fire roads. Bernheim grew up near Germany's famous Black Forest and had a deep love of wild things.

Continuous programs, workshops, lectures, bird censuses, nature walks, and wildlife seminars are conducted in cooperation with universities, the National Audubon Society, the Sierra Club, and other nature groups. Research projects on wildlife, forest ecology, and horticulture have been conducted on the grounds. About 2,000 acres of Bernheim Forest are landscaped. The 225-acre arboretum has flowering trees and hardwoods—crabapples, hollies, nut trees, beeches, ginkgoes, oaks, horse chestnuts, and buckeyes.

Picnic grounds are located at Toms Town, Guerilla Hollow, on the north side of Cedar lake in a pine grove surrounding the forest office and east of Rock Run bridge. Visitors are asked to keep their speed under 25 mph on paved roads. No swimming or boating is allowed on either of the two small lakes. Fishing, under Kentucky Fish and Wildlife regulations, is allowed Monday through Saturdays only. No fishing is permitted on Sundays or federal holidays. Acceptable bait includes artificial lures or crickets, red worms, nightcrawlers, meal worms, cut bait or dough balls; minnows are not allowed. Picnic tables and grills are available at most picnic grounds; visitors may use their own portable grills, tables, and lawn chairs in the Pines Picnic Area. Since Bernheim Forest is a nature preserve, no hunting is allowed, and unleashed dogs, air rifles, guns, and molestation of wildlife are strictly prohibited.

Overlooking Big Meadow is a grove of dogwoods and azaleas surrounding the original bronze statue, "Let there be Light," by George Grey Barnard. All plants are labeled and grouped by seasonal interest; plant collecting is not allowed. Holly Hill is another point of interest in the landscaped arboretum. American, Japanese, and deciduous holly surround the plaque, "Justice."

There are thirteen trails (approximately 23.5 miles) for day-use only; overnight camping isn't allowed. All but two of the trails are located in the 8,000-acre portion of the forest that hasn't been disturbed since Bernheim was established in 1928. The half-mile **Sun and Shade Trail,** which demonstrates how the amount of sun and shade in a forest affects plant communities, is in the arboretum center. The **Bent Twig Nature Trail,** south of the Nature Center, is a 1-mile, self-guided loop trail that features a whitetail deer corral, and a birds-of-prey rehabilitation station for the care of injured hawks and owls. Trees along this footpath are marked with identification plates.

The eleven other day-hiking trails are: The **Poplar Flats Trail,** an easy, three-quarter-mile loop, rises approximately 100 feet. This ridgetop trail passes through stands of oak–hickory woods; ferns and mushrooms are abundant along the trail; no water is available. The Poplar Flats Trail begins south of the Nature Center.

The **Rocky Run Trail** is a three-quarter-mile loop. The trail encircles a gap between two knobs. It is almost level and has short descents into the creek bottoms. Halfway along the trail hikers cross a wet-weather stream. There are numerous woods openings and reverting fields. In the warm months of the year hikers often encounter groundhogs and fox squirrels in the woodlots. The Rocky Run Trail begins opposite the Poplar Flats Trail.

The **Jackson Overlook Trail** is a 2-mile loop that begins and ends at the Jackson Hollow Picnic Area. The trail follows a wet-weather creek bed and has one uphill stretch where there are sandstone cliffs. On the ridgetop the trail passes through mature, open woodlands. At the halfway point there are a couple of benches just perfect for relaxing and enjoying the view of the hills in the distance. From the benches it's all downhill. Be alert for deer!

The **Tower Loop** is a half-mile trail that is primarily an access to the lookout tower (elevation 968), the highest point in the Bernheim Forest. Most of the time hikers are on gravel, both a path and road. The view of the surrounding forest is spectacular, especially in the autumn.

The **Overalls Fork Trail** is another of the trails in the Pauls Point Loop Road Hiking Trails System. The Overalls Fork is blazed in yellow is approximately 3 miles long, and ascends 200 feet. The first few hundred yards of the trail are practically level and pass through some open, mature woods with some impressive stands of oak trees. The trail descends into a creek bottom with numerous switchbacks. It's all uphill back to the trailhead.

The **Fern Valley Trail** is the longest of the day-hiking trails in Bernheim Forest. Expect to spend three to five hours on the trail as it is listed as being 7 miles long, though it seemed shorter. Nonetheless, it is a lengthy walk through woods clearings and open woods. Starting at the parking lot (Pauls Point Loop Road), the trail is a gravel road for about a quarter of a mile. When it comes to an opening, bear to the right. You'll see the trail; the road continues through the field. The 15-mile Big Rock Horse Trail intersects Fern Valley and goes back to the gravel road.

The **Shale Bank Trail** is a 1.5-mile trail (blazed in red) that ascends 200 feet. It descends through a creek bottom to a wet-weather stream; there's a 30-foot-high shale wall beside the trail. The scenic trail then connects to a gravel road that is uphill all the way to the end.

The **Knob Top Trail** is a half-mile loop blazed also in red. It is a level ridgetop trail with no water available. If you wander off the trail, there are some good views of the valley. One important aspect of this trail is that it can be hiked in conjunction with the Double Cabin Hollow Trail, perhaps the most scenic of all the trails in Bernheim Forest.

The **Double Cabin Hollow Trail,** which begins on the Pauls Point Loop Road, is a 4-mile trail (blazed in yellow) that climbs 400 feet. It's downhill in the beginning and passes through some beautiful hollows. After intersecting with the Red Top Trail, it follows a wet-weather creek through open woodlands. It intersects the Iron Ore Hill Trail with some uphill stretches. There are numerous scenic overlooks.

The **High Point Trail** is a half-mile loop within the Pauls Point Loop Road. It leads to the highest knob in the forest (926 feet). The trail is blazed in yellow; there are a few nice views.

The **Iron Ore Hill Trail** is a 2-mile footpath through open forest of maples, oaks, and elms, with some scattered holly trees. Lush vegetation lines sections of the trail. There's one very scenic overlook before the trail intersects the Double Cabin Hollow Trail. The last three-quarters mile of the trail is uphill and rises approximately 100 feet.

There are also numerous unmarked footpaths in the forestlands south of the lookout tower. All trails are for foot travel only, no vehicles. Bernheim Forest, Clermont, Kentucky 40110. (502) 543-2451.

NAME OF TRAIL: Clyde E. Buckley Wildlife Sanctuary Trail Sys-
                        tem
MAP ON PAGE: 304
START: Harm House Nature Center
END: (See map)
TRAIL CONNECTIONS: None
USGS QUADS: Frankfort East
COUNTIES: Woodford
RATING: Easy; 4.0 mi.; footpath and woods road;
                        +100 ft.

Atop the bluffs of the Kentucky River in northwest Woodford County is the
Clyde E. Buckley Wildlife Sanctuary—approximately 280 acres of wooded
hill country and open fields. Rich in native plants and wildlife, the sanctuary is intended to preserve a living heritage of the natural environment and
serve as a center for study.

Operated by the National Audubon Society on land donated by Mrs.
Clyde E. Buckley of Lexington, Kentucky, as a memorial to her late hus-
band, this wildlife refuge is one of the few Audubon Society sanctuaries
located in the interior of the United States.

Points of interest in the sanctuary include the all-weather, glass-enclosed observation building near the birdfeeders by the Marion E. Lindsey
Bird-watching House and the nature center named after Kentucky wildlife
artist–naturalist Ray Harm. Visitors may see a wide variety of wildlife that
may include whitetail deer, cottontail rabbit, raccoon, red and grey fox,
woodchuck, and many species of birds.

The sanctuary lies along the path of the spring and fall migration of
many species of birds—herons, black, mallard and wood ducks, Canada
geese, warblers, and kingfishers. In spring and summer the woodlands and
fields are filled with the calls of colorful songbirds busily building nests and
rearing young. Warden Naturalist Tim Williams conducts programs open
to the public on Saturdays and Sundays at regularly scheduled times that
are sometimes followed by slide presentations and special programs.
Closed Mondays and Tuesdays, the hours the rest of the week for the
grounds and bird blind are Wednesday through Sunday 9:00 A.M. to 5:00
P.M.; and for the museum, Saturdays and Sundays 1:00 to 6:00 P.M. Special
programs are available by reservation only for groups.

There are approximately 3.25 miles of color-coded day-hiking trails
in the Clyde E. Buckley Wildlife Sanctuary. The longest, 2-mile-long **Red
Trail** begins in the woods behind the display barn and ends where it
intersects the White Trail. The trail is level and passes deciduous forest,

meadows, and sinkholes. The display barn features exhibits that include medicinal herbs, lichens, songbirds, and wildflowers.

The quarter-mile-long **White Trail** begins in front of the display barn and ends in the parking lot. It passes through red cedar forests along limestone outcroppings. No water is available on either the Red or White Trails.

The 1-mile-long **Blue Trail** begins at the parking lot and ends in the woods in front of Harm House. The trail winds through deciduous forest and passes 3-acre Apollo Pond and its adjacent wetlands. There are several wet-weather creeks on this trail. Drinking water is available from a fountain in front of the Harm House. There are approximately three-quarters mile of spur trails (most of them are off the Red Trail) that crisscross the interior of the wildlife refuge.

The displays in Harm House include local marine fossils, coal age fossils, the water cycle, food chains of plants and animals, insect collections, local high school science projects, and a large collection of prints and miscellaneous sketches by the man for whom the environmental education center was named.

In addition to these permanent displays are representative prints by other wildlife artists such as Coheleach, Eckelberry, and Ruthven that are housed in the nature center; the sanctuary staff prepares traveling exhibits for local county fairs and career days at high schools. White Trail is being made into a self-interpreting day-hiking trail with signs and a brochure.

The Clyde E. Buckley Wildlife Sanctuary is 12 miles west of Versailles, in Kentucky's Bluegrass Region, and can be reached via U.S. 60, the Glenns Creek–McCracken and German Roads. The mailing address and telephone number are: Route #3, Frankfort, Kentucky 40601. (606) 873-5711.

NAME OF TRAIL: Lilley Cornett Woods Trail System
MAP ON PAGE: Guided tours only
START: KY 1103 at Skyline
END: KY 1103 at Skyline
TRAIL CONNECTIONS: None
USGS QUADS: Tilford
COUNTIES: Letcher
RATING: Strenuous; 6.0 mi.; footpath; +900 ft.

Lilley Cornett Woods, one of the last remaining tracts of virgin timber in the eastern United States, is a prime example of a climax forest at its best. Untouched for thousands of years except by the forces of nature itself, this 554-acre tract of woodland on Linefork Creek in Letcher County near Whitesburg in eastern Kentucky offers the visitor a firsthand look at the last remaining climax portion of one of the greatest forest types of all time, the mixed mesophytic, which was at its finest in the Cumberland Mountains of eastern Kentucky.

Names for the man who spent most of his life personally guarding the forest against all intruders, Lilley Cornett Woods (Lilley's Woods, as they were known to his friends and neighbors), is located on KY 1103 at Skyline, and may be reached via KY 15 from the Mountain Parkway at Campton or by U.S. 25E and U.S. 119 from Interstate 75 at Corbin.

Trees in the virgin portion of the woods are more than 400 years old. Their survival is attributed to Cornett, whose intense devotion prompted him to ensure their safety from fire by sending crews into the woods at his own expense when the danger was great. Cornett steadfastly refused to allow any logging in his woods, even during World War II when lumber was scarce and all his neighbors were selling their trees.

In 1915, Lilley Cornett saw the woods and decided they were worth protecting. He knew that if the trees were cut, Kentuckians probably wouldn't ever have another opportunity to view such a majestic stand of hardwood trees. His resolution to retain the woods in their virgin state was steadfast. Between 1915 and 1933, Cornett bought up the land and set about a lifelong vigil to preserve for all time the last remaining tract of virgin eastern timberland. At his death in 1958, his four sons decided to carry on their father's wish. When mining interests attempted to strip the area in 1969, Cornett's sons sold the land to the Commonwealth of Kentucky with the provision that the land would remain untouched forever. The mining companies subsequently agreed that as long as the woods remained the property of the state and was managed as a forest preserve, they would relinquish their mineral rights.

Lilley Cornett Woods, designated a national natural landmark, is open to visitors from April 1 to October 31, 9:00 A.M. to 4:30 P.M. daily. Since January 1977, Eastern Kentucky University has been responsible for the protection and management of the forest, which now serves as an environmental study area for graduate students at the university. Guided tours of the woods are conducted daily.

There are two day-hiking trails in the Lilley Cornett Woods. All hikers must be accompanied by the forest naturalist; hiking alone in the woods is not allowed. The longest of the two day-hiking trails is the 4-mile long **Big Everidge Trail** that begins at a restored cabin 1 mile southeast of the visitors' center on an unmarked gravel road that was built for access in case of fire. The Big Everidge Trail is rated strenuous and ascends 900 feet. There are numerous switchbacks up narrow, steep hollows. Part of the trail is on the ridgetop. Points of interest on the Big Everidge Trail are rock outcroppings (rockhouses), white oak trees with diameters of more than 50 inches, and 100-foot-tall chestnut trees that have fallen and are carpeted with mosses and ferns. The Big Everidge Trail ends one-half mile southeast of the visitors' center.

The **Shop Hollow Trail** is less strenuous and shorter. The 2-mile trail begins three-quarter miles southeast of the visitors' center on the gravel fire access road and ends at the same place as the Big Everidge Trail. This trail climbs 450 feet and is best known for the large number of wildflowers that bloom at trailside in the spring. Massive stands of tulip poplar, beech, and hemlock shade the moist forest floor from which as many as fifty species of wildflowers grow. Among the most beautiful are the trilliums, several species of uncommon orchids (including the pink lady's slipper), and May apples that carpet the trail in the spring.

In the lower, moist areas, eastern hemlocks grow so densely that the forest floor is in deep shade, allowing only shade-tolerant herbaceous ground plants to grow in rich soil. The black walnut also thrives at the lower elevations; some reach 60 or 70 feet into the air before their trunks branch. At the higher elevations, pitch and scrub pine and chestnut oaks live in the drier sites atop ridges. Smooth-barked beech abounds as one of the most common trees in the hillside, forest slope community. In all there are some ninety species of trees and shrubs, a large variety of animal life, and profusion of wild flowers—trilliums, partridgeberries, pink lady's slipper, trailing arbutus, and May apples. Songbirds and predatory birds such as the broad-winged hawk and barred owl are common in Lilley Cornett Woods.

Botanists speculate that the forests of eastern Kentucky were the seed producers for all the great American forests. Ice ages destroyed most the northern forests, while the plateau land of eastern Kentucky, with a relatively southerly climate and hilly terrain, was a buffer against the advance of glaciers. Pockets of trees survived the onslaught of ice age after ice age to become the seed producers after the cold climate drastically changed more than 10,000 years ago. Lilley Cornett Woods is the last remnant of the great forests that stretched from the Big Sandy River to the Mississippi River in Kentucky. Lilley Cornett Woods, P. O. Box 78, Skyline, Kentucky 41851. (606) 633-5828.

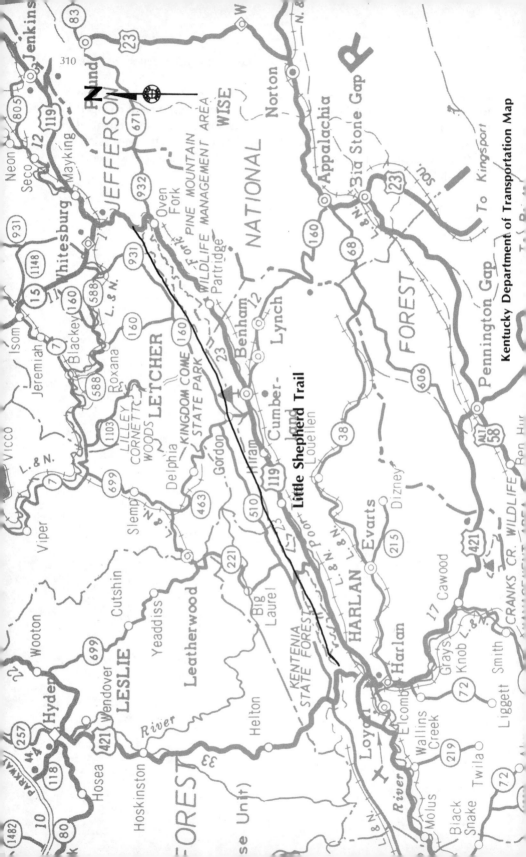

Kentucky Department of Transportation Map

NAME OF TRAIL: Little Shepherd Trail (KY 1679)
MAP ON PAGE: 310
START: 5.5 miles north of Harlan at U.S. 421
END: KY 119, 5 miles south of Whitesburg
TRAIL CONNECTIONS: None
USGS QUADS: Bledsoe, Nolansburg, Benham, Roxana, and
                      Whitesburg
COUNTIES: Harlan and Letcher
RATING: Moderate; 46.0 mi.; gravel road; +500 ft.

The Little Shepherd Trail is a 46-mile gravel road atop Pine Mountain that extends northeastward from Harlan to Whitesburg. The scenic mountain-top trace is used by hikers, horseback riders and four-wheel-drive enthusiasts and parallels seven tracts (a total of 3,624 acres) of Kentenia State Forest.

The only developed campground on the Little Shepherd Trail is at the Putney Lookout Tower on KY 2010 off U.S. 119 at Laden. Open year-round, the campground's facilities include: tent pads, picnic grills, a shelter house, pit toilets, and drinking water. Primitive camping is allowed on state forest lands.

At Cumberland, the Little Shepherd Trail intersects KY 1926 at Kingdom Come State Park. The park and trail were named for John Fox, Jr.'s immortal novel, *The Little Shepherd of Kingdom Come*, the story of a boy who grows to manhood during the Civil War, finds and loses love, and must bear the anguish of divided loyalties caused by the war and his conscience. An outdoor drama based on Fox's book is presented late June through late August at an amphitheater 5 miles north of Whitesburg on KY 15 at 8:30 P.M. on Friday, Saturday, and Sunday nights.

The Little Shepherd Trail also passes through the 5,018-acre Pine Mountain Wildlife Management Area. Other points of interest along the trail include Raven's Rock, a 290-foot rock slab that juts into the air at a 45-degree angle and Log Rock, a small natural arch. Little Shepherd Arts and Crafts Corporation, Box 806, Whitesburg, Kentucky 41858. (606) 633-7503.

Appendix

Topographic Maps

U.S. Geological Survey, Washington, D.C. 20242, Attn: Distribution Section, (202) 867-7000 or 343-8073.

Kentucky Department of Commerce, Map Sales Office, 133 Holmes Street, Frankfort, Kentucky 40601, (502) 564-4715.

Kentucky Geological Survey, Mineral Industries Building, 120 Graham Avenue, Lexington, Kentucky 40506, (606) 258-5863.

Index

References to maps are in boldface type.

About the Author

Arthur B. Lander, Jr. has been a full-time outdoor and travel writer and photographer since 1973. His articles have appeared in *Wilderness Camping, Camping Journal, Outdoors Today, Southern Outdoors, Southern Living, Odyssey, Chevron USA, Pace, Back Home in Kentucky, All Outdoors,* and *Lakeland Boating.* Currently a free-lance writer and photographer, and correspondent for the Lexington *Herald-Leader* newspaper in Lexington, Kentucky, the author is a member of the Outdoor Writer's Association of America. His first book, *A Guide to Kentucky Outdoors,* was published in December 1978.

A native Kentuckian, the author has hiked throughout his home state, California's High Sierra, and the Colorado Rockies. He lives in St. Matthews, a suburb east of Louisville.

Thomas hoc fecit

322

A Canoeing and Kayaking Guide to the Streams of Kentucky

by Bob Sehlinger

"Without doubt [Kentucky] has the best and probably biggest guide to its boatable waters of all the 50 states. . . . In all, about 70 creeks and rivers grace this comprehensive book. . . . The best buy you can make after your canoe, paddle and life jacket." — *Canoe*

"At last, the last word on canoeing in Kentucky. . . . The book's maps and tables give the location, degree of difficulty, gradient, mean monthly water temperature, velocity of the water, width and hazards for each stream. You can find out when a stream is runnable, how difficult it will be and how long it will take to get help in case of an accident–plus highlights, scenery and access points. It even tells you where to get more information. (Can there be more?)" — *Louisville Times*

"But best of all, you know it's been written by someone who has been there and is writing from experience." — *Louisville Courier-Journal*

ISBN 0-89732-000-X   320 pp., paper $12.95

A Guide to Kentucky Outdoors

by Arthur B. Lander, Jr.

"A gold mine of information about wildnerness experiences and recreational possibilities that even native Kentuckians may not know existed . . . The standard by which future outdoors guides will be judged."
— *Louisville Courier-Journal*

"A great book for the great outdoors." — *Louisville Times.*

"Two national and 17 state parks, 25 lakes, 6 state and 1 national forest, and 7 nature and scenic areas are described as potential recreational sites. Opportunities for skiing, scuba diving, hang-gliding, parachuting, and bicycling in Kentucky are also identified. Fishing and hunting get more space, with each major game species having its own section, and there is considerable advice on the techniques found most useful by local sportspeople." — *Library Journal*

ISBN 0-89732-001-8   280 pp., paper, $9.95